KB085113

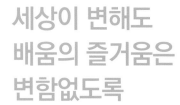

세상이 변해도
배움의 즐거움은
변함없도록

시대는 빠르게 변해도
배움의 즐거움은
변함없어야 하기에

어제의 비상은
남다른 교재부터
결이 다른 콘텐츠
전에 없던 교육 플랫폼까지

변함없는 혁신으로
교육 문화 환경의 새로운 전형을
실현해왔습니다.

비상은 오늘, 다시 한번
새로운 교육 문화 환경을 실현하기 위한
또 하나의 혁신을 시작합니다.

오늘의 내가 어제의 나를 초월하고
오늘의 교육이 어제의 교육을 초월하여
배움의 즐거움을 지속하는 혁신,

바로, 메타인지학습을.

**상상을 실현하는 교육 문화 기업 비상**

**메타인지학습**
초월을 뜻하는 meta와 생각을 뜻하는 인지가 결합된 메타인지는
자신이 알고 모르는 것을 스스로 구분하고 학습계획을 세우도록 하는
궁극의 학습 능력입니다. 비상의 메타인지학습은 메타인지를 키워주어
공부를 100% 내 것으로 만들도록 합니다.

중학 영어의 모든 것

VISANG

# All that

# 중학 영어 2-2

# 구성과 특징

**PART I** 실력 다지기

## All that Grammar

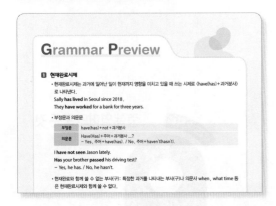

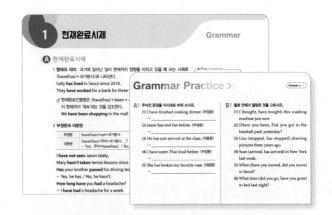

- 단원을 학습하기 전에 꼭 알아야 할 핵심 문법 개념을 소개하는 자기주도적 학습 장치

- 주요 교과서를 철저히 분석하여 구성한 체계적인 문법 목차
- [개념 소개] → [Grammar Practice] → [Grammar Test] 3단계로 구성된 체계적인 문법 학습 시스템
- 출제 빈도가 높은 기출 문항들을 엄선하여 수록한 연습 문제

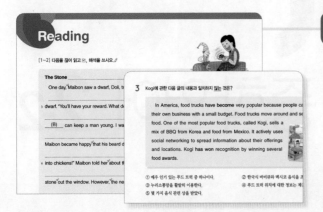

## All that Reading

- 재미있고 다양한 소재의 지문 수록
- 교과서 지문을 이용한 끊어 읽기, 해석 연습
- 실제 시험과 유사한 독해 문항 유형을 다양하게 수록

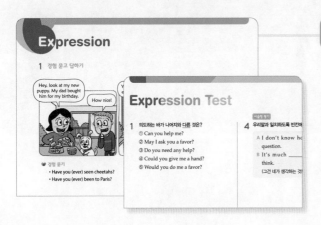

## All that Expression

- 주요 교과서에 소개된 의사소통 기능을 엄선하여 소개
- 대화 상황을 재미있는 만화로 생생하게 제시
- 다양한 유형의 기출 문항들을 엄선하여 수록

## Test & Review

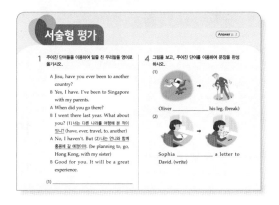

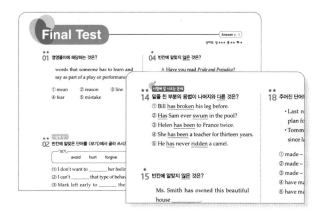

- 문법과 표현을 적용한 서술형 평가 제공
- 학교 서술형 평가 완벽 대비를 위한 다양한 문제 수록

- 실제 시험과 동일한 유형으로 구성된 종합 평가
- 여러 난이도의 문제를 빈출 유형 위주로 수록

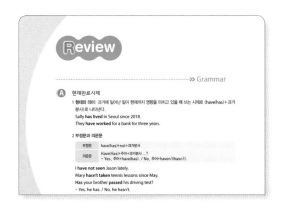

- 단원에서 학습한 문법과 의사소통 기능 복습
- 학습 내용을 도식화하여 신속한 이해 점검 가능

## PART II 듣기 실전 모의고사

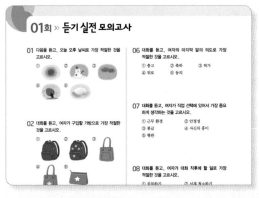

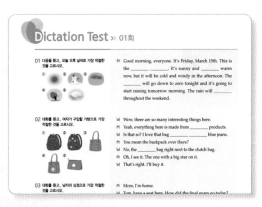

- 시 · 도 교육청 영어 듣기능력평가를 분석하여 반영한 듣기 실전 모의고사 5회 수록
- 실제 시험과 유사한 분량 및 녹음속도의 듣기 자료를 통해 실전 적응력 향상
- 듣기 능력을 향상시켜줄 Dictation Test 제공

# 차 례

## PART I 실력 다지기

# How To Study

* 월간, 주간, 일간 학습 계획을 세운 후 공부하는 습관을 가져 보세요. 무턱대고 공부하는 것보다 훨씬 체계적이고 계획적으로 공부할 수 있어요.
* 먼저, 구체적으로 공부할 분량을 파악한 후에 학습 목표를 세워 보세요. 목표를 세울 때는 막연하거나 장황하지 않게 구체적으로 세우는 것이 중요해요. 그렇게 해야 계획대로 공부할 수 있고 목표한 만큼은 반드시 끝낸다는 마음으로 공부할 수 있어서 효율적이에요.

## 60일 완성 학습 계획표

### Lesson 01 현재완료시제

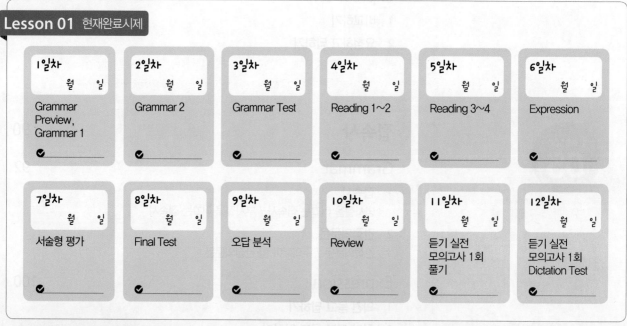

| 1일차 월 일 | 2일차 월 일 | 3일차 월 일 | 4일차 월 일 | 5일차 월 일 | 6일차 월 일 |
|---|---|---|---|---|---|
| Grammar Preview, Grammar 1 | Grammar 2 | Grammar Test | Reading 1~2 | Reading 3~4 | Expression |

| 7일차 월 일 | 8일차 월 일 | 9일차 월 일 | 10일차 월 일 | 11일차 월 일 | 12일차 월 일 |
|---|---|---|---|---|---|
| 서술형 평가 | Final Test | 오답 분석 | Review | 듣기 실전 모의고사 1회 풀기 | 듣기 실전 모의고사 1회 Dictation Test |

### Lesson 02 관계대명사

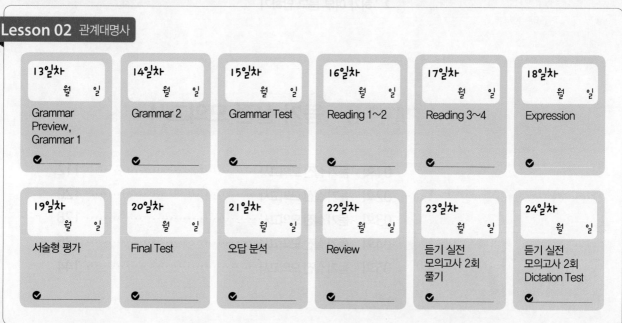

| 13일차 월 일 | 14일차 월 일 | 15일차 월 일 | 16일차 월 일 | 17일차 월 일 | 18일차 월 일 |
|---|---|---|---|---|---|
| Grammar Preview, Grammar 1 | Grammar 2 | Grammar Test | Reading 1~2 | Reading 3~4 | Expression |

| 19일차 월 일 | 20일차 월 일 | 21일차 월 일 | 22일차 월 일 | 23일차 월 일 | 24일차 월 일 |
|---|---|---|---|---|---|
| 서술형 평가 | Final Test | 오답 분석 | Review | 듣기 실전 모의고사 2회 풀기 | 듣기 실전 모의고사 2회 Dictation Test |

## Lesson 03 명사, 대명사

| 25일차<br>월 일<br>Grammar<br>Preview,<br>Grammar 1<br>✔ ___ | 26일차<br>월 일<br>Grammar 2<br><br>✔ ___ | 27일차<br>월 일<br>Grammar Test<br><br>✔ ___ | 28일차<br>월 일<br>Reading 1~2<br><br>✔ ___ | 29일차<br>월 일<br>Reading 3~4<br><br>✔ ___ | 30일차<br>월 일<br>Expression<br><br>✔ ___ |
|---|---|---|---|---|---|
| 31일차<br>월 일<br>서술형 평가<br><br>✔ ___ | 32일차<br>월 일<br>Final Test<br><br>✔ ___ | 33일차<br>월 일<br>오답 분석<br><br>✔ ___ | 34일차<br>월 일<br>Review<br><br>✔ ___ | 35일차<br>월 일<br>듣기 실전<br>모의고사 3회<br>풀기<br>✔ ___ | 36일차<br>월 일<br>듣기 실전<br>모의고사 3회<br>Dictation Test<br>✔ ___ |

## Lesson 04 형용사, 부사, 비교

| 37일차<br>월 일<br>Grammar<br>Preview,<br>Grammar 1<br>✔ ___ | 38일차<br>월 일<br>Grammar 2<br><br>✔ ___ | 39일차<br>월 일<br>Grammar Test<br><br>✔ ___ | 40일차<br>월 일<br>Reading 1~2<br><br>✔ ___ | 41일차<br>월 일<br>Reading 3~4<br><br>✔ ___ | 42일차<br>월 일<br>Expression<br><br>✔ ___ |
|---|---|---|---|---|---|
| 43일차<br>월 일<br>서술형 평가<br><br>✔ ___ | 44일차<br>월 일<br>Final Test<br><br>✔ ___ | 45일차<br>월 일<br>오답 분석<br><br>✔ ___ | 46일차<br>월 일<br>Review<br><br>✔ ___ | 47일차<br>월 일<br>듣기 실전<br>모의고사 4회<br>풀기<br>✔ ___ | 48일차<br>월 일<br>듣기 실전<br>모의고사 4회<br>Dictation Test<br>✔ ___ |

## Lesson 05 접속사

| 49일차<br>월 일<br>Grammar<br>Preview,<br>Grammar 1<br>✔ ___ | 50일차<br>월 일<br>Grammar 2<br><br>✔ ___ | 51일차<br>월 일<br>Grammar Test<br><br>✔ ___ | 52일차<br>월 일<br>Reading 1~2<br><br>✔ ___ | 53일차<br>월 일<br>Reading 3~4<br><br>✔ ___ | 54일차<br>월 일<br>Expression<br><br>✔ ___ |
|---|---|---|---|---|---|
| 55일차<br>월 일<br>서술형 평가<br><br>✔ ___ | 56일차<br>월 일<br>Final Test<br><br>✔ ___ | 57일차<br>월 일<br>오답 분석<br><br>✔ ___ | 58일차<br>월 일<br>Review<br><br>✔ ___ | 59일차<br>월 일<br>듣기 실전<br>모의고사 5회<br>풀기<br>✔ ___ | 60일차<br>월 일<br>듣기 실전<br>모의고사 5회<br>Dictation Test<br>✔ ___ |

# 돌아보는 1학기 차례

# 실력 다지기

# Lesson 01

# 현재완료시제

# Grammar Preview

## 1 현재완료시제

- 현재완료시제는 과거에 일어난 일이 현재까지 영향을 미치고 있을 때 쓰는 시제로 〈have(has)+과거분사〉로 나타낸다.

  Sally **has lived** in Seoul since 2018.

  They **have worked** for a bank for three years.

- 부정문과 의문문

| 부정문 | have(has)+not+과거분사 |
|---|---|
| 의문문 | Have(Has)+주어+과거분사 …?<br>– Yes, 주어+have(has). / No, 주어+haven't(hasn't). |

  I **have not seen** Jason lately.

  **Has** your brother **passed** his driving test?

  – Yes, he has. / No, he hasn't.

- 현재완료와 함께 쓸 수 없는 부사(구): 특정한 과거를 나타내는 부사(구)나 의문사 when, what time 등은 현재완료시제와 함께 쓸 수 없다.

| | | |
|---|---|---|
| ago …전에 | last 지난 | then 그때 |
| yesterday 어제 | just now 지금 막 | |

  They have moved here several years ago. (×)

  → They **moved** here several years **ago**. (○)

## 2 현재완료시제의 용법

| 용법 | 의미 | 자주 쓰이는 부사 |
|---|---|---|
| 완료 | 막 …했다 | just, already, yet |
| 경험 | …해 본 적이 있다 | ever, never, before, once, twice, … times |
| 계속 | (지금까지) …해 왔다 | for, since, how long |
| 결과 | …해 버렸다 (그 결과 지금 …하다) | – |

I **have** just **finished** watering the plants. 〈완료〉

**Have** you ever **eaten** raw fish? 〈경험〉

They**'ve changed** a lot since last spring. 〈계속〉

She **has left** for Italy. (So, she isn't here.) 〈결과〉

# 1 현재완료시제

## Ⓐ 현재완료시제

**1 형태와 의미:** 과거에 일어난 일이 현재까지 영향을 미치고 있을 때 쓰는 시제로 〈have(has)+과거분사〉로 나타낸다.

Sally **has lived** in Seoul since 2018.

They **have worked** for a bank for three years.

> *cf.* 현재완료진행형은 〈have(has)+been+-ing〉의 형태로, 과거에 시작한 동작이 현재까지 '계속'되는 것을 강조한다.
>
> We **have been shopping** in the mall since 2 o'clock.

**2 부정문과 의문문**

| | |
|---|---|
| 부정문 | have(has)+not+과거분사 |
| 의문문 | Have(Has)+주어+과거분사 ...?<br>– Yes, 주어+have(has). / No, 주어+haven't(hasn't). |

I **have not seen** Jason lately.

Mary **hasn't taken** tennis lessons since May.

**Has** your brother **passed** his driving test?

– Yes, he has. / No, he hasn't.

**How long have** you **had** a headache?

– I **have had** a headache for a week.

> **● Plus** Grammar
>
> 현재완료시제 *vs.* 과거시제
> I **have lost** my bag.
> 과거에 가방을 잃어버렸고, 현재에도 가방을 잃어버린 상태임
> I **lost** my bag.
> 과거에 가방을 잃어버렸고, 현재 가방을 찾았는지 알 수 없음

> **● Plus** Grammar
>
> 현재완료시제의 축약형
> • 긍정문
> I have → I've
> You have → You've
> They have → They've
> He has → He's
> • 부정문
> have not → haven't
> has not → hasn't

## Ⓑ 현재완료와 함께 쓸 수 없는 부사(구)

특정한 과거를 나타내는 부사(구)나 의문사 when, what time 등은 현재완료시제와 함께 쓸 수 없다.

| | | |
|---|---|---|
| ago ···전에 | last 지난 | then 그때 |
| yesterday 어제 | just now 지금 막 | |

> **● Plus** Grammar
>
> 완료시제와 함께 자주 쓰이는 단어
> since, for, ever, never, before, once, already, yet, lately, recently 등
> It **has rained since** yesterday.

They have moved here several years ago. (×)

→ They **moved** here several years **ago**. (○)

When have you taken a cooking class? (×)

→ **When did** you **take** a cooking class? (○)

# Grammar Practice >>

Answer p. 1

**A1** 주어진 문장을 지시대로 바꿔 쓰시오.

(1) I have finished cooking dinner. (부정문)

→ _____

(2) Jason has met her before. (부정문)

→ _____

(3) He has just arrived at the class. (의문문)

→ _____

(4) I have eaten Thai food before. (부정문)

→ _____

(5) She has broken my favorite vase. (의문문)

→ _____

**A2** 빈칸에 알맞은 말을 쓰시오.

(1) A Has Yuna bought a pink backpack?

B No, she _____.

(2) A Have you ever been to Paris?

B Yes, I _____.

(3) A Have you ever ridden a horse?

B No, I _____.

**A3** 우리말과 일치하도록 주어진 단어를 이용하여 빈칸에 알맞은 말을 쓰시오.

(1) 어젯밤부터 비가 내렸다. (rain)

→ It _____ _____ since last night.

(2) 우리는 이 컴퓨터를 3년 동안 썼다. (use)

→ We _____ _____ this computer for three years.

(3) 너는 최근에 그를 본 적이 있니? (see)

→ _____ you _____ him lately?

**B1** 괄호 안에서 알맞은 것을 고르시오.

(1) I (bought, have bought) this washing machine just now.

(2) (Have you been, Did you go) to the baseball park yesterday?

(3) Lisa (stopped, has stopped) drawing pictures three years ago.

(4) Sean (arrived, has arrived) in New York last week.

(5) When (have you moved, did you move) to Seoul?

(6) What time (did you go, have you gone) to bed last night?

**B2** 어법상 어색한 부분을 찾아 문장을 다시 쓰시오.

(1) I begin to study English two years ago.

→ _____

(2) He has bought a new car last week.

→ _____

(3) Sam has taught me Korean last month.

→ _____

(4) I finish reading the novel an hour ago.

→ _____

(5) I have run into an old friend of mine yesterday.

→ _____

---

교과서 **pass** 통과하다  **headache** 두통  **finish** 끝내다, 마치다  **break** 깨다, 부수다  **ride** 타다  **washing machine** 세탁기
어휘 **run into** …와 우연히 만나다

## **C** 완료 / 경험

**1 완료:** '막 …했다'라는 뜻으로 과거에 시작된 행동이 현재에 완료되었음을 나타낸다.

- 완료 용법에서 자주 쓰이는 부사

| just 막, 방금 | already 이미 | yet 아직, 벌써 |
|---|---|---|

I **have** just **finished** watering the plants.
Tomas **hasn't done** his homework <u>yet</u>.
**Has** kate **arrived** at the airport <u>yet</u>?

**2 경험:** '…해 본 적이 있다'라는 뜻으로 과거에서 현재까지의 경험을 나타낸다.

- 경험 용법에서 자주 쓰이는 부사

| ever 지금까지, 언젠가 | never 결코 … 않다 | before 전에 |
|---|---|---|
| once 한 번 | twice 두 번 | … times …번 |

**Have** you <u>ever</u> **eaten** raw fish?
James **has been** to Rome <u>before</u>.
Emily **has heard** the song <u>once</u>.

> **Plus Grammar**
>
> **already와 yet**
> - already는 일반적으로 '이미, 벌써'란 뜻으로 긍정문에 쓰인다.
>   Jim has **already** finished the work. (Jim은 이미 일을 마쳤다.)
> - yet은 '아직'이란 뜻으로 부정문에 쓰이거나 '이미, 벌써'란 뜻으로 의문문에서 쓰인다.
>   Jim hasn't finished the work **yet**. (Jim은 아직 일을 마치지 못했다.)

## **D** 계속 / 결과

**1 계속:** '(지금까지) …해 왔다'라는 뜻으로 과거에 시작된 행동이나 상태가 현재까지 계속되고 있음을 나타낸다.

- 계속 용법에서 자주 쓰이는 부사(구)

| for … 동안 | since … 이후로 | how long 얼마나 오랫동안 |
|---|---|---|

They**'ve changed** a lot <u>since</u> last spring.
I **have known** him <u>for</u> three years.
How long **have** you **learned** Spanish?

> **Plus Grammar**
>
> **for**＋일정 기간
> **since**＋과거의 특정 시점
> Mike has studied Chinese **for** <u>three years</u>.
> Tom has been sad **since** <u>last evening</u>.

**2 결과:** '…해 버렸다 (그 결과 지금 …하다)'라는 뜻으로 과거의 행동이 현재 결과에 영향을 주고 있음을 나타낸다.

She **has left** for Italy. (So, she isn't here.)
Jack **has taken** my umbrella, so I don't have one.

*cf.* have been to : …에 가 본 적이 있다 / have gone to : …에 가고 없다
　　Mina **has been to** Europe. 〈경험〉
　　Mina **has gone to** Europe. 〈결과〉

> **Plus Grammar**
>
> have gone to는 '…에 가고 없다'라는 뜻이므로 1, 2인칭 주어와는 쓸 수 없다.

# Grammar Practice >

Answer p. 1

**C1** 밑줄 친 부분의 용법이 〈보기〉와 같으면 S, 다르면 D를 쓰시오.

〈보기〉
Have you ever spoken to a foreigner?

(1) I have just done the dishes. → _____
(2) Alice has been to Chicago. → _____
(3) He has broken his leg, so he can't play soccer. → _____

**C2** 우리말과 일치하도록 빈칸에 알맞은 말을 쓰시오.

(1) 우리는 이미 숙제를 다 했다.
   → We _____ already _____ our homework.
(2) Emily는 프랑스에 두 번 가 본 적이 있다.
   → Emily _____ _____ to France twice.
(3) Tom은 방금 새로운 휴대전화를 구입했다.
   → Tom _____ just _____ a new cell phone.
(4) 아무도 그 소설을 읽어 본 적이 없다.
   → Nobody _____ ever _____ the novel.

**C3** 밑줄 친 부분에 주의하여 문장을 우리말로 옮기시오.

(1) Mom has just come back home from the supermarket.
   → _____
(2) She has already read today's newspaper.
   → _____
(3) I haven't received a letter from him yet.
   → _____

**D1** 밑줄 친 부분의 용법을 〈보기〉에서 고르시오.

〈보기〉
ⓐ 계속        ⓑ 결과

(1) I have lost my textbook.
(2) Jimmy and Anna haven't visited us since last year.
(3) He has been a doctor for ten years.

**D2** 빈칸에 알맞은 말을 쓰시오.

(1) My brother has been sick _____ last Sunday.
(2) Jessica has studied Korean _____ seven years.

**D3** 두 문장이 같은 의미가 되도록 주어진 단어를 이용하여 빈칸에 알맞은 말을 쓰시오.

(1) Brad went to Japan, so he is not here.
   → Brad _____ _____ to Japan. (go)
(2) Jane grew melons last summer, and she still grows them.
   → Jane _____ _____ melons since last summer. (grow)
(3) I lost my camera, so I don't have one.
   → I _____ _____ my camera. (lose)
(4) My mom had a cold a week ago, and she is still sick.
   → My mom _____ _____ a cold for a week. (have)

---

교과서 어휘 ♪ water 물을 주다  airport 공항  raw 날것의  foreigner 외국인  do the dishes 설거지를 하다  receive 받다
have a cold 감기에 걸리다

# Grammar Test

**01** 빈칸에 알맞은 것은?

Yuri _____ a cold for a week.

① have          ② has          ③ having
④ has had       ⑤ has been had

**02** 빈칸에 공통으로 들어갈 말로 알맞은 것은?

- They _____ just fallen off the ladder.
- _____ you ever eaten carrot cakes?

① do           ② did          ③ have
④ are          ⑤ been

**03** 밑줄 친 단어의 형태가 바르게 짝지어진 것은?

- Uncle Joe is an author. He <u>write</u> many books since 2015.
- Hemingway was a great author. He <u>write</u> The Old Man and the Sea in 1952.

① write – wrote
② wrote – wrote
③ have written – write
④ has written – wrote
⑤ wrote – has written

서술형 평가

**04** 우리말과 일치하도록 빈칸에 알맞은 말을 쓰시오.

저 소녀를 본 적이 있니?

→ _____ you ever _____ that girl?

**05** 빈칸에 알맞지 <u>않은</u> 것은?

They have lived here _____.

① before         ② since 2017
③ all their lives   ④ for ten years
⑤ last year

서술형 평가

**06** 빈칸에 알맞은 말을 쓰시오.

A Has Erica visited the museum recently?

B _____, _____ _____. She has been very busy preparing for the exam. Perhaps she will visit there next month.

서술형 평가

**07** 주어진 문장을 괄호 안의 지시대로 바꿔 쓸 때 빈칸에 알맞은 말을 쓰시오.

(1) Jina has broken her arm. (의문문으로)
→ _____ her arm?

(2) David has fixed his bicycle. (부정문으로)
→ David _____ his bicycle.

**08** 괄호 안에서 알맞은 것을 고르시오.

- Andy is not here. He has (been, gone) to Disneyland.
- Tom has (been, gone) to Disneyland before. He wants to visit there again.

---

교과서  **fall off** …에서 떨어지다  **author** 작가  **all one's life** 평생, 일생 내내  **prepare for** …을 준비하다  **perhaps** 아마도
어휘  **fix** 수리하다, 고치다

**09** 어법상 어색한 것은?

① Have you ever driven a car?

② She has already read the poem.

③ Amanda has just done the work.

④ Somebody has eaten all my chocolates.

⑤ June has finished the report two hours ago.

**10** 〈보기〉의 밑줄 친 부분과 용법이 같은 것은?

> ─ 보기 ─
>
> Jane <u>has known</u> him for two years.

① I <u>have</u> already <u>made</u> a kite.

② Tom <u>has been</u> busy since last Monday.

③ My father <u>has been</u> to New York twice.

④ She <u>has cut</u> a lemon in half.

⑤ I <u>have</u> never <u>heard</u> about that test.

서술형 평가

**11** 두 문장을 한 문장으로 바꿔 쓸 때 빈칸에 알맞은 말을 쓰시오.

(1) Justin lost a new toy car. So he doesn't have it now.

→ Justin _____ _____ a new toy car.

(2) Katherine started to study Chinese two years ago. She still studies Chinese.

→ Katherine _____ _____ Chinese _____ two years.

서술형 평가

**12** 주어진 단어들을 이용하여 우리말을 영어로 옮기시오.

나는 작년부터 서울에서 살아 왔다. (live, since)

→ _____

서술형 평가

**13** 어법상 어색한 문장을 찾아 다시 쓰시오.

A I haven't seen Jane for a long time. Where is she?

B She has been to Paris to attend a design school.

A Really? Have you ever been to Paris?

B No, I haven't. I want to see her this summer.

_____

→ _____

**14** 밑줄 친 부분의 용법이 나머지와 <u>다른</u> 것은?

① I <u>have met</u> his older sister before.

② Mary <u>has</u> never <u>learned</u> how to cook.

③ They <u>have</u> just <u>bought</u> a new refrigerator.

④ <u>Have</u> you ever <u>read</u> any English novels?

⑤ I've <u>seen</u> elephants at the zoo many times.

교과서   **poem** 시   **report** 보고서   **kite** 연   **in half** 절반으로   **attend** 다니다; 참석하다
어휘

# Reading

[1~2] 다음을 끊어 읽고 ☑, 해석을 쓰시오. ✏️

**Voices in Our Mind**

Today, Bella looks down. Let's listen to Bella's feelings.

**Day 1**

3 **Anger**    I can't believe ✓ Jenny yelled at Bella ✓ after the school play.

**Sadness**    Well, ✓ that's because Bella ⓐ forgot her lines ✓ on stage.

**Joy**    I'm sure ✓ Jenny didn't mean to ⓑ hurt Bella. They've been best friends ✓ _____

6     elementary school.

**Fear**    I'm ⓒ worried ✓ that they are not going to be friends anymore.

**Day 2**

**Joy**    Whew! I'm so ⓓ depressed ✓ that they are talking again.

9 **Anger**    Yeah, ✓ Bella talked to Jenny first. It turns out Jenny didn't know ✓ how to ⓔ apologize.

**Fear**    I hope ✓ Bella doesn't have any more problems ✓ like this.

**Joy**    Just like this time, ✓ Bella will face the problems, ✓ solve them, ✓ and become wiser ✓ in the end.

**1** 밑줄 친 ⓐ-ⓔ 중 문맥상 의미가 어색한 것은?

① ⓐ      ② ⓑ      ③ ⓒ      ④ ⓓ      ⑤ ⓔ

**2** 빈칸에 알맞은 것은?

① for      ② about      ③ yet      ④ once      ⑤ since

교과서  **down** 우울한  **yell** 소리 지르다  **line** 대사  **stage** 무대  **turn out** …인 것으로 드러나다  **face** 직면하다  **solve** 해결하다
어휘🎧  **in the end** 결국

**3** Kogi에 관한 다음 글의 내용과 일치하지 <u>않는</u> 것은?

세계
문화

In America, food trucks **have become** very popular because people can easily start their own business with a small budget. Food trucks move around and sell a variety of food. One of the most popular food trucks, called Kogi, sells a mix of BBQ from Korea and food from Mexico. It actively uses social networking to spread information about their offerings and locations. Kogi **has won** recognition by winning several food awards.

① 매우 인기 있는 푸드 트럭 중 하나이다.　　② 한국식 바비큐와 멕시코 음식을 조합한 음식을 판다.
③ 누리소통망을 활발히 이용한다.　　④ 푸드 트럭 위치에 대한 정보는 제공하지 않는다.
⑤ 몇 가지 음식 관련 상을 받았다.

**4** 다음 글의 주제로 알맞은 것은?

취미

What do you do when you're stressed out? Everyone has their own way to relieve stress. For me, reading books is a very effective way to relax. Since I was young, reading interesting books **has helped** me reduce stress. It not only makes me feel comfortable and relaxed, but it also gives me a lot of useful information. Therefore, I recommend reading to blow off stress. Just ten minutes of reading is enough. Don't worry about what book to read. Any book is fine. So, if you're looking for a good way to reduce stress, just try reading a book.

① 좋은 책을 고르는 방법　　② 스트레스를 푸는 다양한 방식
③ 청소년들이 스트레스를 받는 원인　　④ 스트레스 해소에 도움이 되는 독서
⑤ 스트레스가 인체에 미치는 부정적인 영향

**3** budget 예산　mix 조합(물)　spread 퍼뜨리다　offering 팔 물건　recognition 인정
**4** relieve 완화하다　effective 효과적인　useful 유용한　recommend 추천하다　reduce 줄이다

# Expression

## 1 경험 묻고 답하기

💜 **경험 묻기**

- Have you (ever) seen cheetahs?
- Have you (ever) been to Paris?

💜 **경험 말하기**

- Yes, I have.
- No, I haven't. / No. I have never ....

## 2 계획 묻고 답하기

💜 **계획 묻기**

- What are you going(planning) to do?
- What will you do?
- Are you going to ...?
- Do you plan to ...?
- Do you have any plans?

💜 **계획 말하기**

- I'm going(planning) to ....
- I will ....
- I have a plan to ....

# Expression Test

Answer p. 2

서술형 평가

**1** 빈칸에 알맞은 말을 쓰시오.

A _____ you ever run a marathon?

B No, I haven't.

**2** 밑줄 친 부분과 바꿔 쓸 수 있는 것은?

A What are you going to do this weekend?

B I'm going to go to the movies.

① I went to the movies.

② I like to go to the movies.

③ I must go to the movies.

④ I can go to the movies.

⑤ I'm planning to go to the movies.

**3** 빈칸에 알맞지 <u>않은</u> 것은?

A Have you been to Singapore?

B _____

① Yes, I have.

② Yes, I've been there once.

③ No, I haven't.

④ No, I've never been there.

⑤ No, I haven't decided yet.

서술형 평가

**4** 우리말과 일치하도록 빈칸에 알맞은 말을 쓰시오.

A Kate, what are you _____ _____

_____ tomorrow?

(Kate, 내일 무엇을 할 계획이니?)

B I'm going to visit a museum.

**5** 밑줄 친 부분의 의미가 나머지와 <u>다른</u> 것은?

① I'm going to learn French.

② I'm going to the gym now.

③ I'm going to go to the concert.

④ I'm going to watch TV tonight.

⑤ I'm going to see a soccer match.

**6** 자연스러운 대화가 되도록 (A)-(D)를 바르게 배열한 것은?

(A) Have you ever been to Spain?

(B) That sounds interesting. I hope to go there someday.

(C) Yes, I have. I went there last year. I attended La Tomatina festival.

(D) No, I haven't. Have you?

① (A) – (B) – (C) – (D)

② (A) – (C) – (B) – (D)

③ (A) – (D) – (C) – (B)

④ (B) – (A) – (C) – (D)

⑤ (D) – (C) – (B) – (A)

# 서술형 평가

**1** 주어진 단어들을 이용하여 밑줄 친 우리말을 영어로 옮기시오.

> **A** Jisu, have you ever been to another country?
>
> **B** Yes, I have. I've been to Singapore with my parents.
>
> **A** When did you go there?
>
> **B** I went there last year. What about you? (1) 너는 다른 나라를 여행해 본 적이 있니? (have, ever, travel, to, another)
>
> **A** No, I haven't. But (2) 나는 언니와 함께 홍콩에 갈 예정이야. (be planning to, go, Hong Kong, with my sister)
>
> **B** Good for you. It will be a great experience.

(1) _____

(2) _____

**2** 주어진 단어를 이용하여 빈칸에 알맞은 말을 쓰시오.

(1)
> **A** How long has Andy studied in Paris?
>
> **B** He _____ _____ since 2017. (study)

(2)
> **A** Has Lisa finished her homework?
>
> **B** No, _____ _____. (have) She was so busy.

**3** 어법상 어색한 부분을 찾아 고쳐 쓰시오.

(1) He has skipped breakfast yesterday.

_____ → _____

(2) They have finished their history project last weekend.

_____ → _____

**4** 그림을 보고, 주어진 단어를 이용하여 문장을 완성하시오.

(1)

Oliver _____ his leg. (break)

(2)

Sophia _____ a letter to David. (write)

**5** 〈보기〉의 단어들을 이용하여 글을 완성하시오. (현재완료시제로 쓸 것)

보기

| raise | be | never | grow |
|---|---|---|---|

This is my pet dog, Lucy. I (1)_____ her since she was a year old. She was very little then. But now, she (2)_____ up. She is very cute and pretty. She is very healthy, too. She (3)_____ sick. I love Lucy very much.

# Final Test

Answer p. 3

난이도: 상 ★★★ 중 ★★ 하 ★

**★★**
**01** 영영풀이에 해당하는 것은?

> words that someone has to learn and say as part of a play or performance

① mean    ② reason    ③ line
④ fear    ⑤ mistake

**★★** 서술형 평가
**02** 빈칸에 알맞은 단어를 <보기>에서 골라 쓰시오.

> ┌ 보기 ┐
> avoid    hurt    forgive

(1) I don't want to _____ her feelings.

(2) I can't _____ that type of behavior.

(3) Mark left early to _____ the rush hour.

**★★**
**03** 짝지어진 대화가 <u>어색한</u> 것은?

① A Have you been to Paris?
   B No, I haven't.
② A What are you planning to do there?
   B I'm planning to go hiking.
③ A Have you ever seen a musical?
   B No. It's my favorite.
④ A Do you have any plans for this Sunday?
   B No, nothing special.
⑤ A Have you ever played baseball before?
   B Yes, I have.

**★**
**04** 빈칸에 알맞지 <u>않은</u> 것은?

> A Have you read *Pride and Prejudice*?
> B _____

① Yes, I have.
② No, I haven't.
③ No. I've never read it.
④ No. I'm not good at it.
⑤ Yes, but I didn't like it.

**★** 서술형 평가
**05** 주어진 단어들을 바르게 배열하여 문장을 완성하시오.

> A _____ Thai food before? (eaten, have, ever, you)
> B Yes, I have.

**★★** 서술형 평가
**06** 그림을 보고, 주어진 단어들을 이용하여 빈칸에 알맞은 말을 쓰시오. (형태 변화 가능)

> A What are you going to do next weekend?
> B I'm _____ for people in need. (plan, make, *gimchi*)

교과서 **performance** 공연   **behavior** 행동   **rush hour** 혼잡 시간대, 러시아워   **prejudice** 편견   **in need** 어려움에 처한
어휘🎧

**07** ★ 빈칸에 알맞지 <u>않은</u> 것은?

> **A** What are you planning to do tomorrow?
>
> **B** _____

① I have no special plan.
② I'm going to go to the bookstore.
③ I'm playing computer games now.
④ I will go to a concert with my sister.
⑤ I have a plan to meet my friends.

**08** ★★ 서술형 평가 자연스러운 대화가 되도록 A의 말에 이어질 (A)–(C) 의 순서를 바르게 배열하시오.

> **A** Have you ever seen a musical?
> (A) Sure, I'd love to.
> (B) I have two tickets for a famous musical. Would you like to go with me?
> (C) Yes, I have. I love musicals.

_____ → _____ → _____

**09** ★★ 시험에 잘 나오는 문제 밑줄 친 부분의 용법을 〈보기〉에서 고르시오.

> ┌─ 보기 ─────────────────────┐
> @ 완료    ⓑ 계속    ⓒ 경험    ⓓ 결과
> └──────────────────────────┘

(1) My mother <u>has</u> never <u>traveled</u> by air.
(2) Fred <u>has taken</u> a yoga class for four months.
(3) He <u>has</u> already <u>eaten</u> lunch in the school cafeteria.

**10** ★ 괄호 안에서 알맞은 것을 고르시오.

> (1) I (knew, have known) Julie since last year.
> (2) I (read, have read) comic books all day long yesterday.

**11** ★ 서술형 평가 밑줄 친 부분을 알맞은 형태로 바꿔 쓰시오.

> **A** Have you lost your dictionary?
> **B** Yes, I have. So I <u>buy</u> a new one last weekend.

→ _____

**12** ★★ 시험에 잘 나오는 문제 두 문장을 한 문장으로 바꿔 쓸 때 빈칸에 알맞은 것은?

> I left my lunchbox on the subway this morning. So I don't have it now.
> → I _____ my lunchbox on the subway.

① leave    ② had left    ③ am leaving
④ have left    ⑤ was leaving

**13** ★★ 밑줄 친 ①–⑤ 중 어법상 <u>어색한</u> 것은?

> **A** How long ①<u>have you been</u> sick?
> **B** I ②<u>have been</u> sick ③<u>since</u> Monday.
> **A** Then you ④<u>have been</u> sick ⑤<u>since</u> four days.

---

교과서   **bookstore** 서점   **cafeteria** 구내식당   **comic book** 만화책   **dictionary** 사전   **lunchbox** 도시락
어휘🎧

**14** 밑줄 친 부분의 용법이 나머지와 <u>다른</u> 것은?

① Bill <u>has broken</u> his leg before.

② <u>Has</u> Sam ever <u>swum</u> in the pool?

③ Helen <u>has been</u> to France twice.

④ She <u>has been</u> a teacher for thirteen years.

⑤ He <u>has</u> never <u>ridden</u> a camel.

**15** 빈칸에 알맞지 <u>않은</u> 것은?

Ms. Smith has owned this beautiful house _____.

① for two years          ② all her life

③ since last fall          ④ two years ago

⑤ since 2018

**16** 두 문장을 한 문장으로 바꿔 쓸 때 빈칸에 알맞은 말을 쓰시오.

John began to make his homepage two hours ago. He is still making it.

→ John _____ _____ _____ his homepage for two hours.

**17** 어법상 <u>어색한</u> 것은?

① When did you finish the work?

② I have run the restaurant for five years.

③ I visited an art museum last week.

④ She has practiced the piano since last year.

⑤ Have you taken a cruise several years ago?

**18** 주어진 단어의 형태가 바르게 짝지어진 것은?

• Last night Tommy and I (make) a plan for Lisa's birthday party.

• Tommy and I (meet) three times since last Friday.

① made – met

② made – meet

③ made – have met

④ have made – met

⑤ have made – have met

**19** 〈보기〉의 밑줄 친 부분과 용법이 같은 것은?

보기
Sue <u>has</u> just <u>bought</u> the sweater.

① He <u>has lost</u> his watch.

② The school bell <u>has</u> already <u>rung</u>.

③ I <u>have known</u> her since childhood.

④ Bob <u>has run</u> in a marathon before.

⑤ How many times <u>has</u> Brazil <u>won</u> the World Cup?

**20** 우리말을 영어로 바르게 옮긴 것은?

James는 작년 이후로 Susie를 좋아해 왔다.

① James likes Susie since last year.

② James liked Susie since last year.

③ James liked Susie for last year.

④ James has liked Susie for last year.

⑤ James has liked Susie since last year.

교과서 어휘  **pool** 수영장  **own** 소유하다  **homepage** (인터넷의) 홈페이지  **run** 운영하다  **cruise** 유람선 여행  **childhood** 어린 시절

**21** 밑줄 친 부분의 용법이 같으면 S, 다르면 D를 쓰시오.

(1) _____ (a) Elizabeth has had stomach problems since 2012.

(b) I have driven a car for six months.

(2) _____ (a) I have just finished my homework.

(b) Chris has never seen a rainbow.

서술형 평가

[22~23] 어법상 어색한 부분을 찾아 고쳐 쓰시오.

**22**

Joe has be playing computer games for more than two hours.

_____ → _____

**23**

Alice has yet written her science report.

_____ → _____

**24** 어법상 어색한 것은?

① The sun has been shining all day.

② Have you met your new neighbor yet?

③ I have gone to Australia.

④ How long has it been raining?

⑤ My mother learned how to bake cookies two months ago.

**25** (A)–(C)의 순서로 알맞은 것은?

Once upon a time, movies and toys had nothing to do with each other.

(A) As a result, the *Star Wars* movies have made $9 billion through the sale of movie products.

(B) George Lucas, the creator of the *Star Wars* series, made special deals with companies to produce movie toys, clothes, and other products.

(C) But things haven't been the same since *Star Wars* came along in 1977.

① (A) – (C) – (B)　　② (B) – (A) – (C)

③ (B) – (C) – (A)　　④ (C) – (A) – (B)

⑤ (C) – (B) – (A)

**26** 빈칸에 알맞은 것은?

I'm currently a volunteer for a project called *Habitat for All*. I have worked for the project for three years. We build houses for people in need. My team's job is to dig the ground and do a safety check. The physical work can be difficult at times. But it is a _____ to see people jump with joy when they see their new houses.

① pleasure　　② sadness

③ pressure　　④ pity

⑤ shame

---

교과서 **stomach** 위, 복부, 배　**rainbow** 무지개　**shine** 빛나다　**neighbor** 이웃　**have nothing to do with** …와 아무 관련이 없다
어휘 **billion** 10억　**deal** 거래, 합의　**volunteer** 자원봉사자　**dig** 파다

**[27~28] 다음을 읽고, 물음에 답하시오.**

For many years doctors have told people that exercising regularly is good for your health. But have you ever thought that working out can be harmful your health? A recent medical report has found proof that exercising too much can have damaging effects on the body. When we exercise, chemicals called endorphins are released into the brain. These endorphins energize the body, and give us a "high." People who exercise too much can become addicted to this "high." Doctors advise them to stop exercising too often. As an old saying goes, "_____"

★★
**27 빈칸에 알맞은 것은?**

① Blood is thicker than water.

② Rome was not built in a day.

③ Patience is the key to paradise.

④ Too much is as bad as too little.

⑤ Empty vessels make the most sound.

★★
**28 밑줄 친 부분과 용법이 같은 것은?**

① I have lost my bag in the bus.

② I have stayed in Rome for a year.

③ They have already finished their work.

④ I have been to the British Museum before.

⑤ Henry has broken a window.

**[29~30] 다음을 읽고, 물음에 답하시오.**

ⓐ Have you ever decided on buying a product just because of its brand name? Then you ⓑ might be affected by the halo effect. The halo effect means ⓒ that one positive impression of a thing can affect your opinion on its overall character, even if you ⓓ have never trying it. For example, if you are happy with your laptop computer, you are more likely ⓔ to buy a cell phone by the same company than one by another company. (A) This concept can be applied to people, too.

★★★
**29 밑줄 친 (A)의 내용에 해당하는 것은?**

① 현아: 주원이의 리더십이 부러워.

② 재민: 항상 친절한 민아와 친해지고 싶어.

③ 중기: 책임감이 강한 예서와 같은 팀이 되고 싶어.

④ 하나: 세미는 체력이 좋고 운동 신경도 뛰어난 것 같아.

⑤ 민지: 지훈이는 얼굴이 잘 생겨서인지 똑똑해 보이고 믿음이 가.

★★
**30 밑줄 친 ⓐ-ⓔ 중 어법상 어색한 것은?**

① ⓐ　　② ⓑ　　③ ⓒ　　④ ⓓ　　⑤ ⓔ

교과서　**harmful** 해로운　**proof** 증거　**damaging** 악영향을 주는　**chemical** 화학 물질　**release** 방출하다　**energize** 활기를 북돋우다
어휘　**high** 황홀감　**impression** 인상　**overall** 전반적인　**apply** 적용하다

**Grammar**

#### A 현재완료시제

**1 형태와 의미:** 과거에 일어난 일이 현재까지 영향을 미치고 있을 때 쓰는 시제로 〈have(has)+과거분사〉로 나타낸다.

Sally **has lived** in Seoul since 2018.

They **have worked** for a bank for three years.

**2 부정문과 의문문**

| 부정문 | have(has)+not+과거분사 |
|---|---|
| 의문문 | Have(Has)+주어+과거분사 ...?<br>– Yes, 주어+have(has). / No, 주어+haven't(hasn't). |

I **have not seen** Jason lately.

Mary **hasn't taken** tennis lessons since May.

**Has** your brother **passed** his driving test?

– Yes, he has. / No, he hasn't.

#### B 현재완료와 함께 쓸 수 없는 부사(구)

특정한 과거를 나타내는 부사(구)나 의문사 when, what time 등은 현재완료시제와 함께 쓸 수 없다.

| ago …전에 | last 지난 | then 그때 |
|---|---|---|
| yesterday 어제 | just now 지금 막 | |

They have moved here several years ago. (×)

→ They **moved** here several years **ago**. (O)

When have you taken a cooking class? (×)

→ **When did** you **take** a cooking class? (O)

28　Part I 실력 다지기

## C 완료 / 경험

**1 완료:** '막 …했다'라는 뜻으로 과거에 시작된 행동이 현재에 완료되었음을 나타낸다.

I **have** just **finished** watering the plants.

Tomas **hasn't done** his homework <u>yet</u>.

**2 경험:** '…해 본 적이 있다'라는 뜻으로 과거에서 현재까지의 경험을 나타낸다.

**Have** you <u>ever</u> **eaten** raw fish?

James **has been** to Rome <u>before</u>.

## D 계속 / 결과

**1 계속:** '(지금까지) …해 왔다'라는 뜻으로 과거에 시작된 행동이나 상태가 현재까지 계속되고 있음을 나타낸다.

They**'ve changed** a lot <u>since</u> last spring.

I **have known** him <u>for</u> three years.

**2 결과:** '…해 버렸다 (그 결과 지금 …하다)'라는 뜻으로 과거의 행동이 현재 결과에 영향을 주고 있음을 나타낸다.

She **has left** for Italy. (So, she isn't here.)

Jack **has taken** my umbrella, so I don't have one.

*cf.* have been to : …에 가 본 적이 있다 / have gone to : …에 가고 없다

Mina **has been to** Europe. 〈경험〉     Mina **has gone to** Europe. 〈결과〉

·········································· >> Expression

## 1 경험 묻고 답하기

❤ 경험 묻기
- Have you (ever) seen cheetahs?
- Have you (ever) been to Paris?

❤ 경험 말하기
- Yes, I have.
- No, I haven't. / No. I have never ….

## 2 계획 묻고 답하기

❤ 계획 묻기
- What are you going(planning) to do?
- What will you do?
- Are you going to …?
- Do you plan to …?
- Do you have any plans?

❤ 계획 말하기
- I'm going(planning) to ….
- I will ….
- I have a plan to ….

# Lesson 02

# 관계대명사

# Grammar Preview

## 1 관계대명사 who, which

- 관계대명사: 서로 관계있는 두 문장을 한 문장으로 연결해 주는 것으로, 두 문장을 연결하는 접속사와 대명사의 역할을 동시에 한다. 선행사의 종류와 관계대명사절에서의 역할에 따라 다른 형태를 쓴다.

| 선행사 \ 격 | 주격 | 목적격 | 소유격 |
|---|---|---|---|
| 사람 | who | who(m) | whose |
| 사물, 동물 | which | which | whose / of which |
| 사람, 사물, 동물 | that | that | – |

- 관계대명사 who: 선행사가 사람인 경우에 쓴다.
  Jane is a famous actress **who** has thousands of fans. 〈주격〉
  Edison is an inventor **who(m)** I admire. 〈목적격〉
  There is a carpenter **whose** wife is also a carpenter. 〈소유격〉

- 관계대명사 which: 선행사가 사물, 동물인 경우에 쓴다.
  These are the shoes **which** are too big for me. 〈주격〉
  Did you find the key **which** you lost yesterday? 〈목적격〉
  Look at the mountain **whose** top is covered with snow. 〈소유격〉

## 2 관계대명사 that, what

- 관계대명사 that: who와 which를 대신하여 선행사가 사람, 사물, 동물인 경우에 모두 쓸 수 있다. 주격과 목적격의 형태는 같으며, 소유격으로는 쓰이지 않는다.
  The man **that** lives next door works at the bank. 〈주격〉
  Peter returned the eraser **that** he borrowed yesterday. 〈목적격〉

- 관계대명사 what: 선행사를 포함하며, '…하는 것'이라는 뜻으로 명사절을 이끌어 문장 내에서 주어, 목적어, 보어의 역할을 한다. what은 the thing(s) which(that)로 바꿔 쓸 수 있다.
  **What** happened yesterday was my fault. 〈주어 역할〉
  Did you hear **what** I heard? 〈목적어 역할〉
  The important thing is not **what** he has. 〈보어 역할〉

## A 관계대명사

**1 관계대명사의 역할:** 서로 관계있는 두 문장을 한 문장으로 연결해 주는 것으로, 두 문장을 연결하는 접속사와 대명사의 역할을 동시에 한다.

> ① I helped the man. + He was very poor.
>            └ 동일인 ┘
> ② I helped the man **who** was very poor.
>      선행사 ←┘ 관계대명사 who: He를 대신하면서 앞의 절과 연결하는 역할
> ①의 두 문장은 the man과 He가 동일인이므로 서로 관계있는 문장이다.
> ②와 같이 관계대명사를 이용해 한 문장으로 나타낼 수 있으며, 이때 꾸밈을 받는 명사를 선행사라고 하고, 관계대명사절은 형용사 역할을 하므로 형용사절이 된다.

**2 관계대명사의 종류:** 선행사의 종류와 관계대명사절에서의 역할에 따라 다른 형태를 쓴다.

| 선행사 〰 격 | 주격 | 목적격 | 소유격 |
|---|---|---|---|
| 사람 | who | who(m) | whose |
| 사물, 동물 | which | which | whose / of which |
| 사람, 사물, 동물 | that | that | – |

## B 관계대명사 who

선행사가 사람인 경우에 쓴다. 관계대명사절에서 주어 역할을 하는 경우에는 who, 목적어 역할을 하는 경우에는 who(m), 소유 관계를 표시할 때는 whose를 쓴다.

Jane is a famous actress **who** has thousands of fans. 〈주격〉
     선행사(사람) └─┘

Edison is an inventor **who(m)** I admire. 〈목적격〉
     선행사(사람) └─┘

There is a carpenter **whose** wife is also a carpenter. 〈소유격〉
     선행사(사람) └─ whose: the carpenter's

> **✦ Plus Grammar**
> • whom은 문어적이어서 전치사 뒤에 오는 경우를 제외하면, whom 대신 who를 쓰는 경우가 많다.
> • 주격 관계대명사절의 동사는 선행사의 인칭과 수에 일치시킨다.
> I like Ms. Parker **who** teaches me English.

## C 관계대명사 which

선행사가 사물, 동물인 경우에 쓴다. 관계대명사절에서 주어, 목적어 역할을 하는 경우에는 which, 소유 관계를 표시할 때는 whose나 of which를 쓴다.

These are the shoes **which** are too big for me. 〈주격〉
     선행사(사물) └─┘

Did you find the key **which** you lost yesterday? 〈목적격〉
     선행사(사물) └─┘

Look at the mountain **whose** top is covered with snow. 〈소유격〉
     선행사(사물) └─ whose: the mountain's

= Look at the mountain **of which** the top is covered with snow.

= Look at the mountain the top **of which** is covered with snow.

# Grammar Practice >>

Answer p. 4

**A1** 관계대명사가 있으면 찾아서 밑줄을 그으시오.

(1) Which shoes are yours?

(2) I like girls whose eyes are blue.

(3) Jennifer likes that boy over there.

(4) Tommy will meet a girl who is his classmate.

(5) I saw a car which was really old.

(6) The pizza which I ate yesterday was delicious.

**B1** 밑줄 친 부분이 맞으면 ○표를 하고, 틀리면 바르게 고치시오.

(1) I have a friend who is a doctor.

(2) I like boys whose smile brightly.

(3) Julia is the woman whom I love most in the whole world.

**B2** 빈칸에 알맞은 말을 〈보기〉에서 골라 쓰시오.

┌─보기─────────────────┐
│   who    whose    whom   │
└───────────────────────┘

(1) Sam _____ dog gave birth to two babies is my neighbor.

(2) Mother Teresa was the nun _____ received the Nobel Prize.

(3) Mr. Smith is my math teacher _____ I like.

(4) This novel is about a girl _____ father is a firefighter.

(5) Jack will date the woman _____ he met last weekend.

**C1** 괄호 안에서 알맞은 것을 고르시오.

(1) There are lots of animals (which, whose, whom) live under the sea.

(2) This is my computer (which, whose, whom) is broken.

(3) The monkey (which, whom, whose) face looks funny is my pet.

(4) Look at that picture (which, whose, whom) I like very much.

(5) Tom bought a car (which, whose, whom) has a turbo engine.

(6) I'm looking for the building (which, whose, whom) roof is blue.

**C2** 두 문장을 한 문장으로 바꿔 쓸 때 빈칸에 알맞은 말을 쓰시오.

(1) The watch is brand new. You gave it to me yesterday.

→ The watch _____ you gave to me yesterday is brand new.

(2) We must protect wild animals. They are in danger.

→ We must protect wild animals _____ are in danger.

(3) We can't afford new cars. Their prices are too expensive.

→ We can't afford new cars _____ prices are too expensive.

(4) They live in a house. Its gate is green.

→ They live in a house _____ gate is green.

---

교과서 **poor** 가난한  **inventor** 발명가  **admire** 존경하다  **carpenter** 목수  **cover** 덮다  **give birth to** …을 낳다  **nun** 수녀
어휘 **protect** 보호하다  **wild animal** 야생 동물  **afford** (…을 할) 여유가 되다

### Ⓓ 관계대명사 that

**1** who와 which를 대신하여 선행사가 사람, 사물, 동물인 경우에 모두 쓸 수 있다.
주격과 목적격의 형태는 같으며, 소유격으로는 쓰이지 않는다.

The man **that** lives next door works at the bank. 〈주격〉
선행사(사람)

Peter returned the eraser **that** he borrowed yesterday. 〈목적격〉
선행사(사물)

*cf.* Give me the shirt that color is blue. (×)
→ Give me the shirt **whose** color is blue. (○)

**2** 항상 that이 쓰이는 경우

> 선행사가 -thing으로 끝나는 부정대명사일 때
> 선행사에 서수, 최상급, all, only, every 등이 포함되어 있을 때
> 선행사가 〈사람＋사물(동물)〉일 때

Everything **that** I told you was true.

He is the only man **that** can save the princess.

This is the tallest building **that** I have ever seen.

Look at the boy and the dog **that** are sleeping on the sofa.

> ● **Plus** Grammar
> **목적격 관계대명사의 생략**
> 목적격 관계대명사로 쓰인 who(m), which, that은 생략할 수 있다.
> The man (**whom**) I met was very rude.
> This is the ring (**that**) Elsa lost yesterday.

### Ⓔ 관계대명사 what

관계대명사 what은 선행사를 포함하며, '…하는 것'이라는 뜻으로 명사절을 이끌어
문장 내에서 주어, 목적어, 보어의 역할을 한다.

**What** happened yesterday was my fault. 〈주어 역할〉
what: 선행사＋주격 관계대명사

Did you hear **what** I heard? 〈목적어 역할〉
what: 선행사＋목적격 관계대명사

The important thing is not **what** he has. 〈보어 역할〉
what: 선행사＋목적격 관계대명사

*cf.* 관계대명사 what은 the thing(s) which(that)로 바꿔 쓸 수 있다.
Give me **what** you have in your bag.
→ Give me **the thing(s) which** you have in your bag.

> ● **Plus** Grammar
> 다른 관계대명사절은 선행사를 꾸미는 형용사절이지만, what이 이끄는 관계대명사절은 선행사를 포함하므로 명사절이다.

# Grammar Practice >

Answer p. 4

**D1** 괄호 안에서 알맞은 것을 고르시오.

(1) He has two sons (whom, that, which) are musicians.

(2) I want to buy the car (whom, whose, that) color is red.

(3) I like to eat food (who, whose, that) my mother cooks.

(4) I'll keep all the letters (whose, that, whom) you sent to me.

(5) He is the best student (that, who, whose) I have ever met.

**D2** 밑줄 친 부분을 어법에 맞게 고쳐 쓰시오.

(1) We bought everything which we need for the trip.

(2) Where are the boy and the dog who were running?

(3) This is my present of which I bought for you.

**D3** 두 문장을 한 문장으로 바꿔 쓸 때 빈칸에 알맞은 말을 쓰시오.

(1) It was the only movie. The director made it.
→ It was the only movie _____ the director made.

(2) The man won the match. The man is Sally's brother.
→ The man _____ is Sally's brother won the match.

(3) The glass is broken. I bought it last week.
→ The glass _____ I bought last week is broken.

**E1** 주어진 단어들을 배열하여 문장을 완성하시오.

(1) Write down _____ in a microscope. (saw, you, what)

(2) That's _____ last year. (I, what, wished)

(3) _____ made me cry. (said, what, he)

(4) _____ is a brilliant leader. (our country, what, needs)

(5) This story is _____ in his diary 10 years ago. (he, wrote, what)

(6) Never put off _____ today. (which, you, do, the things, can)

**E2** 밑줄 친 부분의 쓰임이 〈보기〉와 같으면 S, 다르면 D를 쓰시오.

┌─ 보기 ─────────────────────┐
│ What I want for my birthday is you. │
└────────────────────────────┘

(1) You had better do what you want to do. → _____

(2) I can't understand what is written here. → _____

(3) What he did was a mistake. → _____

(4) What a beautiful sight it is! → _____

(5) What color do you like? → _____

(6) What I dream of is to become a basketball player. → _____

교과서 **return** 돌려주다 **save** 구하다 **fault** 잘못 **musician** 음악가 **director** 감독 **match** 경기 **microscope** 현미경 **brilliant** 훌륭한
어휘 **put off** 미루다, 연기하다

# Grammar Test

>>

**01** 빈칸에 알맞은 것은?

> 내가 수미에게서 들은 것을 너에게 말해 줄게.
> → I'll tell you _____ I heard from Sumi.

① that    ② which    ③ what
④ whom    ⑤ whose

**02** 빈칸에 들어갈 말이 바르게 짝지어진 것은?

> • At first, I didn't like the boy _____ I met at the party.
> • This is a tree _____ leaves turn red and yellow in fall.

① which – that    ② who – what
③ which – which    ④ whom – whose
⑤ whose – that

서술형 평가

**03** 주어진 단어들을 배열하여 문장을 완성하시오.
  (1) These are the shoes _____.
      (buy, want, I, to, which)
  (2) I believe the words _____.
      (that, yesterday, said, she)
  (3) The person _____ most is his mother. (he, whom, respects)

서술형 평가

**04** 어법상 어색한 부분을 찾아 바르게 고치시오.

> He turned off the radio which volume was too high.

_____ → _____

서술형 평가

**05** 두 문장이 같은 의미가 되도록 빈칸에 알맞은 말을 쓰시오.

> Show me what you are keeping in your hand.
> = Show me _____ _____ _____ you are keeping in your hand.

**06** 〈보기〉의 밑줄 친 부분과 쓰임이 다른 것은?

> ┌─보기─
> There are many tourists that like Seoul.

① I lost the watch that was made in Italy.
② These are pears that grow on my farm.
③ The fact is that we don't have much time.
④ The man that they visited was their uncle.
⑤ He is the only person that remembers her face.

서술형 평가

**07** 두 문장을 한 문장으로 바꿔 쓸 때 빈칸에 알맞은 말을 쓰시오.
  (1) I know a man. His name is Brown.
      → I know a man _____ _____ is Brown.
  (2) The dog is very fast. It is running on the playground.
      → The dog _____ is running on the playground is very fast.

---

교과서   **respect** 존경하다   **turn off** 끄다   **tourist** 관광객   **pear** 배   **playground** 운동장
어휘 ♫

**08** 빈칸에 들어갈 말이 바르게 짝지어진 것은?

- The man _____ stole my purse was arrested.
- There are lots of animals _____ live on the land.
- He is the last man _____ can do the work in this company.

① who – who – who
② who – that – whose
③ who – which – that
④ which – which – who
⑤ which – who – that

서술형 평가

**09** 빈칸에 공통으로 들어갈 알맞은 말을 쓰시오.

- I think _____ the movie is very serious.
- He is the only man _____ I can trust.

서술형 평가

**10** 우리말과 일치하도록 빈칸에 알맞은 말을 쓰시오.

그녀는 표지가 매우 두꺼운 책을 가지고 있었다.

→ She had a book _____ _____ the cover was very thick.

**11** 빈칸에 that이 들어갈 수 <u>없는</u> 것은?

① The dish _____ I ordered was very delicious.
② This is the newest computer _____ you can buy in the shops.
③ He found a letter _____ was written in English.
④ A woman _____ name is June came to see me a few minutes ago.
⑤ My hobby is to collect coins _____ were used in America.

**12** 밑줄 친 부분이 어법상 <u>어색한</u> 것은?

① I have a brother <u>who</u> likes pets.
② Michael has a game CD <u>which</u> is very interesting.
③ Edward showed me all stamps <u>that</u> he collected.
④ Mina lives in the house <u>whose</u> roof is blue.
⑤ My present for you is <u>whom</u> you dreamed of.

서술형 평가

**13** 주어진 단어를 이용하여 두 문장을 한 문장으로 바꿔 쓰시오.

I don't believe the thing. My brother said the thing yesterday. (what)

→ _____

교과서 **purse** 지갑 **arrest** 체포하다 **serious** 진지한 **trust** 믿다, 신뢰하다 **dish** 요리 **collect** 모으다, 수집하다
어휘

# Reading

[1~2] 다음을 끊어 읽고 ☑, 해석을 쓰시오. ✎

**The Stone**

One day, Maibon saw a dwarf, Doli, trying to get his leg out from under a log. Maibon freed the

3 dwarf. "You'll have your reward. What do you want?" "I've heard ___(A)___ you have magic stones

___(B)___ can keep a man young. I want one." Doli handed him a magic stone and went away.

Maibon became happy that his beard didn't grow, but his wife got upset. "The eggs don't change

6 into chickens!" Maibon told her about the stone, and she told him to throw it away. He threw the

stone out the window. However, the next morning, he found the stone sitting by the window! He

then found out that his baby wasn't growing any teeth. Maibon began to worry. "There's nothing

9 to look forward to." Maibon tried to destroy the stone, but it kept coming back. Maibon saw the

dwarf again. "Why didn't you warn me about the stone? I want no more of it!" Doli explained how

to get rid of the stone. Maibon did as Doli said. When he arrived home, Maibon saw a tooth in

12 his baby's mouth. The eggs changed into chickens. Maibon was _____ of his long white beard.

**1** 빈칸 (A), (B)에 공통으로 들어갈 알맞은 말을 쓰시오.

_____

**2** 빈칸에 알맞은 것은?

① afraid      ② ashamed      ③ complaining      ④ aware      ⑤ proud

교과서 **dwarf** 난쟁이 **log** 통나무 **free** 풀어 주다, 빼내다 **reward** 보상 **beard** 수염 **throw** 던지다 **look forward to** …을 기대하다
어휘 **destroy** 파괴하다 **explain** 설명하다

Answer p. 5

**3** 다음 글의 내용과 일치하지 <u>않는</u> 것은?

동물

Koalas spend a lot of time eating. They eat only the leaves of eucalyptus trees. However, they cannot eat every kind of eucalyptus leaf. The leaves of some trees are poisonous, and some have an unpleasant taste. Koalas' large, sensitive noses help them pick the best leaves. The leaves give koalas all the water **that** they need. In fact, the name koala **which** comes from one of the languages of the Aborigines means *no drink*.

*Aborigine 오스트레일리아 원주민

① 코알라는 유칼립투스 잎만 먹는다.　　　② 독성이 있는 유칼립투스 잎이 있다.

③ 어떤 유칼립투스 잎은 불쾌한 맛이 난다.　　④ 코알라는 눈으로 최상의 잎을 골라낼 수 있다.

⑤ 유칼립투스 잎은 코알라가 필요로 하는 모든 수분을 제공한다.

**4** 필자가 주장하는 바로 알맞은 것은?

실험

In a famous experiment **that** began in 1968, children were given the choice of eating one marshmallow whenever they wanted or waiting for the researcher to return with two marshmallows. Participants **who** had the patience to wait were better able to handle the frustration **that** comes with failure. They went on to attend better colleges and have more rewarding careers. The lesson here is that good things come to those **who** wait. The fast, easy solution isn't always best. A little patience goes a long way in solving problems and achieving long-term success.

① 빠르고 쉬운 해결책을 찾아야 한다.　　　② 작은 일에도 끊임없이 의문을 던져야 한다.

③ 한꺼번에 많이 먹는 것은 건강에 좋지 않다.　④ 좋은 직업을 갖기 위해 지속적으로 노력해야 한다.

⑤ 장기적인 문제 해결을 위해서는 인내심을 가져야 한다.

---

3　**poisonous** 독성이 있는　**unpleasant** 불쾌한　**sensitive** 예민한, 민감한　**language** 언어

4　**experiment** 실험　**participant** 참가자　**patience** 인내심　**go a long way** …에 도움이 되다　**long-term** 장기적인

# Expression

## 1 금지하기 / 충고하기

🍎 금지하기

- Don't ....
- You must(should) not ....
- ... is not allowed.
- You are not allowed to ....
- You are not supposed to ....

🍎 충고하기

- Why don't you ...?
- You'd better ....
- (I think) You should(ought to) ....
- If I were you, I'd ....

## 2 동의하기 / 이의 제기하기

🍎 동의하기

- Me, too.
- Same here.
- Okay! / Good! / Fine! / Great!
- I agree.
- I couldn't agree more.
- I'm with you on that.
- That's a good idea.

🍎 이의 제기하기

- I don't think so.
- I don't believe so.
- I don't agree (with you).
- I'm against ....
- I'm not with you on that.

# Expression Test

Answer p. 6

**1** 빈칸에 알맞은 것은?

A You _____ take photos here.

B Oh! I'm sorry. I didn't know that.

① should     ② must     ③ may

④ shouldn't    ⑤ didn't

서술형 평가

**2** 우리말과 일치하도록 빈칸에 알맞은 말을 쓰시오.

A The music is so loud that Mom is very angry. You _____ _____ turn down the volume. (너는 소리를 줄이는 게 좋겠어.)

B I see.

**3** 밑줄 친 부분과 바꿔 쓸 수 있는 것은?

A I think Robert is good at computers.

B I agree with you. He knows many computer programs.

① I'm sorry but I can't.

② I don't need it.

③ I don't know that.

④ I couldn't agree more.

⑤ It doesn't make sense.

**4** 의도하는 바가 나머지와 <u>다른</u> 것은?

① You'd better go to bed early.

② I think you should go to bed early.

③ Why do you go to bed early?

④ If I were you, I'd go to bed early.

⑤ It might be a good idea to go to bed early.

**5** 빈칸에 알맞지 <u>않은</u> 것은?

A The Chinese restaurant is very good.

B _____ The food is delicious and waiters are very kind.

① I think so, too.

② That's right.

③ I agree with you.

④ You're wrong.

⑤ I'm with you on that.

서술형 평가

**6** 자연스러운 대화가 되도록 (A)–(D)를 바르게 배열하시오.

(A) Excuse me?

(B) You shouldn't take your umbrella into the museum.

(C) Could you put your umbrella here, please?

(D) Oh, I see.

_____ → _____ → _____ → _____

**1** 밑줄 친 단어들을 바르게 배열하여 대화를 완성하시오.

> A Hey, Lisa. I've got over a hundred comments for one of my SNS posts.
>
> B Oh, I wouldn't feel comfortable to share my posts with so many people.
>
> A Really? I think it's great that a lot of people see my posts.
>
> B I am, that, on, with, not, you. I only want to share my posts with close friends.

_____

**2** 관계대명사를 이용하여 두 문장을 한 문장으로 바꿔 쓰시오.

(1) I'll take my camera. I bought it yesterday.

→ _____

(2) I saw a man. His costume was very unique.

→ _____

**3** 표를 보고, 관계대명사를 이용하여 문장을 완성하시오.

| 인물 | 직업 | 업적 |
|---|---|---|
| Thomas Edison | inventor | He invented the light bulb. It brightens the darkness. |

(1) Thomas Edison is the inventor

_____.

(2) We can work at night thanks to the light bulb _____.

**4** 그림을 보고, 주어진 단어들을 배열하여 문장을 완성하시오.

(1)

Jane is _____ soft and chewy. (that, making, are, cookies)

(2)

Bob is an artist _____.
(draws, beautiful scenery, who)

**5** 밑줄 친 ①-⑤ 중 어법상 어색한 것을 찾아 바르게 고쳐 쓰시오.

> One day, Mrs. Johnson said to her son, "You just sit around, ① play computer games and watch TV all day. That's not ② that you should do. You should ③ spend more time enjoying the nice summer weather. There are a lot of things ④ who you can do outdoors." Then, her son said, "I don't want ⑤ to get tanned."

( ) _____ → _____

( ) _____ → _____

★★
**01** 영영풀이에 해당하는 것은?

> to damage something so badly that it no longer exists or cannot be used

① show　　② hand　　③ change
④ destroy　　⑤ throw

★★ 서술형 평가
**02** 빈칸에 공통으로 들어갈 알맞은 말을 쓰시오.

- Put your _____ up if you know the answer.
- Give me a _____ with this ladder.
- Please _____ me the book.

★
**03** 의도하는 바가 나머지와 다른 것은?

① I agree.
② I'm with you on that.
③ I think so, too.
④ I couldn't agree more.
⑤ I'm afraid you're wrong.

★★
**04** 빈칸에 알맞은 것은?

> A I borrowed Mike's book, but I lost it. What do you think I should do?
> B I think _____.

① I have to thank him
② you should not buy it for him
③ you should say sorry to him
④ I don't need to say sorry to him
⑤ you need to borrow one more

★★
**05** 걱정거리와 그에 대한 충고가 <u>잘못</u> 연결된 것은?

① I feel very cold.
　→ You'd better drink some warm milk.
② I had a quarrel with my best friend.
　→ If I were you, I'd say, "I'm sorry."
③ I don't know what to buy for Sue's birthday.
　→ Shall we go to Sue's birthday party?
④ I lost Jacob's dictionary.
　→ I advise you to buy him a new one.
⑤ I have nothing to do in my free time.
　→ I think you should find a hobby.

★★ 서술형 평가
**06** 그림을 보고, 주어진 단어들을 이용하여 빈칸에 알맞은 말을 쓰시오.

A There are so many famous paintings here. Let's take pictures of them.
B Wait, Nick. Didn't you see the sign?
A What sign?
B That one over there. You _____ _____ _____ _____ here.
(should, take, photos)
A Oh, I didn't know that.

교과서 **damage** 훼손하다　**exist** 존재하다　**ladder** 사다리　**quarrel** 다툼, 언쟁　**advise** 충고하다　**sign** 표지판
어휘🎧

# Final Test

**07** 서술형 평가

빈칸에 알맞은 말을 쓰시오.

A What do you think of Jane?

B I think she is very kind. What about you?

A I _____ with you. She often helps her friends.

**08** 밑줄 친 우리말을 영어로 바르게 옮긴 것은?

A Can I swim here?

B No. 여기서 수영은 허용되지 않습니다.

① You must swim here.

② You ought to swim here.

③ You're allowed to swim here.

④ You're supposed to swim here.

⑤ You're not allowed to swim here.

[09~10] 빈칸에 알맞은 것을 고르시오.

**09**

He is the writer _____ book won a prize last year.

① which ② that ③ what

④ whose ⑤ whom

**10**

_____ he cooked yesterday was very delicious.

① That ② What ③ Which

④ Who ⑤ Whom

**11** 서술형 평가

밑줄 친 부분을 바르게 고치시오.

Look at the girl and the dog <u>which</u> are taking a walk in the park.

→ _____

**12** 밑줄 친 부분과 공통으로 바꿔 쓸 수 있는 것은?

• I have a friend <u>who</u> is good at math.

• Did you see the letter <u>which</u> came yesterday?

① that ② what ③ whose

④ whom ⑤ of which

**13** 서술형 평가

우리말과 일치하도록 빈칸에 알맞은 말을 쓰시오.

당신이 그녀에 대해 아는 모든 것을 저에게 말해 주세요.

→ Please tell me everything _____ _____ _____ about her.

**14** 서술형 평가

어법상 어색한 부분을 찾아 바르게 고치시오.

There are many people who is good at many things.

_____ → _____

교과서 어휘 🎧  **prize** 상  **take a walk** 산책하다  **be good at** …을 잘하다

**15** 빈칸에 공통으로 들어갈 알맞은 말을 쓰시오.

서술형 평가

- _____ do you like better, cats or dogs?
- Find the word _____ has two different meanings.

**16** 밑줄 친 부분의 쓰임이 나머지와 다른 것은?

시험에 잘 나오는 문제

① Who do you want to meet?
② He is the boy who is honest.
③ I met the woman who came from France.
④ He is the driver who works hard.
⑤ Look at the girl who is singing very well.

[17~18] 관계대명사 which(that)가 들어갈 알맞은 위치를 고르시오.

**17**

The cat ① I ② bought ③ was ④ a Persian ⑤ cat.

**18**

Barbara ① works ② for a company ③ makes ④ washing ⑤ machines.

**19** that의 쓰임이 어색한 것은?

① He scolded the boy that broke the vase.
② This is that I don't understand well.
③ Is there anything that I can do?
④ The boy that sits next to Mary is Sam.
⑤ I know a girl that plays soccer.

**20** 밑줄 친 부분 중 어법상 어색한 것은?

① I have a friend who has a baby sister.
② That's the girl whom I like most in my class.
③ I like the girl who is sitting on the bench.
④ The man whom was singing looked happy.
⑤ He is the only man that she has ever loved.

**21** 〈보기〉의 밑줄 친 부분과 쓰임이 같은 것은?

시험에 잘 나오는 문제

/보기/
This is the nicest seashore that I've ever seen.

① I think that boy is smart.
② Joe said that he was unhappy.
③ Everything that Jason said was false.
④ It is a pity that he couldn't sleep enough.
⑤ The problem is that I can't remember her.

교과서 **meaning** 의미, 뜻  **scold** 꾸짖다  **vase** 꽃병  **seashore** 해변, 해안  **false** 틀린  **pity** 유감
어휘

★★★
## 22 어법상 옳은 것은?

① The doll I loved was stolen.

② I lost the bag what I bought last week.

③ He met the woman whom wrote this novel.

④ The bus which it goes to the airport hasn't come.

⑤ Eric was surprised at the news what he heard yesterday.

★★
## 23 우리말을 영어로 바르게 옮긴 것은?

저것이 그녀가 사고 싶어 하는 것이니?

① Is that she wants to buy?

② Is that what she wants to buy?

③ Is that which she wants to buy?

④ Is that of which she wants to buy?

⑤ Is that what does she want to buy?

★★★
## 24 어법상 어색한 것은?

① I like the earrings which you are wearing.

② He is the last man which came here.

③ I have a goldfish which looks pretty.

④ The car which he wants to buy is very expensive.

⑤ English is a language which is used all over the world.

★★
## 25 ⓐ–ⓔ중 글의 흐름에 어울리지 않는 것은?

ⓐThere are many advantages that wind energy has. ⓑFirst, unlike fossil fuels, wind is an unlimited, free and renewable resource. ⓒWind power is also a clean form of energy since it does not make gases that cause air pollution. ⓓIn addition, wind energy creates jobs in manufacturing, installation and supporting services. ⓔWind energy has been a threat to wildlife because birds are often killed by flying into spinning wind turbine.

① ⓐ    ② ⓑ    ③ ⓒ    ④ ⓓ    ⑤ ⓔ

★★
## 26 빈칸에 알맞은 것은?

Robots do various jobs nowadays. Robot vacuums clean the house from bottom to top. Some robots put together electronic devices. Other robots are used for jobs that are too difficult or too dangerous for humans. _____, they were used to explore the planet Mars, to investigate the interior of the great pyramids in Egypt, and to search the wreckage of the World Trade Center in New York City.

① In addition     ② Nevertheless

③ For example     ④ However

⑤ On the other hand

---

교과서 **advantage** 장점 **fossil fuel** 화석 연료 **unlimited** 무제한의 **renewable** 재생 가능한 **resource** 자원 **cause** 유발하다
어휘 **air pollution** 대기 오염 **threat** 위협 **investigate** 조사하다 **wreckage** 잔해

[27~28] 다음을 읽고, 물음에 답하시오.

Many children today start watching educational videos before they are two years old. But research shows that babies learn best from interacting with others. Videos cannot provide them with this kind of interaction. Also, rapid scene changes and bright colors ___(A)___ are typical in educational videos may negatively affect the development of a baby's attention. In addition, children ___(B)___ watched violent videos at an early age are more likely to have difficulty concentrating as they get older.

★
**27** 위 글의 주제로 알맞은 것은?

① 유아에게 적합한 비디오 시청 시간
② 유아에게 비디오 시청이 필요한 이유
③ 연령별 적절한 비디오를 고르는 법
④ 집중력 향상에 도움이 되는 비디오
⑤ 비디오 시청이 유아에게 미치는 부정적 영향

★★
**28** 빈칸 (A)와 (B)에 들어갈 말이 바르게 짝지어진 것은?

① who – who          ② which – who
③ that – whom        ④ which – whose
⑤ that – whose

[29~30] 다음을 읽고, 물음에 답하시오.

There are some awesome animals _____ exist only in and around the Galapagos Islands. Locusts are similar to grasshoppers since both of them share a great jumping ability. But locusts in Galapagos can leap about 3 meters, and this ability can be helpful when escaping from predators. Galapagos penguins are the only penguins _____ reside in the Northern Hemisphere. They've found their own creative ways to adapt to their isolated habitat. They build their nests with lava rocks!          *locust 황충  *hemisphere 반구

★★
**29** 위 글의 내용과 일치하지 <u>않는</u> 것은?

① 갈라파고스 황충은 3미터 가까이 뛰어오를 수 있다.
② 갈라파고스 황충의 점프력은 포식자로부터 도망갈 때 유용하다.
③ 갈라파고스 펭귄은 북반구에 서식하는 여러 펭귄들 중 하나이다.
④ 갈라파고스 펭귄은 서식지에 적응하기 위한 방법을 찾아냈다.
⑤ 갈라파고스 펭귄은 화산암으로 둥지를 만든다.

★★
**30** 빈칸에 공통으로 들어갈 말로 알맞은 것은?

① who          ② whom          ③ which
④ that          ⑤ what

교과서 **interact** 상호 작용을 하다  **development** 발달  **attention** 주의 (집중)  **violent** 폭력적인  **concentrate** 집중하다  **escape** 탈출하다
어휘 ∩  **predator** 포식자  **adapt** 적응하다

### A 관계대명사

**1 관계대명사의 역할:** 서로 관계있는 두 문장을 한 문장으로 연결해 주는 것으로, 두 문장을 연결하는 접속사와 대명사의 역할을 동시에 한다.

> ① I helped the man. + He was very poor.
>          └─ 동일인 ─┘
> ② I helped the man **who** was very poor.
>        선행사 └─── 관계대명사 who: He를 대신하면서 앞의 절과 연결하는 역할
> ①의 두 문장은 the man과 He가 동일인이므로 서로 관계있는 문장이다.
> ②와 같이 관계대명사를 이용해 한 문장으로 나타낼 수 있으며, 이때 꾸밈을 받는 명사를 선행사라고 하고, 관계대명사절은 형용사 역할을 하므로 형용사절이 된다.

**2 관계대명사의 종류**

| 선행사＼격 | 주격 | 목적격 | 소유격 |
|---|---|---|---|
| 사람 | who | who(m) | whose |
| 사물, 동물 | which | which | whose / of which |
| 사람, 사물, 동물 | that | that | – |

### B 관계대명사 who

선행사가 사람인 경우에 쓴다. 관계대명사절에서 주어 역할을 하는 경우에는 who, 목적어 역할을 하는 경우에는 who(m), 소유 관계를 표시할 때는 whose를 쓴다.

Jane is a famous actress **who** has thousands of fans. 〈주격〉
Edison is an inventor **who(m)** I admire. 〈목적격〉
There is a carpenter **whose** wife is also a carpenter. 〈소유격〉

### C 관계대명사 which

선행사가 사물, 동물인 경우에 쓴다. 관계대명사절에서 주어, 목적어 역할을 하는 경우에는 which, 소유 관계를 표시할 때는 whose나 of which를 쓴다.

These are the shoes **which** are too big for me. 〈주격〉
Did you find the key **which** you lost yesterday? 〈목적격〉
Look at the mountain **whose** top is covered with snow. 〈소유격〉
= Look at the mountain **of which** the top is covered with snow.
= Look at the mountain the top **of which** is covered with snow.

**D** 관계대명사 that

**1** who와 which를 대신하여 선행사가 사람, 사물, 동물인 경우에 모두 쓸 수 있다.
주격과 목적격의 형태는 같으며, 소유격으로는 쓰이지 않는다.
The man **that** lives next door works at the bank. 〈주격〉
Peter returned the eraser **that** he borrowed yesterday. 〈목적격〉

**2** 항상 that이 쓰이는 경우

> 선행사가 -thing으로 끝나는 부정대명사일 때
> 선행사에 서수, 최상급, all, only, every 등이 포함되어 있을 때
> 선행사가 〈사람＋사물(동물)〉일 때

**E** 관계대명사 what

관계대명사 what은 선행사를 포함하며, '…하는 것'이라는 뜻으로 명사절을 이끌어
문장 내에서 주어, 목적어, 보어의 역할을 한다.
**What** happened yesterday was my fault. 〈주어 역할〉
Did you hear **what** I heard? 〈목적어 역할〉
The important thing is not **what** he has. 〈보어 역할〉
*cf.* 관계대명사 what은 the thing(s) which(that)로 바꿔 쓸 수 있다.

**≫ Expression**

## 1 금지하기 / 충고하기

❤ 금지하기
- Don't ....
- You must(should) not ....
- ... is not allowed.
- You are not allowed to ....
- You are not supposed to ....

❤ 충고하기
- Why don't you ...?
- You'd better ....
- (I think) You should(ought to) ....
- If I were you, I'd ....

## 2 동의하기 / 이의 제기하기

❤ 동의하기
- Me, too.
- Same here.
- Okay! / Good! / Fine! / Great!
- I agree.
- I couldn't agree more.
- I'm with you on that.
- That's a good idea.

❤ 이의 제기하기
- I don't think so.
- I don't believe so.
- I don't agree (with you).
- I'm against ....
- I'm not with you on that.

# Lesson 03

# 명사, 대명사

# Grammar Preview

## ❶ 명사, 관사

• 명사의 종류와 수량 표현

| 셀 수 있는 명사 | a(an)를 붙이거나 복수로 쓸 수 있다. many, (a) few 등의 형용사로 꾸민다. | There are three **books** on the desk. Jessica typed in **a few words**. |
|---|---|---|
| 셀 수 없는 명사 | a(an)를 붙이거나 복수로 쓰지 않는다. much, (a) little 등의 형용사로 꾸민다. | **Love** cannot be bought with **money**. There was **little doubt** in my mind. |

• 부정관사 a(an) / 정관사 the

| 부정관사 a(an) | 셀 수 있는 단수명사 앞에 온다. 정해지지 않은 막연한 것을 가리킨다. | We have **a** problem. They bought **an** umbrella. |
|---|---|---|
| 정관사 the | 특정한 것을 가리키는 명사 앞에 온다. | That is an album. **The** album is expensive. |

• 관사를 쓰지 않는 경우

| play + 운동경기 | play baseball | 식사·과목·나라 앞 | lunch, math, Korea |
|---|---|---|---|
| by + 교통수단 | by subway | 건물이 본래의 목적으로 쓰일 때 | go to school |

## ❷ 대명사

• 재귀대명사: 인칭대명사에 -self나 -selves를 붙여서 '…자신(들)'이라는 뜻을 나타낸다.
  The players are proud of **themselves**. 〈재귀 용법〉
  Yuri **herself** thinks that she is very pretty. 〈강조 용법〉

• 부정대명사 one: 앞에 나온 명사와 같은 종류의 불특정한 것을 가리킨다.

• one, other, another

| one / the other | (둘 중) 하나 / 나머지 하나 |
|---|---|
| one / another / the other | (셋 중) 하나 / 또 다른 하나 / 나머지 하나 |
| one / the others | (여럿 중) 하나 / 나머지 모두 |
| some / others | (여럿 중) 어떤 것들 / 또 다른 어떤 것들 |
| some / the others | (여럿 중) 어떤 것들 / 나머지 모두 |

• all, each

| all | 모든 것(사람), 모두 | 대명사, 형용사 | 뒤에 복수명사가 오면 복수 취급 뒤에 단수명사가 오면 단수 취급 |
|---|---|---|---|
| each | 각각(의) | 대명사, 형용사 | 단수명사와 함께 쓰임 / 단수 취급 |

# 1 명사, 관사

## A 명사의 종류와 수량 표현

**1 셀 수 있는 명사**: a(an)를 붙일 수 있고, 복수 형태로 쓸 수 있다. many, (a) few 등의 형용사로 꾸민다.

There are three **books** on the desk.

Jessica typed in **a few words**.

**2 셀 수 없는 명사**: a(an)를 붙일 수 없고, 복수 형태로 쓸 수 없다. much, (a) little 등의 형용사로 꾸민다.

| 고유명사 | 사람, 나라, 바다, 요일 등 고유한 이름 | Edison, January, Seoul |
| 물질명사 | 일정한 형태가 없거나 작아서 셀 수 없는 것 | sugar, bread, water |
| 추상명사 | 보거나 셀 수 없는 추상적인 개념 | love, peace, happiness |

**Love** cannot be bought with **money**.

There was **little doubt** in my mind.

> **● Plus Grammar**
> · 물질명사는 용기나 단위 등을 나타내는 말을 이용하여 수량을 표현한다.
> **a glass of** water
> **a piece of** paper
> **a slice of** bread
> · 두 개가 하나의 쌍을 이루는 명사(pants, shoes, socks 등)의 수량은 a pair of로 표현한다.
> **a pair of** gloves
> **two pairs of** shoes

## B 부정관사 a[an] / 정관사 the

**1 부정관사 a(an)**: 셀 수 있는 단수명사 앞에 오며 정해지지 않은 막연한 것을 가리킨다. 뒤에 오는 단어의 첫 발음이 자음일 때는 a, 모음일 때는 an을 쓴다.

We have **a** problem.　　　　　　He wears **a** uniform.

They bought **an** umbrella.　　　Amy is **an** honest girl.
　　　　　　　　　　　　　　　　　　　　　 h는 묵음

> **● Plus Grammar**
> 묵음은 문자상으로는 드러나지만 실제 발음이 되지 않는 음이다.
> <u>h</u>onest, <u>k</u>now, <u>k</u>nife, clim<u>b</u>, com<u>b</u>, <u>h</u>onor, We<u>d</u>nesday 등

**2 정관사 the**: 특정한 것을 가리키는 명사 앞에 온다. 뒤에 오는 단어의 첫 발음이 자음일 때는 [ðə], 모음일 때는 [ði]로 발음된다.

| 앞에 나온 명사를 다시 말할 때 | That is an album. **The** album is expensive. |
| 서로가 알고 있는 대상을 뜻할 때 | Please sit on **the** chair. |
| 세상에 하나밖에 없는 것 앞 | **The** Earth is round. |
| 연주하는 악기 이름 앞 | My younger brother plays **the** piano. |
| 수식어구가 명사를 꾸밀 때 | **The** cat on the bench is very cute. |

> **● Plus Grammar**
> · 세상에 하나밖에 없는 것
> the sun, the moon, the sea, the Earth, the world, the universe 등
> · 아침, 점심, 저녁을 나타낼 때 관용적으로 the를 쓴다.
> in the morning (아침에)
> in the afternoon (점심에)
> in the evening (저녁에)

## C 관사를 쓰지 않는 경우

| play+운동경기 | play baseball, play basketball, play soccer |
| by+교통수단 | by subway, by bus, by bicycle |
| 식사 · 과목 앞 | breakfast, lunch, dinner, science, math |
| 나라 · 도시 · 사람 이름 앞 | Korea, England, Seoul, Paris, Jim, Amy |
| 소유격과 함께 쓰인 명사 앞 | my car, his desk, her pen |
| 건물 · 장소가 본래의 목적으로 쓰일 때 | go to school, go to church |

Chris plays **baseball** on Saturday.　　　I eat **breakfast** at 7:30.

# Grammar Practice >

Answer p. 8

**A1** 밑줄 친 부분을 바르게 고쳐 쓰시오.

(1) How about buying these shoe?

(2) I look for a woman with intelligence and a beauty.

(3) Is there any waters in the pot?

(4) We don't have many milk in the refrigerator.

(5) John has few hair on his head.

**A2** 주어진 문장을 바꿔 쓸 때 빈칸에 알맞은 말을 쓰시오.

(1) They need a bottle of red wine.

→ They need three _____ _____ red wine.

(2) Please hand me a piece of paper.

→ Please hand me thirteen _____ _____ _____.

(3) I want to buy a pair of hiking boots.

→ I want to buy two _____ _____ hiking boots.

**B1** 괄호 안에서 알맞은 것을 고르시오.

(1) He likes swimming in (a, the) sea.

(2) I always exercise in (a, the) morning.

(3) This is (a, an) exciting movie.

(4) Ms. White always wears (a, an) uniform.

(5) Anna plays (a, the) violin very well.

(6) (A, The) bag on my desk is very big.

(7) Bill visits his grandmother once (a, an) week.

**B2** 빈칸에 a(an) 또는 the를 쓰시오.

(1) My mom has _____ pretty hat.

(2) My brother is _____ English teacher.

(3) _____ sun rises in the east.

(4) He studies at _____ university.

(5) _____ girls in this class are smart.

(6) It takes _____ hour and _____ half.

(7) My father plays _____ guitar for me.

(8) Please open _____ door.

**C1** 밑줄 친 부분을 바르게 고쳐 쓰시오.

(1) I go to the beach by a train.

(2) I have the lunch at 12.

(3) It is a her doll.

(4) Mary goes to the school from Monday to Friday.

(5) I play the soccer every day.

**C2** 빈칸에 알맞은 관사를 쓰고, 필요 없는 경우에는 ×를 쓰시오.

(1) I like _____ my aunt.

(2) That is _____ good idea.

(3) My favorite subject is _____ math.

(4) I eat _____ dinner at 8 p.m.

(5) Are you in _____ Seoul now?

(6) We play _____ basketball after school.

(7) Let's go by _____ subway.

---

교과서 어휘 **type in** 입력하다 **doubt** 의심 **uniform** 제복, 교복 **intelligence** 지성, 지혜 **rise** 뜨다, 올라가다

### D 재귀대명사

**1 의미와 형태:** 인칭대명사에 -self나 -selves를 붙여서 '…자신(들)'이라는 뜻을 나타낸다.

| | 단수 | 재귀대명사 | 복수 | 재귀대명사 |
|---|---|---|---|---|
| 1인칭 | I | myself | we | ourselves |
| 2인칭 | you | yourself | you | yourselves |
| 3인칭 | he | himself | | |
| | she | herself | they | themselves |
| | it | itself | | |

> **Plus Grammar**
>
> **재귀대명사의 관용 표현**
> • by oneself: 혼자서 (= alone)
> • for oneself: 혼자 힘으로
> • of itself: 저절로
> • in itself: 본질적으로
> • enjoy oneself: 즐거운 시간을 보내다
> • beside oneself: 제정신이 아닌
> • between ourselves: 우리끼리 이야기지만

**2 용법**

• 재귀 용법: 문장의 주어와 목적어가 같을 때 목적어를 대신하여 쓰며 생략할 수 없다.

The players are proud of **themselves**.

• 강조 용법: 강조하고자 하는 말 뒤나 문장의 맨 끝에 쓰며 생략할 수 있다.

Yuri **herself** thinks that she is very pretty.

### E 부정대명사

**1 one:** 앞에 나온 명사와 같은 종류의 불특정한 것을 가리킨다.

This cup is dirty. Can I have a clean **one**?

Don't buy those oranges. Buy these **ones**. 〈복수형〉

**2 one, other, another**

| one / the other | (둘 중) 하나 / 나머지 하나 |
|---|---|
| one / another / the other | (셋 중) 하나 / 또 다른 하나 / 나머지 하나 |
| one / the others | (여럿 중) 하나 / 나머지 모두 |
| some / others | (여럿 중) 어떤 것들 / 또 다른 어떤 것들 |
| some / the others | (여럿 중) 어떤 것들 / 나머지 모두 |

> **Plus Grammar**
>
> **부정대명사 one vs. 대명사 it**
> one은 앞에 나온 명사와 같은 종류의 불특정한 것을, it은 앞에 나온 바로 그것을 가리킨다.
> Anna bought a pen. She liked it very much. (동일한 사물)
> Anna lost the pen. She had to buy a new one. (동일한 종류의 불특정한 사물)

There are two boxes. **One** of them weighs 1 kg more than **the other**.

I have been to three countries. **One** is America, **another** is China, and **the other** is England.

**Some** people live in the city, while **others** don't.

**3 all, each**

| all | 모든 것(사람), 모두 | 대명사, 형용사 | 뒤에 복수명사가 오면 복수 취급<br>뒤에 단수명사가 오면 단수 취급 |
|---|---|---|---|
| each | 각각(의) | 대명사, 형용사 | 단수명사와 함께 쓰임 / 단수 취급 |

> **Plus Grammar**
>
> every는 '모든, …마다'의 뜻으로 단수명사와 함께 쓰여 단수 취급한다.
> **Every** dog **has** his day.

**All** (of) the students <u>were</u> excited.     **Each** person <u>has</u> different looks.

# Grammar Practice >

Answer p. 8

**D1** 밑줄 친 부분의 쓰임이 같으면 S, 다르면 D를 쓰시오.

(1) _____ (a) He thinks himself a poet.

　　　　　 (b) She wrote the song herself.

(2) _____ (a) Tommy himself packed the package.

　　　　　 (b) Anna drove the school bus herself.

(3) _____ (a) Did you hurt yourself?

　　　　　 (b) The old man made this toy ship himself.

**D2** 빈칸에 알맞은 말을 <보기>에서 골라 쓰시오.

┌─ 보기 ─────────────────────┐
| myself　　　herself　　　himself |
| yourself　　themselves　 ourselves |
└─────────────────────────┘

(1) James introduced _____ to Jessica.

(2) She enjoyed _____ in London.

(3) I'm not angry with you. I'm angry with _____.

(4) Sam and I enjoyed _____ at the party.

(5) You should be proud of _____.

**D3** 두 문장이 같은 의미가 되도록 빈칸에 알맞은 말을 쓰시오.

(1) She went there alone.

　 = She went there _____ _____.

(2) I can't decide without other's help.

　 = I can't decide _____ _____.

**E1** 괄호 안에서 알맞은 것을 고르시오.

(1) (All, Every) the birds in the cage don't look happy.

(2) I've got four presents. One is from my aunt, and (the other, the others) are from my friends.

(3) My father and I go hiking (all, every) Sunday.

(4) Sally bought two backpacks. One is white and (the other, the others) is red.

(5) I need a ruler. Do you have (one, it)?

(6) Three of the twelve boys stayed and (another, the others) went out.

**E2** 우리말과 일치하도록 빈칸에 알맞은 부정대명사를 쓰시오.

(1) 어떤 사람들은 스파게티를 좋아하는 반면, 또 어떤 사람들은 그것을 싫어한다.

　 →Some people love spaghetti, while _____ hate it.

(2) 우리들 각각은 새로운 모자를 사야 한다.

　 →_____ of us needs to buy a new hat.

(3) Kate는 자매가 셋이다. 한 명은 여덟 살, 또 한 명은 열 살, 나머지 한 명은 열다섯 살이다.

　 →Kate has three sisters; one is eight, _____ is ten, and _____ is fifteen.

---

교과서　**weigh** 무게가 …이다　**look** 외모　**poet** 시인　**pack** (짐을) 싸다　**introduce** 소개하다　**cage** 우리　**ruler** 자
어휘⌂

# Grammar Test

**01** 빈칸에 알맞은 것은?

> A Do you want something cold?
> B Yes. Please give me _____.

① a water
② waters
③ a glass of waters
④ two glasses of water
⑤ two glasses of waters

서술형 평가

**02** 생략할 수 있는 부분을 찾아 쓰시오.

> A Who repaired your bicycle?
> B I repaired it myself.

_____

**03** 빈칸에 알맞지 <u>않은</u> 것은?

> I'd like to buy her a pair of _____.

① socks       ② gloves       ③ skirts
④ shoes       ⑤ blue jeans

**04** 빈칸에 a(an)를 쓸 수 <u>없는</u> 것은? (2개)

① Joe is _____ handsome man.
② This is _____ new MP3 player.
③ She buys _____ umbrella.
④ I live in _____ Washington now.
⑤ I go to _____ school on foot.

**05** 밑줄 친 부분과 바꿔 쓸 수 있는 것은?

> Does Jack read <u>a lot of</u> novels?

① many       ② much       ③ some
④ any         ⑤ plenty

**06** 우리말을 영어로 바르게 옮긴 것은?

> 각각의 집에 작은 마당이 있다.

① Each house have a small yard.
② Each houses have a small yard.
③ Each house has a small yard.
④ Every house have a small yard.
⑤ All the houses have a small yard.

서술형 평가

**07** 어법상 어색한 부분을 찾아 고쳐 쓰시오.

(1) Alice has few money.

_____ → _____

(2) There are three rooms in my house.
One is mine, another is my sister's,
and other is my parents'.

_____ → _____

---

교과서   **repair** 수리하다, 고치다   **handsome** 멋진, 잘생긴   **on foot** 걸어서   **novel** 소설   **yard** 마당
어휘 🎧

Answer p. 8

**08** 밑줄 친 부분 중 어법상 옳은 것은?

① Let me give you some advices.

② How many tomato do you need?

③ I ate piece of pizza for lunch.

④ I bought a pair of shoes yesterday.

⑤ I want to read today's newspaper. This is an old it.

**09** 밑줄 친 부분의 쓰임이 나머지와 다른 것은?

① He made this table himself.

② She fell down and hurt herself.

③ Ann runs to the mirror and looks at herself.

④ I started to introduce myself to the crowd.

⑤ Luckily they found empty seats and could seat themselves.

[10~11] 밑줄 친 부분 중 어법상 어색한 것을 고르시오.

**10**

Look at ①a bag on ②the chair. It's ③my sister's bag. It's ④very nice. She loves ⑤the bag very much.

**11**

There ①are ②a little apples and ③some water ④on ⑤the table.

서술형 평가

**12** 어법상 어색한 부분을 찾아 문장을 고쳐 쓰시오.

A How about these black pants?

B They are too small. Please show me bigger one.

→ _____

**13** 어법상 어색한 문장의 개수는?

ⓐ Each girls likes the dog.

ⓑ Every child loves chocolate.

ⓒ All of the milk was spilt.

ⓓ All the people has left the room.

① 0개        ② 1개        ③ 2개

④ 3개        ⑤ 4개

**14** 밑줄 친 부분 중 어법상 어색한 것은?

① I don't like this shirt. Show me another.

② I have many friends. Some are kind and others are unkind.

③ Here are five balls. One is mine and others are Mary's.

④ There are two notebooks. One is mine and the other is my brother's.

⑤ She bought three umbrellas. One is red, another is yellow, and the other is blue.

교과서
어휘 ♪    **advice** 충고  **empty** 비어 있는  **seat** 자리; 앉히다  **spill** 흘리다, 쏟다  **leave** 떠나다

# Reading

[1~2] 다음을 끊어 읽고 ☑, 해석을 쓰시오. ✐

**Possible or Impossible?** _____

In animation movies,✓ amazing things are possible. But are they

_____

3 actually possible✓ in real life?

_____

**Up, Up and Away!** _____

The house is lifted and flown✓ by thousands of balloons✓ in the

_____

6 animation. Could that actually work? Let's say✓ that a house weighs

_____

about 50,000 kg. A normal balloon at an amusement park✓ can lift

_____

about 14 g. So we need about 3,570,000 balloons✓ to lift up the house.

_____

9 We also have to think about the weight of the balloons _____ and

_____

the strings. Then,✓ we need to add a few more thousand balloons.

_____

Now,✓ the biggest challenge is pumping up all those balloons!

_____

## 1 빈칸에 알맞은 것은?

① oneself　　② itself　　③ them　　④ it　　⑤ themselves

## 2 다음 영영풀이에 해당하는 단어를 위 글에서 찾아 쓰시오.

_____ : to be effective or successful

교과서 **lift** 들어 올리다　**normal** 보통의　**weight** 무게　**string** 줄, 끈　**challenge** 도전　**pump up** 주입하다, 채워 넣다
어휘 ∩

**3** 다음 글과 관련이 있는 속담은?

교훈

Everyone wants to be the best at something. However, it is impossible to master a skill in one day. If you want to **play golf** well, for example, you should watch experienced players and learn the basic skills. But this is not enough to be a good golfer. You have to practice every day. You cannot just pick up a club, hit a ball, and hope to be a world champion in a week or two. You need to put in **a lot of** time and effort to be a good player.

① No news is good news.
② Practice makes perfect.
③ Two heads are better than one.
④ A sound mind in a sound body.
⑤ A friend in need is a friend indeed.

**4** 다음 글의 내용과 일치하지 <u>않는</u> 것은?

세계
문화

The Maya civilization in central America is one of the world's most well-known ancient civilizations. Though far from Europe, the Maya civilization had a lot in common with the ancient Greek and Egyptian civilizations. Just like the Greeks, the Maya built stone buildings and they worshipped gods. They also had **many** independent city-states similar to those of ancient Greece. Like the Egyptians, the Maya built very tall pyramids. The Maya pyramids had temple rooms at the top but had the same steep sides and steps as the Egyptian **ones**.

① 마야 문명은 중앙아메리카를 중심으로 이루어졌다.
② 마야 문명은 그리스, 이집트 문명과 비슷한 점이 있다.
③ 마야인들은 신을 숭배했다.
④ 마야 문명과 고대 그리스에는 도시 국가가 있었다.
⑤ 마야 문명과 이집트의 피라미드는 꼭대기에 사원이 있다.

---

3  **master** …을 완전히 익히다, 숙달하다  **experienced** 숙련된  **practice** 연습하다  **club** 골프채
4  **civilization** 문명  **worship** 숭배하다  **independent** 독립적인  **city-state** 도시 국가  **steep** 가파른

# Expression

## 1 약속 정하기

**약속 정하기**

- Can you make it at ...?
- Can we meet at ...?
- Why don't we meet at ...?
- Shall we meet(make it) at ...?

- How(What) about meeting at ...?
- What time and where should we meet?
- Let's meet(make it) at ....

## 2 알고 있는지 묻기 / 궁금증 표현하기

**알고 있는지 묻기**

- Do you know about ...?
- Have you heard about(of) ...?
- Are you aware of ...?
- Do you happen to know ...?

**궁금증 표현하기**

- I'm curious about ....
- I wonder (about) ....
- I'd like to know about ....
- Can you tell me (more) about ...?

# Expression Test

Answer p. 9

**1** 빈칸에 알맞은 말을 쓰시오.

   A How about riding a bike this afternoon?
   B Good. I'd love to. _____ _____ shall we make it?
   A How about two?
   B No problem.

**2** 의도하는 바가 나머지와 <u>다른</u> 것은?

① I wonder about the blue whale.
② I'm curious about the blue whale.
③ I'm worried about the blue whale.
④ I want to know about the blue whale.
⑤ I'd like to know about the blue whale.

**3** 밑줄 친 부분과 바꿔 쓸 수 있는 것은?

   A <u>Have you heard about upcycling?</u>
   B Yes. But I don't know much about it.

① Have you ever tried upcycling?
② Do you know about upcycling?
③ Are you reading about upcycling?
④ Could you explain about upcycling?
⑤ Would you like to know about upcycling?

**4** 우리말과 일치하도록 주어진 단어들을 바르게 배열하시오.

   A 나는 Paulo Coelho에 대해 궁금해.
     (I'm, Paulo Coelho, about, curious)
   B He wrote *The Alchemist*.

→ _____

**5** 빈칸에 알맞은 것은?

   A When do you want to meet?
   B _____
   A Sounds good.

① Let's meet at the bus stop.
② Do you have the time?
③ Can you make it at five?
④ What time do you want to meet?
⑤ What about meeting in front of the bank?

**6** 자연스러운 대화가 되도록 (A)~(D)를 바르게 배열한 것은?

   (A) How about six in front of my school?
   (B) That's fine with me. See you tomorrow.
   (C) Of course. What time should we meet?
   (D) Would you like to come to our school festival tomorrow?

① (A) – (B) – (C) – (D)
② (A) – (B) – (D) – (C)
③ (D) – (B) – (A) – (C)
④ (D) – (C) – (A) – (B)
⑤ (D) – (C) – (B) – (A)

**1** 밑줄 친 단어들을 바르게 배열하여 대화를 완성하시오.

> A What are you watching, Sally?
> B I'm watching the Sci-Magic show. It's a new program. (1) <u>you, have, about, heard it</u>?
> A No, I haven't. What's it about?
> B The program uses science to explain magic tricks.
> A Oh, it sounds interesting. (2) <u>how, curious, I'm, about</u> magic tricks work. Can I watch it with you?
> B Sure.

(1) _____

(2) _____

**2** 그림을 보고, 주어진 단어들을 배열하여 문장을 완성하시오.

(1)

Anne _____ in the mirror. (looking, herself, is, at)

(2)

I did _____.
(by, homework, my, myself)

**3** 밑줄 친 부분을 바르게 고쳐 문장을 다시 쓰시오.

(1) We don't have <u>many snow</u> in winter.

→ _____

(2) <u>Loves are</u> actually all around.

→ _____

**4** 빈칸에 알맞은 말을 〈보기〉에서 골라 쓰시오.

> 보기
> a    an    the

> A Dad, I'm hungry. Can I have (1) _____ hamburger? A cheese burger would be great.
> B Sure. Here's a tomato and there's (2) _____ egg and (3) _____ slice of cheese in the fridge.
> A Can I also have (4) _____ glass of coke?
> B Sure. It's in (5) _____ fridge, too.

**5** 그림을 보고, 빈칸에 알맞은 말을 〈보기〉에서 골라 쓰시오.

> 보기
> one    other    others    some

(1) There are many people in the park. _____ are playing badminton and others are jogging.

(2) There is a woman walking her dogs. _____ is black and the _____ is white.

(3) Some flowers are red and the _____ are yellow.

Answer p. 9

난이도: 상 ★★★ 중 ★★ 하 ★

★
## 01 영영풀이에 해당하는 것은?

usual, typical, or expected

① actual    ② single    ③ normal
④ helpful    ⑤ entire

★★
## 02 영영풀이를 완성할 때 빈칸에 알맞은 것은?

**lift**: to _____ something or someone upwards into the air

① add    ② change    ③ move
④ weigh    ⑤ fly

★★ 시험에 잘 나오는 문제
## 03 짝지어진 대화가 <u>어색한</u> 것은?

① A What time shall we meet?
　 B How about four o'clock?
② A I'm curious about who created this work.
　 B Rebecca created it.
③ A I wonder how long it will take to solve this problem.
　 B Maybe one or two minutes.
④ A Have you heard about the new phone from ABC?
　 B No, I have already bought it.
⑤ A I watched a video clip about friendship between an old man and a lion.
　 B Really? I'm curious about the story.

★ 서술형 평가
## 04 주어진 단어를 이용하여 빈칸에 알맞은 말을 쓰시오.

A Look at this. This bird laughs like a person.
B Oh, I'm _____.
(curious, the bird)

★★
## 05 빈칸에 알맞은 것은?

A Will you go shopping with me tomorrow?
B Sounds good. _____
A How about four o'clock?
B That's fine with me.

① Let's meet tomorrow.
② Can we make it at four?
③ Where do you want to meet?
④ What time shall we make it?
⑤ Shall we meet in front of the theater?

★★ 서술형 평가
## 06 자연스러운 대화가 되도록 (A)–(C)를 바르게 배열하시오.

(A) Yes, but I don't know much about it.
(B) What are you doing?
(C) I'm reading a book. Have you heard about impressionism art?

_____ → _____ → _____

교과서 **upwards** 위쪽으로　**create** 만들어 내다, 창작하다　**solve** 해결하다　**laugh** 웃다　**impressionism** 인상주의
어휘

★
## 07 빈칸에 알맞지 <u>않은</u> 것은?

A When do you want to meet?

B _____

① Can you make it at five?
② Is next weekend all right?
③ Let's make it at three.
④ How about this Monday?
⑤ All right. See you then.

★★ 서술형 평가
## 08 주어진 단어들을 배열하여 대화를 완성하시오.

A I _____.
(how, wonder, high, is, Mt. Everest)

B I don't know exactly. Let's search on the Internet.

★
## 09 빈칸에 알맞지 <u>않은</u> 것은?

David has _____ close friends.

① few        ② a few        ③ many
④ little       ⑤ a lot of

★ 서술형 평가
## 10 빈칸에 알맞은 대명사를 쓰시오.

(1) A Are you planning to buy a sweater?
   B No, I don't need _____.

(2) A Your shoes are too old.
   B I think so too. I want new _____.

★ 서술형 평가
## 11 빈칸에 알맞은 말을 〈보기〉에서 골라 쓰시오.

보기
a loaf of     a pair of     a glass of

(1) I ate _____ bread for breakfast.
(2) I'm full. Just order _____ juice.
(3) Let's buy her _____ pants.

★★
## 12 밑줄 친 부분 중 어법상 어색한 것은?

I know ①<u>a boy</u> in my town. He is
②<u>my son's best friend</u>. My son likes
③<u>the boy</u> very much. The boy's name
is ④<u>an Alex</u>. Alex is ⑤<u>a very handsome
boy</u>.

★ 서술형 평가
## 13 주어진 단어를 알맞은 형태로 쓰시오.

(a) Some people are very selfish. They only think of (them).

(b) Don't worry about Mary. She will take care of (she).

(a) _____ (b) _____

★ 서술형 평가
## 14 우리말과 일치하도록 빈칸에 알맞은 말을 쓰시오.

마당의 모든 꽃들이 아름답다.

→ _____ of the flowers in the yard are beautiful.

교과서  **exactly** 정확히   **search** 검색하다   **order** 주문하다   **selfish** 이기적인   **take care of** …을 돌보다
어휘

**15** 어법상 어색한 것은?

① Eric has an old car.

② A day has twenty four hours.

③ Ann goes to London by airplane.

④ She goes to the church on Sundays.

⑤ I play the piano every day.

★★ 서술형 평가

**16** 빈칸에 알맞은 대명사를 쓰시오.

A How many uncles do you have?

B I have two uncles. _____ is a
doctor, and _____ is a teacher.

★★

**17** 주어진 단어의 형태가 바르게 짝지어진 것은?

The professor introduced (he). He
wanted to know more about (us).

① him – our          ② himself – us

③ him – ourselves    ④ himself – our

⑤ himself – ourselves

★★ 서술형 평가

**18** 빈칸에 공통으로 들어갈 알맞은 말을 쓰시오.

• I have three sisters. One is 10,
_____ is 12, and the other is 18.

• I don't like this one. Show me
_____.

★★ 서술형 평가

**19** 두 문장이 같은 의미가 되도록 빈칸에 알맞은 말을
쓰시오.

(1) Mina reads a lot of books.

= Mina reads _____ books.

(2) There are some people in the park.

= There are a _____ people in the
park.

★★

**20** 정관사 the가 들어갈 수 없는 것은?

① I travel by _____ train.

② We can see _____ moon at night.

③ _____ coin in his pocket is very old.

④ Please close _____ window right now.

⑤ I have a bag. _____ bag is very large.

★★ 서술형 평가

**21** 그림을 보고, 빈칸에 알맞은 말을 쓰시오.

You need _____ bread,
_____ cheese and a tomato
to make a sandwich.

교과서   **professor** 교수   **travel** 여행하다   **coin** 동전   **pocket** 주머니
어휘

★★★
## 22 어법상 옳은 것은?

① All of them looks tired.

② All my money was gone.

③ Each of them are special to me.

④ I know every students in the school.

⑤ Each person learn in a slightly different way.

★★
## 23 빈칸에 들어갈 말이 바르게 짝지어진 것은?

> • Some visit Paris on business, and _____ visit Paris for pleasure.
> • Here are five roses. One is red and _____ are white.

① other – another

② another – others

③ others – the other

④ the other – others

⑤ others – the others

★★ 시험에 잘 나오는 문제
## 24 밑줄 친 부분 중 생략할 수 있는 것은?

① Do you sometimes talk to yourself?

② We'll keep this between ourselves.

③ Can he find the way by himself?

④ Sue herself doesn't think she'll get the job.

⑤ Peter and Anna are very selfish. They only think of themselves.

★★
## 25 빈칸에 알맞은 것은?

> Can you buy happiness with money? Well, ask yourself. Do you think a conversation with your friend is more enjoyable when you are in expensive clothes? Is the TV show funnier on a 60 inch TV than on a 32 inch one? The answer is no. Happy moments do not come from what money can buy. In other words, your happiness does not depend on _____.

① how much money you have

② how often you get along with others

③ how much you can enjoy your life itself

④ how much money you donate

⑤ how much you feel grateful

★
## 26 글쓴이의 심정으로 알맞은 것은?

> Last Sunday, I went to the *Amazing Show*. It started with tightrope walking. A man walked along a thin rope up in the sky. The man once nearly fell off the rope but he was able to keep his balance. There were many other exciting performances. But my favorite one was the skateboarding trick. I was amazed when ten boys jumped into the air on their skateboards.

① nervous    ② thrilled    ③ upset

④ confused    ⑤ bored

교과서 **slightly** 약간  **conversation** 대화  **get along with** …와 잘 지내다  **tightrope walking** 줄타기  **balance** 균형
어휘 ∩

**[27~28] 다음을 읽고, 물음에 답하시오.**

A teacher named Miranda Smith plays (A) a / the piano and guitar for her students. Well, it looks like a normal music class, except for the fact (B) that / what the teacher can't see anything. Miranda was born blind, but her parents didn't want to send her to a special school. So she attended the local high school. She was a good student and went to college. After graduating from college, Miranda has worked (C) during / for twenty years as a skilled teacher at a school for the blind.

**★**
**27** 위 글의 내용과 일치하도록 할 때, 빈칸에 공통으로 들어갈 말로 알맞은 것은?

Although Miranda Smith was _____, she successfully finished her school and became a teacher for the _____.

① normal ② kind ③ poor
④ blind ⑤ skilled

**★★**
**28** (A)−(C)에서 어법에 맞는 말이 바르게 짝지어진 것은?

|  | (A) | (B) | (C) |
|---|---|---|---|
| ① | a | that | during |
| ② | a | what | for |
| ③ | the | what | during |
| ④ | the | that | for |
| ⑤ | the | that | during |

**[29~30] 다음을 읽고, 물음에 답하시오.**

Of all the planets in the solar system, Mars has been ⓐ the most popular choice as a new planet to live on. ( ① ) It is very similar to Earth and this is why humans living on Mars might be easier than ⓑ on other planets. ( ② ) Even though Mars has ⓒ an atmosphere, it is very thin and is mainly carbon dioxide. ( ③ ) There ⓓ is not enough oxygen for humans to breathe! ( ④ ) There is ⓔ few water on Mars and it can be very difficult to find. ( ⑤ ) Also, it is very cold on Mars and the gravity is weaker.

**★★**
**29** 주어진 문장이 들어가기에 알맞은 곳은?

However, the differences between Mars and Earth make living on Mars challenging.

① ② ③ ④ ⑤

**★★**
**30** 밑줄 친 ⓐ-ⓔ 중 어법상 어색한 것은?
① ⓐ ② ⓑ ③ ⓒ ④ ⓓ ⑤ ⓔ

---

교과서 **except for** …을 제외하고는 **local** 지역의 **graduate** 졸업하다 **planet** 행성 **solar system** 태양계 **atmosphere** 대기
어휘∩ **carbon dioxide** 이산화탄소 **breathe** 숨을 쉬다 **gravity** 중력

**A** 명사의 종류와 수량 표현

**1 셀 수 있는 명사:** a(an)를 붙일 수 있고, 복수 형태로 쓸 수 있다. many, (a) few 등의 형용사로 꾸민다.

There are three **books** on the desk.          Jessica typed in **a few words**.

**2 셀 수 없는 명사:** a(an)를 붙일 수 없고, 복수 형태로 쓸 수 없다. much, (a) little 등의 형용사로 꾸민다.

**Love** cannot be bought with **money**.          There was **little doubt** in my mind.

**B** 부정관사 a(an) / 정관사 the

**1 부정관사 a(an):** 셀 수 있는 단수명사 앞에 오며 정해지지 않은 막연한 것을 가리킨다. 뒤에 오는 단어의 첫 발음이 자음일 때는 a, 모음일 때는 an을 쓴다.

We have **a** problem.          They bought **an** umbrella.

**2 정관사 the:** 특정한 것을 가리키는 명사 앞에 온다. 뒤에 오는 단어의 첫 발음이 자음일 때는 [ðə], 모음일 때는 [ði]로 발음된다.

| 앞에 나온 명사를 다시 말할 때 | That is an album. **The** album is expensive. |
|---|---|
| 서로가 알고 있는 대상을 뜻할 때 | Please sit on **the** chair. |
| 세상에 하나밖에 없는 것 앞 | **The** Earth is round. |
| 연주하는 악기 이름 앞 | My younger brother plays **the** piano. |
| 수식어구가 명사를 꾸밀 때 | **The** cat on the bench is very cute. |

**C** 관사를 쓰지 않는 경우

| play+운동경기 | play baseball, play basketball, play soccer |
|---|---|
| by+교통수단 | by subway, by bus, by bicycle |
| 식사 · 과목 앞 | breakfast, lunch, dinner, science, math |
| 나라 · 도시 · 사람 이름 앞 | Korea, England, Seoul, Paris, Jim, Amy |
| 소유격과 함께 쓰인 명사 앞 | my car, his desk, her pen |
| 건물 · 장소가 본래의 목적으로 쓰일 때 | go to school, go to church |

### D 재귀대명사

인칭대명사에 -self나 -selves를 붙여서 '…자신(들)'이라는 뜻을 나타낸다.

- 재귀 용법: 문장의 주어와 목적어가 같을 때 목적어를 대신하여 쓰며 생략할 수 없다.
  The players are proud of **themselves**.
- 강조 용법: 강조하고자 하는 말 뒤나 문장의 맨 끝에 쓰며 생략할 수 있다.
  Yuri **herself** thinks that she is very pretty.

### E 부정대명사

**1 one**: 앞에 나온 명사와 같은 종류의 불특정한 것을 가리킨다.
This cup is dirty. Can I have a clean **one**?

**2 one, other, another**

| one / the other | (둘 중) 하나 / 나머지 하나 |
|---|---|
| one / another / the other | (셋 중) 하나 / 또 다른 하나 / 나머지 하나 |
| one / the others | (여럿 중) 하나 / 나머지 모두 |
| some / others | (여럿 중) 어떤 것들 / 또 다른 어떤 것들 |
| some / the others | (여럿 중) 어떤 것들 / 나머지 모두 |

**3 all, each**

| all | 모든 것(사람), 모두 | 대명사, 형용사 | 뒤에 복수명사가 오면 복수 취급<br>뒤에 단수명사가 오면 단수 취급 |
|---|---|---|---|
| each | 각각(의) | 대명사, 형용사 | 단수명사와 함께 쓰임 / 단수 취급 |

---

## >> Expression

### 1 약속 정하기

- Can you make it at …?
- Can we meet at …?
- Why don't we meet at …?
- Shall we meet(make it) at …?

- How(What) about meeting at …?
- What time and where should we meet?
- Let's meet(make it) at ….

### 2 알고 있는지 묻기 / 궁금증 표현하기

❤️알고 있는지 묻기
- Do you know about …?
- Have you heard about(of) …?
- Are you aware of …?
- Do you happen to know …?

❤️궁금증 표현하기
- I'm curious about ….
- I wonder (about) ….
- I'd like to know about ….
- Can you tell me (more) about …?

# Lesson 04

# 형용사, 부사, 비교

# Grammar Preview

## 1 형용사, 부사

- -thing＋형용사: -thing으로 끝나는 대명사(something, anything, nothing, everything 등)를 꾸미는 형용사는 꾸밈을 받는 대상의 뒤에 위치한다.
  I'll make you <u>something</u> **useful**.

- the＋형용사: '…한 사람들'의 뜻으로 보통명사처럼 쓸 수 있으며, 대개 복수 취급한다.
  **The wise**(= Wise people) are always thoughtful.

- 형용사와 부사의 형태가 같은 경우

  | | | |
  |---|---|---|
  | fast (빠른 – 빨리) | early (이른 – 일찍) | long (오래된 – 오래) |
  | far (먼 – 멀리) | late (늦은 – 늦게) | high (높은 – 높게) |
  | near (가까운 – 가까이) | close (가까운 – 가까이) | pretty (예쁜 – 꽤, 매우) |
  | hard (딱딱한, 어려운, 열심히 하는 – 열심히) | | |

- -ly가 붙어서 의미가 달라지는 부사

  | | | |
  |---|---|---|
  | hardly (거의 … 않는) | lately (최근에) | highly (매우) |
  | nearly (거의) | closely (밀접하게, 주의 깊게) | |

## 2 비교

- 원급, 비교급, 최상급

  | | | |
  |---|---|---|
  | **원급 비교** | as＋형용사(부사) 원급＋as | …만큼 …한(하게) |
  | **비교급 비교** | 비교급＋than | …보다 더 …한(하게) |
  | **최상급 비교** | the＋최상급(＋명사)＋ in＋단수명사(장소, 단체) / of＋복수명사(비교 대상) | …(중)에서 가장 …한(하게) |

- 여러 가지 비교 표현

  배수사(twice, three times 등)＋as＋원급＋as …　…보다 몇 배 …한(하게)

  as＋원급＋as possible (＝ as＋원급＋as＋주어＋can(could))　가능한 한 …한(하게)

  비교급＋and＋비교급　점점 더 …한(하게)

  The＋비교급 …, the＋비교급 …　…하면 할수록 더 …하다

  배수사＋비교급＋than …　…보다 몇 배 더 …한(하게)

  one of the＋최상급＋복수명사　가장 …한 것들 중 하나

## A 형용사

**1** 형용사는 사람이나 사물의 모양, 성질, 상태, 수량 등을 나타내는 말로, 명사를 꾸미거나 주어나 목적어를 보충 설명한다.

My family had a **wonderful** time in Spain. 〈명사 time 수식〉

The population growth is so **rapid**. 〈주어 The population growth 설명〉

I found the towel **dirty**. 〈목적어 the towel 설명〉

> **◆ Plus** Grammar
>
> 감각동사＋형용사
> look, sound, smell, feel, taste 등의 감각동사는 형용사를 보어로 취한다.
> You **look fantastic** today.
> The cake **smelled sweet**.

**2** -thing＋형용사: -thing으로 끝나는 대명사(something, anything, nothing, everything 등)를 꾸미는 형용사는 꾸밈을 받는 대상의 뒤에 위치한다.

I'll make you something **useful**.

**3** the＋형용사: '…한 사람들'의 뜻으로 보통명사처럼 쓸 수 있으며, 대개 복수 취급한다.

| the rich | rich people | the wise | wise people |
|---|---|---|---|
| the poor | poor people | the young | young people |
| the brave | brave people | the blind | blind people |

**The wise**(= Wise people) are always thoughtful.

## B 부사

**1** 부사는 장소, 방법, 시간, 정도 등을 나타내는 말로, 동사, 형용사, 다른 부사, 또는 문장 전체를 꾸민다. 보통 〈형용사＋ly〉의 형태이다.

He closed the door **softly** so as not to wake the sleeping baby. 〈동사 수식〉

**Unfortunately**, I can't meet you tomorrow. 〈문장 전체 수식〉

> **◆ Plus** Grammar
>
> 빈도부사
> 동작, 사건이 얼마나 자주 일어나는지 나타내는 부사로, be동사와 조동사 뒤에, 일반동사 앞에 쓰인다.
> He is **always** nice to his friends.
> I will **never** help them again.

**2** 혼동하기 쉬운 부사

- 형용사와 부사의 형태가 같은 경우

> fast (빠른 – 빨리)　　early (이른 – 일찍)　　long (오래된 – 오래)
> far (먼 – 멀리)　　late (늦은 – 늦게)　　high (높은 – 높게)
> near (가까운 – 가까이)　　close (가까운 – 가까이)　　pretty (예쁜 – 꽤, 매우)
> hard (딱딱한, 어려운, 열심히 하는 – 열심히)

I always jog in the **early** morning. 〈형용사〉

It's very difficult to get up **early** every day. 〈부사〉

- -ly가 붙어서 의미가 달라지는 부사

> hardly (거의 … 않는)　　lately (최근에)　　highly (매우)
> nearly (거의)　　closely (밀접하게, 주의 깊게)

I haven't seen him **lately**.

Philip is a **highly** successful politician.

# Grammar Practice >

Answer p. 11

**A1** 괄호 안에서 알맞은 것을 고르시오.

(1) A (cute, cutely) girl wants to see you.

(2) My mother is (angry, angrily) with me.

(3) That sounds (great, greatly).

(4) He'll do (everything possible, possible everything) to help you.

(5) Doctors should take care of the (sick, sickly).

(6) Tom always looks (happy, happily).

(7) They talk about (strange something, something strange).

(8) We should help (a weak, the weak) and the poor.

**A2** 주어진 단어들을 배열하여 문장을 완성하시오.

(1) We went to _____.
(restaurant, Chinese, a)

(2) The twins sitting _____.
(alike, on, are, the sofa)

(3) I'll buy _____ to wear.
(comfortable, something)

**A3** 우리말과 일치하도록 주어진 단어들을 이용하여 빈칸에 알맞은 말을 쓰시오.

(1) 자고 있는 아기가 귀여워 보인다.
→ The sleeping baby _____.
(look, cute)

(2) 뜨거운 마실 것 좀 주세요.
→ Give me _____.
(something, hot, drink)

(3) 부상자들이 병원으로 옮겨졌다.
→ _____ were taken to the hospital. (injured)

**B1** 우리말과 일치하도록 괄호 안에서 알맞은 것을 고르시오.

(1) 나는 어젯밤에 거의 잠을 잘 수 없었다.
→ I could (hard, hardly) sleep last night.

(2) Jenny는 내일 늦게까지 일을 해야 한다.
→ Jenny has to work (late, lately) tomorrow.

(3) 그의 성격은 매우 긍정적이다.
→ His character is (high, highly) positive.

(4) 그는 너무 빨리 말한다.
→ He speaks so (fast, fastly).

(5) 작은 새들이 높이 날고 있다.
→ Small birds are flying (high, highly).

**B2** 밑줄 친 부분을 바르게 고쳐 쓰시오.

(1) I got up lately in the morning.

(2) Bob drives a car very careful.

(3) I could hard say anything.

(4) You cook very perfect.

(5) She was high disappointed by his big mistake.

**B3** 두 문장의 의미가 같으면 S, 다르면 D를 쓰시오.

(1) _____ (a) You've worked hard.
(b) You've hardly worked.

(2) _____ (a) I've been unwell recently.
(b) I've been unwell lately.

교과서 어휘 **wonderful** 아주 멋진  **population** 인구  **thoughtful** 사려 깊은  **unfortunately** 불행히도  **comfortable** 편안한  **positive** 긍정적인

## C 원급, 비교급, 최상급

**1 원급 비교:** 둘을 비교하여 정도가 같을 때 쓰며, 형용사나 부사의 원급을 쓴다.

| | |
|---|---|
| as + 형용사(부사) 원급 + as | …만큼 …한(하게) |
| not as(so) + 형용사(부사) 원급 + as | …만큼 …하지 않은(않게) |

This chair is **as comfortable as** that sofa.

My bag is**n't as(so) heavy as** yours.

**2 비교급 비교:** 둘 중 하나가 '더 …하다'라고 말할 때 쓰며, 형용사나 부사의 비교급을 쓴다.

| | |
|---|---|
| 비교급 + than | …보다 더 …한(하게) |

Janet is **more intelligent than** Sam.

**3 최상급 비교:** 셋 이상을 비교하여 '가장 …하다'라고 말할 때 쓰며, 형용사나 부사의 최상급을 쓴다.

| | |
|---|---|
| the + 최상급( + 명사) + ⌈ in + 단수명사(장소, 단체) <br> ⌊ of + 복수명사(비교 대상) | …(중)에서 가장 …한(하게) |

Alan is **the nicest of the three boys**.

The Pacific is **the biggest** ocean **in the world**.

## D 여러 가지 비교 표현

**1 원급을 이용한 표현**

> 배수사(twice, three times 등) + as + 원급 + as ...    …보다 몇 배 …한(하게)
>
> as + 원급 + as possible (= as + 원급 + as + 주어 + can(could))   가능한 한 …한(하게)

Our garden is **twice as** large **as** yours.

Can you send me your digital camera **as soon as possible**?
                                            = as soon as you can

**2 비교급을 이용한 표현**

> 비교급 + and + 비교급   점점 더 …한(하게)
>
> The + 비교급 ..., the + 비교급 ...   …하면 할수록 더 …하다
>
> 배수사 + 비교급 + than ...   …보다 몇 배 더 …한(하게)

Your work is getting **better and better**.

**The higher** you go up, **the more** you can see.

**3 최상급을 이용한 표현**

> one of the + 최상급 + 복수명사   가장 …한 것들 중 하나

He took **one of the most important roles** in the play.

---

**⬤ Plus Grammar**

- **the same (명사) as ...**
'…와 똑같은'의 뜻으로 비교하는 대상의 정도가 같음을 나타낸다.
I made **the same** mistake as Peter. (나는 Peter와 똑같은 실수를 했다.)
- **비교급 강조**
비교급 앞에 much, still, even, far, a lot이 오면 '훨씬 더 …한'이라는 뜻이 된다.
Today is **even** colder than yesterday. (오늘은 어제보다 훨씬 더 춥다.)

---

**⬤ Plus Grammar**

**비교급을 이용한 최상급 표현**
〈부정 주어 + 비교급 + than ...〉: 어떤 것도 …보다 더 …하지 못한
**Nothing** is **faster than** light in the world.
〈비교급 + than any other + 단수명사〉: 다른 어떤 것보다 더 …한
Light is **faster than any other** thing in the world.

# Grammar Practice >>

Answer p. 11

**C1** 괄호 안에서 알맞은 것을 고르시오.

(1) This city is (as, so, than) large as Seoul.

(2) Ross doesn't eat as (much, more, most) as Joe.

(3) Bob has the same hobby (as, so, than) his brother.

(4) He is (richer, the richest) man in the world.

(5) Health is (more important, the most important) thing in life.

(6) Mary is the cutest (of, in, than) the three sisters.

(7) I can cook (well, better, best) than Sujin.

**C2** 우리말과 일치하도록 빈칸에 알맞은 말을 쓰시오.

(1) 고래는 상어보다 더 크다.

→ A whale is _____ _____ a shark.

(2) Sally는 수미만큼 빨리 달린다.

→ Sally runs _____ _____ _____ Sumi.

(3) 이 빨간 의자는 저 노란 의자만큼 편하지 않다.

→ This red chair isn't _____ _____ _____ that yellow one.

**C3** 주어진 단어들을 배열하여 문장을 완성하시오.

(1) This book is _____.
(useful, than, more, one, that)

(2) I have _____.
(the, hers, watch, same, as)

(3) He is _____ the world.
(in, man, the, richest)

**D1** 우리말과 일치하도록 주어진 단어들을 이용하여 빈칸에 알맞은 말을 쓰시오.

(1) 그 구멍은 점점 더 커졌다.

→ The hole became _____ _____ _____. (big and big)

(2) 나에게 가능한 한 빨리 이메일을 보내라.

→ Send me an e-mail _____ _____ _____ _____. (soon)

(3) 이 방은 저 방보다 두 배 크다.

→ This room is _____ as large as that one. (two)

(4) 내가 그를 알게 될수록 그를 더 좋아하게 되었다.

→ The more I got to know him, _____ _____ I liked him. (more)

**D2** 어법상 어색한 부분을 찾아 문장을 다시 쓰시오.

(1) Our world is getting small and small.

→ _____

(2) The bee is one of the busiest insect.

→ _____

(3) My book is three time thicker than yours.

→ _____

**D3** 주어진 문장과 같은 의미가 되도록 빈칸에 알맞은 말을 쓰시오.

Greenland is the biggest island in the world.

= No other island in the world is _____ than Greenland.

= Greenland is _____ than _____ _____ island in the world.

교과서 어휘 🎧 **intelligent** 똑똑한  **ocean** 대양  **insect** 곤충  **thick** 두꺼운  **island** 섬

# Grammar Test

## 01 빈칸에 공통으로 들어갈 말로 알맞은 것은?

- He scored as high _____ Jason.
- Taking a taxi isn't so slow _____ walking.

① as ② so ③ the
④ than ⑤ more

서술형 평가

## 02 우리말과 일치하도록 빈칸에 알맞은 말을 쓰시오.

이 소설은 저 소설보다 더 흥미롭다.
→ This novel is _____ _____
_____ that novel.

## 03 빈칸에 알맞지 않은 것은?

My friend spoke _____.

① fast ② quietly ③ politely
④ friendly ⑤ very loud

## 04 빈칸에 알맞은 것은?

I have been busy _____ due to my work.

① late ② later ③ latest
④ lately ⑤ more late

## 05 괄호 안에서 알맞은 것을 고르시오.

(1) There was (important nothing, nothing important) in what she heard.
(2) Finally, he became (high, highly) successful in the field.
(3) The game looks really (complicated, complicatedly).

## 06 빈칸에 알맞지 않은 것은?

Space travel in the future will be _____ more common than now.

① much ② very ③ even
④ still ⑤ far

서술형 평가

## 07 그림을 보고, 주어진 단어를 이용하여 빈칸에 알맞은 말을 쓰시오.

→ Math is _____ _____ _____
English for Minjun. (difficult)

---

교과서 **score** 점수를 받다 **due to** … 때문에 **field** 분야 **common** 흔한
어휘

**08** 밑줄 친 부분이 어법상 어색한 것은?

① He tried to throw the ball slowly.

② I can hardly wait to see them again.

③ The house on the hill is high expensive.

④ She sometimes reads books late at night.

⑤ I was surprised because the tree grew too fast.

**09** 주어진 내용을 바르게 설명한 것은?

- A sofa is more expensive than a table.
- A chair is as expensive as a table.

① A sofa is the same price as a table.

② A table is as expensive as a sofa.

③ A chair is as expensive as a sofa.

④ A sofa is the most expensive of all.

⑤ A chair is more expensive than a sofa.

**10** 어법상 옳은 것은?

① He is one of the best actor in France.

② This stick is much longer than that one.

③ His room is three times as larger as mine.

④ You have to come back as sooner as possible.

⑤ More and most people are using smartphones.

**11** 우리말을 영어로 바르게 옮긴 것을 모두 고르면?

현명한 사람들이 항상 오류가 없는 것은 아니다.

① Wise are not always free from errors.

② The wise are always free from errors.

③ The wise are not always free from errors.

④ The wise person is not always free from errors.

⑤ Wise people are not always free from errors.

서술형 평가

**12** 우리말과 일치하도록 주어진 단어들을 배열하여 문장을 완성하시오.

차가운 것을 드시고 싶으세요?

(would, to, have, cold, you, something, like)

→ _____

**13** 어법상 어색한 것은?

① Suri is much taller than her sister.

② His hands are twice as small as my hands.

③ The air pollution is getting worse and worse.

④ This is the most wonderful movie in the world.

⑤ Mary is more beautiful than any other girls in the town.

교과서 **throw** 던지다 **price** 가격 **free from** ···을 면한, ···의 염려가 없는 **error** 오류
어휘

# Reading

[1~2] 다음을 끊어 읽고 ☑, 해석을 쓰시오. ✎

**The Footprints of a Baby Elephant**

**Date/Time: July 8th / 2:35 p.m.**

3 Today was my first day in Africa. This morning, I found an elephant group by a small water hole.

I saw ⓐa baby elephant drinking water beside her mother. ⓑHer eyes were as (A)brighter as

stars. I gave ©her a name, Stella.

6 **Date/Time: July 12th / 7:20 p.m.**

Around sunset, I found Stella crying next to her mom. ⓓShe was lying dead. I called the

elephant shelter and asked for help. I decided to stay by ⓔher until the rescue team came.

9 **Date/Time: July 13th / 6:00 a.m.**

A new elephant group appeared and Stella approached them. An elephant, probably the oldest

female allowed Stella to become part of the group. Unbelievably, one of the female elephants

12 cared for Stella as (B)warm as Stella's mom did. This was such an amazing moment!

**1** 밑줄 친 ⓐ~ⓔ 중 가리키는 대상이 나머지와 다른 것은?

① ⓐ      ② ⓑ      ③ ©      ④ ⓓ      ⑤ ⓔ

**2** 밑줄 친 (A)와 (B)를 알맞은 형태로 쓰시오.

(A) _____          (B) _____

교과서 **footprint** 발자국   **water hole** 물웅덩이   **shelter** 보호소   **rescue** 구조   **appear** 나타나다   **approach** 다가가다
어휘 ∩   **female** 암컷; 암컷의

**3** 밑줄 친 Octopus Friend가 의미하는 바로 알맞은 것은?

친구

Angela is an <u>Octopus Friend</u>. She has a friend, Vanessa, who she wants to stay **close** to. Like an octopus, Angela tries to hold on to Vanessa very **tight**. However, Vanessa might not like this situation. No one likes to feel trapped. If Angela keeps trying to control Vanessa, Vanessa is going to want to escape. Angela is afraid of losing Vanessa as a friend, but the way she's acting could end up pushing Vanessa away. Keep in mind that you don't have to have just one friend. Having different kinds of friends will surely make your school life fun and interesting.

① 대화의 화제가 끊이지 않는 친구
② 친구 수를 늘리는 데에 급급한 친구
③ 한 친구를 옭아매고 통제하려는 친구
④ 남의 말은 듣지 않고 자기 말만 하는 친구
⑤ 리더십이 강하여 무슨 일이든 앞장서서 하는 친구

**4** 글의 흐름으로 보아, 주어진 문장이 들어가기에 알맞은 곳은?

사회 변화

People **often** spend a lot of time trying to buy bigger things. ( ① ) They want bigger houses and bigger cars, and sometimes even bigger beds. ( ② ) Take computers, for example. The earliest computers were so large and heavy that they took up several rooms. ( ③ ) Now, some computers are **smaller than** a book and are completely wireless. ( ④ ) Cars are also getting smaller. A small car is easier to drive in busy traffic and **a lot** easier to park. ( ⑤ ) Small cars also use **far less** gas **than** large cars, and it makes owning a small car more economical.

> But sometimes bigger isn't always better.

①      ②      ③      ④      ⑤

**3** **hold on to** …을 붙잡다, …에 매달리다  **trap** 가두다  **escape** 탈출하다  **keep in mind** …을 명심하다
**4** **take up** …을 차지하다  **wireless** 무선의  **traffic** 교통  **own** 소유하다  **economical** 경제적인

# Expression

## 1 비교하기

### 💗 비교하기

- The dog is as small as my hand.
- It is longer than a basketball court.
- The blue whale is the biggest sea animal in the world.

## 2 요청하고 답하기

### 💗 요청하기

- (Please,) Open the door.
- Can you ...(, please)?
- Could I ask you to ...?
- Can(May) I ask you a favor?
- Would(Could) you do me a favor?
- Do(Would) you mind closing the window?

### 💗 요청에 답하기

- Yes! / Okay! / Sure! / All right!
- No problem.
- Not at all.
- (I'm) Sorry, but I can't.
- I'm afraid I can't.

# Expression Test

Answer p. 12

**1** 의도하는 바가 나머지와 <u>다른</u> 것은?

① Can you help me?

② May I ask you a favor?

③ Do you need any help?

④ Could you give me a hand?

⑤ Would you do me a favor?

**2** 빈칸에 알맞은 것은?

A I bought a new tablet PC yesterday.

B Oh, it's so small!

A Yeah. It's as _____ my hand.

① small

② small as

③ smaller

④ smaller than

⑤ smallest

**3** 빈칸에 알맞지 <u>않은</u> 것은?

A I can't solve this problem. Could you do me a favor?

B _____ Which one were you having trouble with?

① Of course.

② No problem.

③ I'd be glad to.

④ Yes, with pleasure.

⑤ I'm sorry, but I can't.

서술형 평가

**4** 우리말과 일치하도록 빈칸에 알맞은 말을 쓰시오.

A I don't know how to solve this question.

B It's much _____ _____ you think.

(그건 네가 생각하는 것보다 훨씬 더 쉬워.)

서술형 평가

**5** 빈칸에 알맞은 말을 쓰시오.

A Can you lend me your dictionary?

B I'm afraid _____ _____. I lost it. I have to buy new one.

**6** 자연스러운 대화가 되도록 (A)–(D)를 바르게 배열한 것은?

(A) Sure. What is it?

(B) No problem.

(C) Will you do me a favor?

(D) Can you help me with the science project?

① (A) – (D) – (C) – (B)

② (C) – (A) – (D) – (B)

③ (C) – (B) – (D) – (A)

④ (D) – (A) – (B) – (C)

⑤ (D) – (C) – (A) – (B)

**1** 주어진 단어들을 이용하여 밑줄 친 우리말을 영어로 옮기시오.

> A George, that red house over there is my grandparents' house.
> B Wow, the tree by the house is really big.
> A Actually, 저 나무는 나만큼 나이를 먹었어 (that tree, as, old, me), thirteen years old.
> B How do you know that?
> A My grandfather planted the tree in 2004 when I was born.

_____

**2** 〈보기〉에서 알맞은 말을 골라 우리말에 맞게 문장을 다시 쓰시오.

> 보기
> always   never   usually

(1) He is at his office. (그는 보통 그의 사무실에 있다.)

→ _____

(2) She will come. (그녀는 절대 오지 않을 것이다.)

→ _____

**3** 주어진 단어들을 이용하여 비교급 문장을 완성하시오.

(1) Sarah is _____ than Mark. (much, young)

(2) The test was _____ the last one. (far, difficult)

(3) The food was _____ it looked. (even, good)

**4** 주어진 표현을 배열하여 그림 속 인물의 말을 완성하시오.

(1)

The more I exercise, _____. (healthier, I, the, become)

(2)

The sooner I finish it, _____. (go home, the, I, can, earlier)

**5** 표를 보고, 〈조건〉에 맞게 두 사람을 비교하는 문장을 완성하시오.

| Name | Mark | Louis |
|---|---|---|
| Age | 20 | 27 |
| Height | 175 cm | 182 cm |
| 100 m record | 11 sec. | 11 sec. |

> 조건
> (1) 원급 비교를 이용할 것
> (2) 주어진 단어를 이용할 것

(1) Mark is _____. (old)

(2) Mark is _____. (fast)

(3) Mark is _____. (tall)

난이도: 상 ★★★ 중 ★★ 하 ★

★★
**01** 영영풀이에 해당하는 것은?

to remain in a place rather than leave

① decide  ② lay  ③ take
④ stay  ⑤ approach

★★ 서술형 평가
**02** 빈칸에 알맞은 단어를 〈보기〉에서 골라 쓰시오.
(형태 변화 가능)

보기
lie    beside    care

(1) He sat _____ her all night.
(2) She moved back home to _____ for her parents.
(3) Snow was _____ thick on the ground.

★★
**03** 짝지어진 대화가 어색한 것은?

① A Would you do me a favor?
   B Sure. What is it?
② A Can I ask you a favor?
   B Of course.
③ A Can you open the window?
   B I'm sorry I'm late.
④ A This puppy is so small!
   B Yeah. He's as small as my hand.
⑤ A The movie is not as interesting as the book.
   B Yeah. The original book has a better storyline.

★
**04** 밑줄 친 부분과 바꿔 쓸 수 있는 것은?

A Can I ask you a favor?
B Sure. What is it?
A Can I borrow your pen?
B No problem.

① May I help you?
② How are you doing?
③ What can I do for you?
④ Would you do me a favor?
⑤ Would you say that again?

★★ 서술형 평가
**05** 주어진 단어들을 배열하여 대화를 완성하시오.

A His new book _____ his last one. (well, as, sold, as)
B Yeah, he is a great writer.

★★ 서술형 평가
**06** 그림을 보고, 주어진 단어들을 이용하여 빈칸에 알맞은 말을 쓰시오. (형태 변화 가능)

A Will you do me a favor?
B Sure. What is it?
A Would _____ this picture on the wall? (help, hang)
B Okay.

교과서   **remain** 남다, 계속 …이다   **rather than** …보다는   **original** 원작의, 원래의   **hang** 걸다
어휘

# Final Test

**07** 빈칸에 알맞은 것은?

> **A** Can you come over to my house today?
> **B** _____ I have a test tomorrow.

① Of course.
② How was it?
③ I remember it well.
④ Yes, I can.
⑤ I'm afraid I can't.

★★

**08** 밑줄 친 부분 중 의미상 <u>어색한</u> 것은?

> **A** ①I'm thinking of buying secondhand books.
> **B** ②You mean used ones?
> **A** Yeah. ③They're almost new. ④They are also more expensive than new ones.
> **B** ⑤Oh, that's a good idea.

①        ②        ③        ④        ⑤

★★ 시험에 잘 나오는 문제

**09** 두 문장의 의미가 같도록 할 때 빈칸에 알맞은 것은?

> Kevin skips breakfast almost every day.
> = Kevin _____ eats breakfast.

① lately        ② highly        ③ mostly
④ hardly        ⑤ certainly

★★ 시험에 잘 나오는 문제

**10** 빈칸에 공통으로 들어갈 알맞은 말을 쓰시오.

> • 이 쿠키는 너무 딱딱해.
>   → This cookie is too _____.
> • 그는 일생 동안 열심히 일해 왔다.
>   → He has worked _____ all his life.

★★ 서술형 평가

**11** 주어진 단어들을 배열하여 문장을 완성하시오.
(1) The sun is _____.
    (bigger, the, than, earth)
(2) This is _____.
    (one, the, of, interesting, most, books)

★★

**12** 우리말을 영어로 바르게 옮긴 것은?

> 이 다리는 저 다리보다 두 배 더 길다.

① This bridge is as long as that one.
② This bridge is longer than that one.
③ This bridge is the longest of all.
④ This bridge is two as longer as that one.
⑤ This bridge is twice as long as that one.

★★

**13** 밑줄 친 부분이 어법상 <u>어색한</u> 것은?
① Your car is <u>the same color</u> as mine.
② This skirt is <u>more longer</u> than that one.
③ This test is <u>less difficult</u> than I thought.
④ This book is <u>three times</u> as expensive as that one.
⑤ That was <u>the most interesting</u> painting in the museum.

---

교과서   **come over to** …에 들르다   **secondhand** 중고의   **skip** 거르다   **museum** 미술관, 박물관
어휘🎧

**14** ★★ 서술형 평가 우리말과 일치하도록 주어진 단어들을 바르게 배열하시오.

그 집은 매우 아름다워 보인다.
(looks, the house, beautiful, so)

→ _____

**15** ★★ 밑줄 친 ①~⑤ 중 어법상 어색한 것은?

One of ① the most famous ② writer is ③ my friend, James. He is ④ the most popular writer ⑤ in my country.

**16** ★★ 밑줄 친 단어의 형태가 바르게 짝지어진 것은?

· The days are becoming longer and long.
· The higher we climb up the mountain, hard the wind blows.

① longer – hard        ② long – harder
③ longer – harder      ④ longer – the harder
⑤ the longer – the harder

**17** ★★ 서술형 평가 우리말과 일치하도록 빈칸에 알맞은 말을 쓰시오.

가족보다 더 중요한 것은 없다.

→ _____ is more important than family.

**18** ★★ 빈칸에 알맞은 것은?

Mr. Brown is taller than _____ in this town.

① other person
② any other person
③ any other people
④ any another person
⑤ any another people

**19** ★★ 시험에 잘 나오는 문제 어법상 어색한 것은?

① The moon is smaller than the earth.
② Sally walked so slowly as she could.
③ The patient is getting better and better.
④ The higher we climb, the colder it becomes.
⑤ His room is three times as big as mine.

**20** ★★ 빈칸에 들어갈 말이 바르게 짝지어진 것은?

· She has never seen him _____.
· A kite was flying _____ in the sky.
· I've worked here for _____ two years.

① late – high – near
② late – highly – nearly
③ lately – high – nearly
④ lately – highly – nearly
⑤ lately – high – near

교과서 **popular** 인기 있는  **climb** 오르다  **blow** 불다  **patient** 환자  **kite** 연
어휘

**★★**

**21** 어법상 옳은 것은?

① You look happily.

② The cookies smell delicious.

③ Do you have special anything in mind?

④ He read a book interesting yesterday.

⑤ The young is interested in popular singers.

서술형 평가

[22~23] 어법상 어색한 부분을 찾아 고쳐 쓰시오.

**★**

**22**

Bella passed the exam successful last Friday.

_____ → _____

**★★**

**23**

A Did you hear of wrong anything with Jack?

B I heard that he had a bad cold.

_____ → _____

**★★★** 서술형 평가

**24** 어법상 어색한 부분을 찾아 문장을 고쳐 쓰시오.

(1) He wanted much more so he needed.

→ _____

(2) This box is four time as heavy as that one.

→ _____

**★★**

**25** 빈칸에 알맞은 것은?

Some people like computer games because of the colorful graphics and sound effects. But I like board games more than computer games. The main reason is that I like to play board games with my family. My family's favorite game is Monopoly. It's similar to the actual buying, selling and rental of properties. Playing board games is a great way to bond with my family. You know what? This is exactly what _____ cannot offer.

① family      ② friends      ③ books

④ money      ⑤ computers

**★★**

**26** 밑줄 친 질문에 대한 답으로 알맞은 것은?

What is the tallest mountain on Earth? Is it Mt. Everest? Surprisingly, it's Mauna Loa, an active volcano in Hawaii. At 56,000 feet from its peak to its base, Mauna Loa is almost twice as tall as Mt. Everest's 29,035 feet. So why doesn't it look like it? It's because only a quarter of Mauna Loa is above water! Its base is sunk 26,200 feet below the ocean floor.

① 수시로 높이와 모양이 변하기 때문에

② 에베레스트산이 더 높기 때문에

③ 아랫부분이 해저에 가라앉아 있기 때문에

④ 해수면 윗부분만 산으로 인정하기 때문에

⑤ 해저에 있는 부분은 측정이 불가능하기 때문에

교과서 **pass** 통과하다  **sound effect** 음향 효과  **rental** 대여  **property** 소유지, 부동산  **offer** 제공하다  **active volcano** 활화산
어휘 **base** 맨 아랫부분

[27~28] 다음을 읽고, 물음에 답하시오.

Elephants are known to be one of the ___(A)___ animals in the world. However, a female elephant called Hong in Thailand showed that elephants can be as artistic ___(B)___ human beings. Born in Thailand in 2001, Hong started learning how to paint when she was four years old. She could paint a picture of an elephant walking along or holding a flower in its trunk. This elephant used a paintbrush on the tip of her trunk to please tourists by beautifully painting her self-portrait and the Thai flag.

**★★**
**27** 위 글을 읽고 답할 수 <u>없는</u> 것은?

① When was Hong born?
② When did Hong begin learning to paint?
③ Who did Hong learn to paint from?
④ What did Hong paint with?
⑤ What did Hong paint?

**★★**
**28** 빈칸 (A)와 (B)에 들어갈 말이 바르게 짝지어진 것은?

① smart – as      ② smart – than
③ smarter – as    ④ smartest – than
⑤ smartest – as

[29~30] 다음을 읽고, 물음에 답하시오.

It's natural for people to make mistakes especially when they do something for the first time. You have probably blamed (A) you / yourself for stupid things you have done. (B) To recover / Recover from mistakes just give a short apology as soon as possible. Just say, "I'm sorry. I didn't handle that very well." or "I want to apologize for what I've done." The sooner you do this after you recognize your mistake, the (C) good / better . It makes things worse if you wait a long time to apologize.

**★★**
**29** 위 글의 요지로 알맞은 것은?

① 실수를 하지 않도록 주의해야 한다.
② 실수를 통해 배울 수 있는 것이 많다.
③ 실수를 하고 나면 빨리 사과하는 것이 좋다.
④ 상대방의 사과를 받아들이는 너그러움이 필요하다.
⑤ 먼저 실수를 수습한 후 사과하는 것이 효과적이다.

**★★★**
**30** (A)–(C)에서 어법에 맞는 말이 바르게 짝지어진 것은?

|   | (A) | (B) | (C) |
|---|-----|-----|-----|
| ① | you | – To recover | – good |
| ② | you | – Recover | – better |
| ③ | yourself | – Recover | – good |
| ④ | yourself | – To recover | – good |
| ⑤ | yourself | – To recover | – better |

교과서 어휘🔊　**paint** 그리다　**paintbrush** 붓　**self-portrait** 자화상　**blame** …을 탓하다　**recover** 만회하다　**handle** 처리하다　**recognize** 인식하다

·············································· **» Grammar**

### Ⓐ 형용사

**1** 형용사는 사람이나 사물의 모양, 성질, 상태, 수량 등을 나타내는 말로, 명사를 꾸미거나 주어나 목적어를 보충 설명한다.

My family had a **wonderful** time in Spain.　　　The population growth is so **rapid**.

**2** **-thing + 형용사**: -thing으로 끝나는 대명사(something, anything, nothing, everything 등)를 꾸미는 형용사는 꾸밈을 받는 대상의 뒤에 위치한다.

I'll make you something **useful**.

**3** **the + 형용사**: '…한 사람들'의 뜻으로 보통명사처럼 쓸 수 있으며, 대개 복수 취급한다.

**The wise**(= Wise people) are always thoughtful.

### Ⓑ 부사

**1** 부사는 장소, 방법, 시간, 정도 등을 나타내는 말로, 동사, 형용사, 다른 부사, 또는 문장 전체 를 꾸민다. 보통 〈형용사 + ly〉의 형태이다.

He closed the door **softly** so as not to wake the sleeping baby.

**2 혼동하기 쉬운 부사**

• 형용사와 부사의 형태가 같은 경우

| | | |
|---|---|---|
| fast (빠른 – 빨리) | early (이른 – 일찍) | long (오래된 – 오래) |
| far (먼 – 멀리) | late (늦은 – 늦게) | high (높은 – 높게) |
| near (가까운 – 가까이) | close (가까운 – 가까이) | pretty (예쁜 – 꽤, 매우) |
| hard (딱딱한, 어려운, 열심히 하는 – 열심히) | | |

• -ly가 붙어서 의미가 달라지는 부사

| | | |
|---|---|---|
| hardly (거의 … 않는) | lately (최근에) | highly (매우) |
| nearly (거의) | closely (밀접하게, 주의 깊게) | |

### Ⓒ 원급, 비교급, 최상급

| | | |
|---|---|---|
| 원급 비교 | as + 형용사(부사) 원급 + as | …만큼 …한(하게) |
| | not as(so) + 형용사(부사) 원급 + as | …만큼 …하지 않은(않게) |
| 비교급 비교 | 비교급 + than | …보다 더 …한(하게) |
| 최상급 비교 | the + 최상급( + 명사) + ⎰ in + 단수명사(장소, 단체)<br>⎱ of + 복수명사(비교 대상) | …(중)에서 가장 …한(하게) |

## D 여러 가지 비교 표현

### 1 원급을 이용한 표현

> 배수사(twice, three times 등)+as+원급+as ...   ...보다 몇 배 ...한(하게)
> as+원급+as possible (= as+원급+as+주어+can(could))   가능한 한 ...한(하게)

Our garden is **twice as** large **as** yours.

Can you send me your digital camera **as** soon **as possible**?

### 2 비교급을 이용한 표현

> 비교급+and+비교급   점점 더 ...한(하게)
> The+비교급 ..., the+비교급 ...   ...하면 할수록 더 ...하다
> 배수사+비교급+than ...   ...보다 몇 배 더 ...한(하게)

Your work is getting **better and better**.

**The higher** you go up, **the more** you can see.

### 3 최상급을 이용한 표현

> one of the+최상급+복수명사   가장 ...한 것들 중 하나

He took **one of the most important roles** in the play.

---

## >> Expression

### 1 비교하기

- The dog is as small as my hand.
- It is longer than a basketball court.
- The blue whale is the biggest sea animal in the world.

### 2 요청하고 답하기

💬 요청하기
- (Please,) Open the door.
- Can you ...(, please)?
- Could I ask you to ...?
- Can(May) I ask you a favor?
- Would(Could) you do me a favor?
- Do(Would) you mind closing the window?

💬 요청에 답하기
- Yes! / Okay! / Sure! / All right!
- No problem.
- Not at all.
- (I'm) Sorry, but I can't.
- I'm afraid I can't.

# Lesson 05

# 접속사

# Grammar Preview

## ❶ 접속사

- 명사절을 이끄는 접속사

| that | 명사절을 이끌어 문장에서 주어, 보어, 목적어 역할을 한다. |
|------|------------------------------------------------------|
| if | '…인지 아닌지'의 뜻으로 명사절을 이끌며, 주로 동사 know, tell, ask 등의 목적어 역할을 한다. 이때 if는 whether와 바꿔 쓸 수 있다. |

**That** Sumin won the tennis match is true. 〈주어〉

→ **It** is true **that** Sumin won the tennis match. 〈가주어 − 진주어〉

Can you look out the window and see **if** he is coming? 〈목적어〉

→ Can you look out the window and see **whether** he is coming **or not**?

- 부사절을 이끄는 접속사

| 시간 | when, while, as, after, before, until, since 등 |
|------|-------------------------------------------------|
| 이유 | because, since, as 등 |
| 결과 | so, so … that 등 |
| 조건 | if, unless (= if … not) 등 |
| 양보 | (al)though, even if, even though 등 |

## ❷ 간접의문문

- 간접의문문은 다른 문장의 일부인 명사절(주어, 목적어, 보어)로 쓰이는 의문문이다.

| 의문사가 없는 간접의문문 | 〈if(whether)＋주어＋동사〉의 어순으로 나타낸다. |
|--------------------------|---------------------------------------------|
| 의문사가 있는 간접의문문 | 〈의문사＋주어＋동사〉의 어순으로 나타낸다. |

I don't know **if(whether) she will come** to my birthday party.

I wonder **when you can show** me the pictures.

- 주의해야 할 간접의문문: 동사 think, imagine, suppose, guess 등이 쓰인 의문문이, 의문사가 있는 간접의문문을 목적어로 쓰는 경우, 간접의문문의 의문사는 문장의 맨 앞에 쓴다.

**Where** do you <u>guess</u> **they will go** this Sunday?

**Why** do you <u>think</u> **we have to learn** foreign languages?

## Ⓐ 명사절을 이끄는 접속사

**1 that**: 명사절을 이끌어 문장에서 주어, 보어, 목적어 역할을 한다. that이 이끄는 절이 주어 역할을 할 때에는 가주어 it을 이용하여 나타낼 수 있다.

**That** Sumin won the tennis match is true. 〈주어〉

→ **It** is true **that** Sumin won the tennis match.
　　가주어　　　　　　　진주어

My dream is **that** our team will win the game. 〈보어〉

Justin thinks (**that**) keeping pets teaches us responsibility. 〈목적어〉
　　　　　목적절을 이끄는 that은 생략 가능

**2 if**: '…인지 아닌지'의 뜻으로 명사절을 이끌며, 주로 동사 know, tell, ask 등의 목적어 역할을 한다. 이때 if는 whether와 바꿔 쓸 수 있다.

Tony doesn't know **if** Emma remembers his birthday. 〈목적어〉

Can you look out the window and see **if** he is coming? 〈목적어〉

→ Can you look out the window and see **whether** he is coming **or not**?

> ◆ **Plus** Grammar
>
> 주어절에는 whether만 쓸 수 있다.
> **Whether** he is smart is not important. (○)
> If he is smart is not important. (×)

## Ⓑ 부사절을 이끄는 접속사

### 1 시간을 나타내는 접속사

| when | …할 때 | **When** you take notes, use your own words. |
|---|---|---|
| while | …하는 동안 | **While** I was sleeping, I heard a strange sound. |
| as | …하면서 | She listened to music **as** she took a walk. |
| | …할 때 | **As** I was going out, the telephone rang. |
| after | …한 후에 | I went out **after** I did my homework. |
| before | …하기 전에 | **Before** it gets dark, we should start back to the city. |
| until | …할 때까지 | My uncle took care of me **until** I found a job. |
| since | … 이후로 | I have known her **since** she was a child. |

> ◆ **Plus** Grammar
>
> 시간과 조건을 나타내는 부사절에서는 현재시제가 미래시제를 대신한다.
> **When** I **get** home this evening, I will have a shower. (나는 오늘 저녁에 집에 도착하면 샤워를 할 것이다.)
> **If** he **knows** this, he will be angry. (만약 그가 이것을 안다면, 그는 화를 낼 것이다.)

### 2 이유 · 결과를 나타내는 접속사

| 이유 | because | … 때문에 | I touched it **because** I was curious. |
|---|---|---|---|
| | since | … 때문에 | **Since** it's raining, we should stay home. |
| | as | … 때문에 | **As** I was tired, I couldn't finish the work. |
| 결과 | so | 그래서 | School was over, **so** I played basketball. |
| | so ... that | 너무 …해서 …하다 | The box is **so** heavy **that** I can't lift it. |

### 3 조건 · 양보를 나타내는 접속사

| 조건 | if | 만약 …라면 | **If** you see Ann, can you call me? |
|---|---|---|---|
| | unless (= if ... not) | 만약 …하지 않으면 | I can't hear you **unless** you speak loudly. |
| 양보 | (al)though, even if, even though | 비록 …일지라도 | **Though** I'm sitting in the sun, I still feel cold. |

# Grammar Practice >

Answer p. 14

**A1** 밑줄 친 부분의 역할을 〈보기〉에서 고르시오.

> 보기
> ⓐ 주어   ⓑ 목적어   ⓒ 보어

(1) It was true that Tom was a liar.

(2) The fact is that I don't like Juliet.

(3) He thinks that the young should offer their seats to the old.

(4) I heard that you broke the window.

(5) The news is that she passed the test.

**A2** 두 문장이 같은 의미가 되도록 빈칸에 알맞은 말을 쓰시오.

(1) That Henry loves Jessica is certain.

= _____ is certain that Henry loves Jessica.

(2) I don't know if he is tired.

= I don't know _____ he is tired or not.

**A3** 우리말과 일치하도록 빈칸에 알맞은 말을 쓰시오.

(1) 나는 그가 이곳에 올 것이라고 믿는다.

→ I believe _____ he will come here.

(2) 그것이 사실인지 아닌지는 내게 중요하지 않다.

→ _____ it is true or not doesn't matter to me.

(3) 사실은 James가 시험에 떨어졌다는 것이다.

→ The fact is _____ James failed the exam.

**B1** 우리말과 일치하도록 괄호 안에서 알맞은 것을 고르시오.

(1) 당신의 개인 정보를 제공할 때는 조심해라.

→ Be careful (when, after) you give out your personal information.

(2) 네가 돌아올 때까지 나는 여기서 기다리겠다.

→ I'll wait here (if, until) you come back.

(3) 나는 떠나기 전에 작별 인사를 했다.

→ I said goodbye (before, after) I left.

(4) 너는 그 일을 한 후에 후회할 것이다.

→ You'll be sorry (before, after) you have done the work.

(5) 그는 너무 많이 먹어서 뚱뚱하다.

→ He is fat (though, because) he eats too much.

**B2** 우리말과 일치하도록 빈칸에 알맞은 말을 쓰시오.

(1) 너는 열심히 연습한다면 시합에서 이길 것이다.

→ _____ you practice hard, you'll win the game.

(2) 그는 비록 나이 들었지만 힘이 아주 세고 건강하다.

→ _____ he is old, he is very strong and healthy.

(3) 비록 나는 실패할지라도 다시 시도할 것이다.

→ _____ I fail, I will try again.

(4) 너는 더 빨리 걷지 않으면 버스를 놓칠 것이다.

→ You'll miss the bus _____ you walk more quickly.

---

교과서  **start back** …로 돌아가기 시작하다  **liar** 거짓말쟁이  **offer** 제공하다  **certain** 확실한, 틀림없는  **matter** 중요하다
어휘  **give out** …을 나눠 주다

# 2 간접의문문

## ⓒ 간접의문문

간접의문문은 다른 문장의 일부인 명사절(주어, 목적어, 보어)로 쓰이는 의문문이다. 직접적인 질문을 피하고 부드러운 어조로 물을 때 주로 쓰인다.

**1 의문사가 없는 간접의문문**: 〈if(whether)＋주어＋동사〉의 어순으로 나타낸다.

> Tell me.＋Did Harry win the gold medal?
> → Tell me **if(whether) Harry won** the gold medal.
>                       주어   동사

I don't know **if(whether) she will come** to my birthday party.
Do you know **if(whether) he will visit** Paris next month?

**2 의문사가 있는 간접의문문**: 〈의문사＋주어＋동사〉의 어순으로 나타낸다.

> Nobody knows.＋When did the fire break out?
> → Nobody knows **when the fire broke out**.
>                  의문사   주어      동사

I wonder **when you can show** me the pictures.
Amy doesn't understand **why Jack should leave** Korea.

*cf.* 의문사구 how often, what time, how old 등은 간접의문문에서 분리하지 않고 하나의 의문사처럼 쓴다.
David wants to know.＋How many legs does an ant have?
→ David wants to know **how many legs** an ant has.

### ⓓ 주의해야 할 간접의문문

동사 think, imagine, suppose, guess 등이 쓰인 의문문이, 의문사가 있는 간접의문문을 목적어로 쓰는 경우, 간접의문문의 의문사는 문장의 맨 앞에 쓴다.

> Do you suppose?＋When will they finish the report?
> → **When** do you suppose **they will finish** the report?
>   의문사가 문장의 맨 앞으로 이동

**Where** do you guess **they will go** this Sunday?
**Why** do you think **we have to learn** foreign languages?

**Plus Grammar**

**조건의 접속사 if**
'만약 …라면'이라는 뜻으로 조건의 부사절을 이끈다.
**If** you are hungry, you can have these cookies. (배가 고프면, 이 쿠키를 먹으렴.)
I'll stay at home **if** it rains tomorrow. (내일 만약 비가 온다면, 나는 집에 있을 거야.)

# Grammar Practice >

Answer p. 14

**C1** 주어진 단어들을 배열하여 문장을 완성하시오.

(1) Do you know _____?
   (if, can, here, park, I)

(2) Please tell me _____.
   (the party, when, begins)

(3) I wonder _____.
   (they, the park, to, how, go)

(4) Does she know _____?
   (works, how, the machine)

(5) I don't know _____.
   (likes, whether, he, the story)

**C2** 두 문장을 한 문장으로 바꿔 쓸 때 빈칸에 알맞은 말을 쓰시오.

(1) I'd like to know. + Did he buy the computer?
   → I'd like to know _____ _____ _____ the computer.

(2) Could you tell me? + Why is the baby crying?
   → Could you tell me _____ _____ _____ _____ _____?

(3) Please tell me. + What is your name?
   → Please tell me _____ _____ _____ _____.

(4) I'm not sure. + Does Jane ride her bike to school?
   → I'm not sure _____ _____ _____ her bike to school.

**C3** 밑줄 친 부분이 어법에 맞으면 ○표를 하고, 틀리면 알맞은 형태로 고쳐 쓰시오.

(1) Tell me how <u>is the weather</u> in Seoul now.

(2) I'd like to know <u>how often she practiced</u> playing the violin.

(3) I'm not sure if <u>did Jack win</u> the game.

(4) I wonder <u>how did long you stayed</u> in Prague last summer.

(5) I don't remember <u>where I bought my</u> hats.

**D1** 우리말과 일치하도록 주어진 단어들을 이용하여 빈칸에 알맞은 말을 쓰시오.

(1) 너는 Elsa가 어디 출신이라고 추측하니?
   → _____ Elsa comes from? (where, suppose)

(2) 너는 누가 그녀를 행복하게 해 주었다고 생각하니?
   → _____ her happy?
   (who, think, make)

(3) 너는 누가 우승할 거라고 추측하니?
   → _____ the winner?
   (who, guess, will, be)

(4) 너는 그 책이 무엇에 관한 거라고 생각하니?
   → _____ is about?
   (what, think, the book)

(5) 너는 Sam이 거기에 언제 갔다고 생각하니?
   → _____ there?
   (when, think, Sam, go)

교과서 어휘 **break out** 발생하다 **foreign** 외국의 **park** 주차하다; 공원 **practice** 연습하다 **hat** 모자

# Grammar Test

**01** 두 문장을 한 문장으로 바꿔 쓸 때 빈칸에 알맞은 것은?

> I don't know.+Does Sora like Italian food?
> →I don't know _____ Italian food.

① Sora likes
② does Sora like
③ if does Sora like
④ whether does Sora like
⑤ whether Sora likes

**02** 빈칸에 들어갈 말이 바르게 짝지어진 것은?

> • Will you send me letters _____ I give you my address?
> • You'll miss the bus _____ you hurry up.

① if – while
② while – whether
③ whether – if
④ if – unless
⑤ unless – whether

서술형 평가

**03** 빈칸에 알맞은 말을 〈보기〉에서 골라 쓰시오.

> 보기
> because    though    if    unless

(1) _____ he was smiling, he was worried about it.
(2) We went for a walk by the sea _____ it was a nice day.
(3) _____ you press this button, the machine will start.

**04** 괄호 안에서 알맞은 것을 고르시오.

(1) It was stupid (that, what) you believed Jenny.
(2) He asked me (what, when) the movie would start.

**05** 두 문장의 의미가 같도록 할 때 빈칸에 알맞은 것은?

> Justin looked both ways before he crossed the road.
> = Justin crossed the road _____ he looked both ways.

① by
② until
③ after
④ though
⑤ because

**06** 빈칸에 when이 들어갈 수 <u>없는</u> 것은?

① _____ I go to school, I have to wear a school uniform.
② _____ they arrived at the hotel, there were no rooms.
③ I always go to the same place _____ I go on holiday.
④ _____ the program ended, I turned off the TV.
⑤ I still ride my bicycle _____ it is too old.

---

교과서  **hurry up** 서두르다   **worry about** …에 대해 걱정하다   **press** (버튼 등을) 누르다   **stupid** 어리석은   **both** 둘 다의   **cross** 건너다
어휘  **go on holiday** 휴가를 가다   **turn off** …을 끄다

Answer p. 14

**07** 밑줄 친 부분이 어법상 어색한 것은?

① I don't know who the lady is.

② Do you know where does Bill live?

③ Please tell me if he comes from Canada.

④ Ask Tony whether he likes his coach.

⑤ What do you think Ann will do tonight?

**08** 빈칸에 들어갈 말이 바르게 짝지어진 것은?

- It's true _____ we were a little late for the meeting.
- I wonder _____ you're free this evening.

① what – if
② that – if
③ if – that
④ that – what
⑤ what – that

서술형 평가

**09** 두 문장이 같은 의미가 되도록 빈칸에 알맞은 말을 쓰시오.

(1) Amy didn't have breakfast because she got up too late.

= Amy got up too late, _____ she didn't have breakfast.

(2) I was wearing a coat, but it was very cold.

= _____ I was wearing a coat, it was very cold.

**10** 밑줄 친 ①–⑤ 중 어법상 어색한 것은?

Julia ①is going away soon. ②I'll be very ③sad ④when she ⑤will leave.

**11** 밑줄 친 부분의 쓰임이 나머지와 다른 것은?

① It is true that Amy came back home.

② Do you know that frogs cannot see colors?

③ Man is the only creature that can speak.

④ Her hope is that she will master Chinese in a year.

⑤ I didn't know that so many people speak good English.

**12** 어법상 어색한 것은?

① I don't know if it's safe.

② Do you know what he likes?

③ I wonder whether she is American.

④ I don't know when she will arrive.

⑤ Do you think why she bought the backpack?

서술형 평가

**13** 어법상 어색한 부분을 찾아 바르게 고쳐 쓰시오.

(1) I don't know if or not the news is true.

_____ → _____

(2) It is certain whether James is angry at me.

_____ → _____

교과서 **go away** 떠나다   **creature** 생물, 창조물   **be angry at** …에 대해 화가 나다
어휘

# Reading

[1~2] 다음을 끊어 읽고 ☑, 해석을 쓰시오. ✏

---

### The More You See, The More You Know

Welcome to the World Art Museum tour. Look

<sup>3</sup> at this painting ˅first. The seaside landscape is

so peaceful and beautiful, ˅isn't it? The title of

this painting is *Landscape with the Fall of Icarus*.

<sup>6</sup> So, ˅can you ⓐ Icarus, see, where, is? Do you see two legs ˅that are sticking out of the water ˅near

the ship? This is Icarus ˅in the famous myth in Greece. In the myth, ˅Icarus' father made wings for

him ˅with feathers and wax ˅and told him ˅to stay away from the sun. However, ˅Icarus didn't listen.

<sup>9</sup> He flew too close ˅to the sun. So, ˅the wax melted ˅and he fell into the water. Now, ˅look at the entire

painting ˅again. Despite the tragedy of Icarus, ˅people are going on with their everyday activities.

Does the painting still look peaceful? What do you think the artist is trying to tell us?

---

**1** 밑줄 친 ⓐ를 어순에 맞게 배열하시오.

_____

**2** 밑줄 친 Icarus에 관한 내용과 일치하는 것은?
① 날개를 직접 만들었다.
② 날개는 종이와 밀랍으로 만들어졌다.
③ 아버지의 말대로 따랐다.
④ 태양에 가까이 다가갔다.
⑤ 밀랍이 녹아 땅으로 추락했다.

---

교과서    **seaside** 바닷가    **landscape** 풍경    **stick out of** …에서 툭 튀어나오다    **myth** 신화    **stay away from** …에서 떨어져 있다    **melt** 녹다
어휘🎧    **entire** 전체의

## 3 (A)–(C)의 순서로 알맞은 것은?

일상

Last week was awful for me. I overslept on Monday morning and was late for school. I missed the teacher's instruction on what to study for the test on Wednesday.

(A) Today, I felt sad **when** I heard my friends talk about **how much fun they had** during the weekend.

(B) The next day, **when** my mom saw my test score, she got very angry. I wasn't allowed to go out with my friends over the weekend.

(C) Of course, I didn't know what to study and so I got a very low score.

① (A) – (C) – (B)　　　　② (B) – (A) – (C)　　　　③ (B) – (C) – (A)

④ (C) – (A) – (B)　　　　⑤ (C) – (B) – (A)

## 4 다음 글의 내용을 요약할 때, 빈칸 (A)와 (B)에 들어갈 말이 바르게 짝지어진 것은?

학습
방법

**When** you study, do you usually write study notes by hand or type on a computer keyboard? In a study, one group was asked to memorize unknown alphabet letters by writing by hand **while** the other used a keyboard. After six weeks, the students were tested to see **if** they still could remember these letters.

The study found **that** students who wrote by hand did better than those who typed. The researchers concluded **that** putting a pen to paper seemed more effective for the brain to remember things than using a keyboard.

It is better to write ___(A)___ than to ___(B)___ when learning something new.

① letters – remember　　　② bigger – type　　　③ by hand – type

④ by hand – use a pen　　　⑤ letters – study

---

3　awful 끔찍한　oversleep 늦잠 자다　miss 놓치다　instruction 설명　allow 허락하다, 허용하다

4　unknown 알려지지 않은　letter 글자, 문자　see 알아보다　conclude 결론을 내리다

# Expression

## 1 의견 묻고 답하기

💗 **의견 묻기**

- What do you think of(about) ...?
- How do you like ...?
- How do you feel about ...?
- What is your view(opinion)?

💗 **의견 표현하기**

- (Well,) I think(feel / believe) ....
- It seems to me (that) ....
- In my view(opinion), ....

💗 **선호 표현하기**

- I prefer ... to ....
- I like ... better than ....

## 2 허가 여부 묻고 답하기

💗 **허가 여부 묻기**

- May(Can) I ...?
- Is it okay if I ...?
- Do you mind if I ...?
- Would it be possible to ...?

💗 **허가하기**

- (Yes,) You may(can) ....
- Sure. / Okay. / All right. / Of course.
- I don't mind (at all).

💗 **불허하기**

- (No,) You can't(may not) ....
- (I'm afraid) That's(It's) not possible.
- You're not allowed(supposed) to ....

# Expression Test

Answer p. 15

**1** 빈칸에 알맞지 <u>않은</u> 것은?

> A _____ touch this?
>
> B No, you're not allowed to do that.

① Can I
② Will you
③ Is it okay if I
④ Am I allowed to
⑤ Is it okay for me to

서술형 평가

**2** 우리말과 일치하도록 빈칸에 알맞은 말을 쓰시오.

> 음식은 어떠니?
> → How do you _____ the food?

**3** 밑줄 친 부분과 바꿔 쓸 수 있는 것은?

> A Can I pick some flowers in the garden?
>
> B No. <u>You can't do that.</u>

① You may do that.
② I can't wait to do that.
③ I don't mind if you do that.
④ You're not allowed to do that.
⑤ I'm not sure if you can do that.

**4** 빈칸에 공통으로 들어갈 말로 알맞은 것은?

> A What is your _____ of this project?
>
> B In my _____, we needs more money to finish the project.

① dream          ② expression
③ action         ④ opinion
⑤ talk

**5** 밑줄 친 부분과 바꿔 쓸 수 있는 것은?

> A Which color do you <u>like better</u>, red or blue?
>
> B I like blue better.

① agree          ② hope
③ prefer         ④ dislike
⑤ improve

**6** 자연스러운 대화가 되도록 (A)-(D)를 바르게 배열한 것은?

> (A) It's very interesting.
> (B) Why do you think it's interesting?
> (C) It makes everybody laugh.
> (D) What do you think of this book?

① (A) – (B) – (C) – (D)
② (A) – (B) – (D) – (C)
③ (B) – (C) – (D) – (A)
④ (D) – (A) – (B) – (C)
⑤ (D) – (C) – (B) – (A)

**1** 밑줄 친 단어들을 바르게 배열하여 대화를 완성하시오.

> A What are you reading, Jina?
> B The novel, *Life of Pi*. It's a story about a boy and a tiger.
> A It's a great book. I've seen the movie too.
> B (1) you, did, how, feel, about the movie?
> A Well, I (2) the movie, better, liked, than the novel. The scenes are very beautiful. And the tiger looks real.

(1) _____

(2) _____

**2** 두 문장을 접속사 that을 이용하여 한 문장으로 바꿔 쓰시오.

(1) He likes her. It is obvious.

→ It is obvious _____.

(2) She was in hospital. We didn't know that.

→ We didn't know _____.

**3** 밑줄 친 부분을 어법에 맞게 고쳐 쓰시오.

> Have you ever made toy cars or planes? Surprisingly, there is a miniature city made up of toys. Do you know (1) where is it? It's in the Netherlands. There are lots of small toy buildings and you can walk around them. Do you know (2) how are they big? The houses only come up to your waist. But the little city has everything such as shops, farms, schools and so on.

(1) _____

(2) _____

**4** 두 문장이 같은 의미가 되도록 빈칸에 알맞은 말을 〈보기〉에서 골라 쓰시오.

> ┌─보기─────────────────────┐
> because    though    while
> └──────────────────────────┘

(1) When I was walking, I heard something strange.

= _____ I was walking, I heard something strange.

(2) I did my best, but I got a bad grade in math yesterday.

= _____ I did my best, I got a bad grade in math yesterday.

(3) This soup is so hot that I can't eat it.

= I can't eat this soup _____ it is so hot.

**5** 그림을 보고, 주어진 단어들을 배열하여 문장을 완성하시오.

(1)

I wonder _____.
(the robot, if, can, the house, clean)

(2)

I'm not sure _____.
(he, my present, will, whether, like)

# Final Test

Answer p. 15

난이도: 상 ★★★ 중 ★★ 하 ★

★
**01** 짝지어진 단어의 관계가 나머지와 <u>다른</u> 것은?

① peace – peaceful

② beauty – beautiful

③ fame – famous

④ art – artist

⑤ harm – harmful

★★ 서술형 평가
**02** 빈칸에 알맞은 단어를 〈보기〉에서 골라 쓰시오.

┌─보기─────────────────────┐
　　　close　　look　　listen
└────────────────────────┘

(1) He lives _____ to the park.

(2) _____ to what he says on the matter.

(3) _____ at the beautiful buildings.

★★ 시험에 잘 나오는 문제
**03** 짝지어진 대화가 <u>어색한</u> 것은?

① A Can I go with you?

　 B Of course.

② A Do you mind if I swim here?

　 B Just relax. They're just kids.

③ A How do you like my new cell phone?

　 B It's very nice.

④ A What do you think about that red backpack?

　 B Well, I don't like it.

⑤ A Is it okay if I practice the guitar?

　 B Okay, but you're not allowed to practice after 9 p.m.

★
**04** 빈칸에 공통으로 들어갈 말로 알맞은 것은?

A Which do you _____, science or math?

B I _____ science to math.

① like　　　② think　　　③ love

④ prefer　　⑤ hate

★★ 서술형 평가
**05** 주어진 단어들을 배열하여 대화를 완성하시오.

A _____ use your cell phone? (mind, do, you, I, if)

B Of course not. Here it is.

★
**06** 밑줄 친 부분과 바꿔 쓸 수 있는 것은?

A <u>What do you think of the movie?</u>

B It's great. The music was so amazing.

① Will you go to the movies?

② How do you like the movie?

③ Why do you like the movie?

④ Do you like watching moves?

⑤ How often do you go to the movies?

★ 서술형 평가
**07** 우리말과 일치하도록 빈칸에 알맞은 말을 쓰시오.

A Can I use your computer, Dad?

B I'm afraid _____ _____. (안 될 것 같구나.) I have to finish my work.

교과서 **relax** 진정하다　**amazing** 놀라운　**finish** 끝내다, 마치다　**work** 일, 업무
어휘∩

**08** 빈칸에 알맞은 것은?

> A _____
>
> B I prefer swimming because I'm a good swimmer.

① Do you like running?

② Are you good at swimming?

③ Why do you like running?

④ Do you prefer running than swimming?

⑤ Which do you prefer, running or swimming?

[09~10] 밑줄 친 부분과 바꿔 쓸 수 있는 것을 고르시오.

**09**

> I've never seen him even though I live near his house.

① until　　② since　　③ although

④ so that　　⑤ whether

**10**

> When I smiled at him, he turned red.

① As　　② That　　③ Unless

④ Though　　⑤ During

**11** 빈칸에 알맞지 <u>않은</u> 것은?

> When do you _____ the woman will come back?

① think　　② imagine　　③ suppose

④ know　　⑤ guess

**12** 두 문장을 한 문장으로 바꿔 쓸 때 빈칸에 알맞은 것은?

> Can you tell me? What will you do after school?
>
> → Can you tell me _____?

① what will you do after school

② what you will do after school

③ if will you do after school

④ if you will do after school

⑤ whether you will do after school

★ 시험에 잘 나오는 문제

**13** 두 문장의 의미가 같도록 할 때 빈칸에 들어갈 말이 바르게 짝지어진 것은?

> We are tired _____ we walked so long.
>
> = We walked so long, _____ we are tired.

① because – so　　② by – until

③ if – unless　　④ when – as

⑤ because – while

**14** 밑줄 친 부분 중 생략할 수 있는 것은?

> ① Do you ② know ③ that tomorrow ④ is ⑤ my birthday?

**15** 빈칸에 알맞은 것을 모두 고르면?

> You'd better check _____ there are any errors.

① if　　② so　　③ what

④ after　　⑤ whether

---

교과서 어휘 🎧　**turn** (…한 상태로) 변하다　**had better** …하는 편이 낫다　**check** 살피다, 점검하다　**error** 오류

**★★**

**16** 우리말을 영어로 바르게 옮긴 것은?

내일 날씨가 좋으면 우리는 소풍을 갈 것이다.

① If it's fine tomorrow, we'll go on a picnic.
② Until it's fine tomorrow, we'll go on a picnic.
③ As it'll be fine tomorrow, we'll go on a picnic.
④ After it's fine tomorrow, we'll go on a picnic.
⑤ When it'll be fine tomorrow, we'll go on a picnic.

**★★★**

**17** 밑줄 친 부분의 쓰임이 〈보기〉와 같으면 S, 다르면 D를 쓰시오.

┌─보기─
When Ann passed the exam, she was very happy.
└─

(1) David doesn't know <u>when</u> his brother's birthday is. → _____
(2) They were very surprised <u>when</u> they heard the news. → _____

**★★★**

**18** 어법상 어색한 것은?

① I'll stay here until Jane comes back.
② If there is a fire, the alarm will ring.
③ I'm going to bed when I'll finish my work.
④ Please close the window before you go out.
⑤ We're going to play tennis unless it rains.

**★★**

**19** 빈칸에 들어갈 말이 나머지와 <u>다른</u> 것은?

① It is certain _____ Sue cheated on the test.
② Do you think _____ Ann will agree to this plan?
③ I'm sure _____ air pollution is bad for people.
④ It is possible _____ Sumi will win the first prize.
⑤ I'll see _____ Jessica is at home or not.

**★★** 서술형 평가

**20** 빈칸에 알맞은 말을 〈보기〉에서 골라 쓰시오.

┌─보기─
since    before    while    although
└─

(1) Eric went running _____ it was very cold.
(2) Emma has enjoyed green tea _____ she first tasted it.
(3) June has to finish her homework _____ her mom comes home.

**★★** 서술형 평가

**21** 두 문장을 한 문장으로 바꿔 쓸 때 빈칸에 알맞은 말을 쓰시오.

I wonder.+How much money did you spend to buy this jacket?
→ I wonder _____ to buy this jacket.

교과서 어휘∩　**fine** 맑은　**ring** 울리다　**cheat** 속이다, 부정행위를 하다　**agree** 동의하다　**green tea** 녹차　**spend** 쓰다, 소비하다

**22** 빈칸에 공통으로 들어갈 말로 알맞은 것은? ★★

- I'm not sure _____ she will come to the party.
- I'll be surprised _____ Martin and Julia get married.

① because   ② though   ③ if
④ as       ⑤ after

**23** 두 문장이 같은 의미가 되도록 빈칸에 알맞은 말을 쓰시오. ★★ [서술형 평가]

If you don't have the receipt, we can't give you a refund.
= _____ you have the receipt, we can't give you a refund.

**24** 어법상 어색한 것은? ★★★

① Do you know when the film begins?
② Please tell me how your brother old is.
③ I'm not sure if Paul likes the blue backpack.
④ She asked me whether I could do the work.
⑤ I wonder how he finished the work.

**25** 다음 글의 주제로 알맞은 것은? ★★

Why do you think we should learn history? Some students complain that history is a boring subject. However, they should know that everything happening in the world today is based on something that already happened in the past. We can only truly understand the present by learning about the past. Nobody knows what will happen in the future, but historical facts will help guide us into the future.

① 역사 공부의 필요성     ② 역사 공부 방법
③ 다양한 역사 해석     ④ 왜곡된 역사
⑤ 미래 기술

**26** 글쓴이에 관한 내용과 일치하지 않는 것은? ★★

My name is Jaden. I work for part-time job at a chocolate factory in London. What do I do here? I taste a variety of flavor of chocolate and predict which one might be popular with teenagers. I sometimes share my ideas for making new chocolate in a meeting. Although it sounds like an unhealthy job, I love my sweet job!

① 초콜릿 공장에서 아르바이트를 한다.
② 다양한 맛의 초콜릿을 시식해 본다.
③ 어떤 초콜릿이 인기가 있을지 예측한다.
④ 새로운 초콜릿에 대한 의견을 나누기도 한다.
⑤ 자신의 일이 건강에 해로운 것 같아 아쉬워한다.

교과서   **get married** 결혼하다   **history** 역사   **complain** 불평하다   **be based on** …에 근거를 두다   **understand** 이해하다   **flavor** 맛
어휘   **predict** 예측하다

[27~28] 다음을 읽고, 물음에 답하시오.

When babies cry, most parents rush to them to check what's wrong. But what if the parents are deaf and cannot hear? It's possible (A) | that / what | they might not notice the baby's cries. So, they aren't able to give them an immediate response. That is when a signal dog can _____. If there's something wrong with the baby, the dog quickly wakes its owner. (B) | Unless / When | its owner wakes up, the dog runs to the baby. But if the owner does not follow, the dog repeats this (C) | until / after | its owner gets to the baby.

★★
**27** 빈칸에 알맞은 것은?

① survive　　② attack　　③ whistle
④ help　　　⑤ sleep

★★★
**28** (A)–(C)에서 어법에 맞는 말이 바르게 짝지어진 것은?

|  | (A) | (B) | (C) |
|---|---|---|---|
| ① | that | – Unless | – until |
| ② | that | – When | – until |
| ③ | that | – When | – after |
| ④ | what | – Unless | – until |
| ⑤ | what | – When | – after |

[29~30] 다음을 읽고, 물음에 답하시오.

Daniel is often forgetful. For example, he frequently leaves things like caps or books at places he visits and loses them. One day, he was wearing a cap. While he was on the bus, he fell asleep. When he opened his eyes, he realized he had to get off. He stood up and rushed out the door. _____ he got off the bus, he thought he had left the cap on the bus. So he ran after the bus to get it back. Then something fell off his head. It was his cap.

★★
**29** 빈칸에 알맞은 것은?

① Unless　　② If　　　③ Before
④ After　　　⑤ Though

★★
**30** (A)–(D)를 일어난 순서대로 배열하시오.

(A) As soon as he woke up, he rushed to get off the bus.
(B) He ran after the bus because he thought he had left the cap there.
(C) Daniel fell asleep on the bus with his cap on.
(D) He realized that the cap was still on his head.

_____ → _____ → _____ → _____

교과서  **rush** 급히 움직이다  **deaf** 청각 장애가 있는  **notice** 알아차리다, 인지하다  **immediate** 즉각적인  **response** 반응  **repeat** 반복하다
어휘  **forgetful** 잘 잊어 먹는  **fall asleep** 잠들다

## A 명사절을 이끄는 접속사

**1 that**: 명사절을 이끌어 문장에서 주어, 보어, 목적어 역할을 한다.

**That** Sumin won the tennis match is true. 〈주어〉

→ **It** is true **that** Sumin won the tennis match. 〈가주어 – 진주어〉

My dream is **that** our team will win the game. 〈보어〉

Justin thinks (**that**) keeping pets teaches us responsibility. 〈목적어〉

**2 if**: '…인지 아닌지'의 뜻으로 명사절을 이끌며, 주로 동사 know, tell, ask 등의 목적어 역할을 한다. 이때 if는 whether와 바꿔 쓸 수 있다.

Can you look out the window and see **if** he is coming? 〈목적어〉

→ Can you look out the window and see **whether** he is coming **or not**?

## B 부사절을 이끄는 접속사

### 1 시간을 나타내는 접속사

| | | |
|---|---|---|
| when …할 때 | while …하는 동안 | as …하면서, …할 때 |
| after …한 후에 | before …하기 전에 | until …할 때까지 |
| since … 이후로 | | |

**When** you take notes, use your own words.

I went out **after** I did my homework.

I have known her **since** she was a child.

### 2 이유 · 결과를 나타내는 접속사

| | | |
|---|---|---|
| because … 때문에 | since … 때문에 | as … 때문에 |
| so 그래서 | so ... that 너무 …해서 …하다 | |

I touched it **because** I was curious.

The box is **so** heavy **that** I can't lift it.

### 3 조건 · 양보를 나타내는 접속사

| | |
|---|---|
| if 만약 …라면 | unless (= if ... not) 만약 …하지 않으면 |
| (al)though 비록 …일지라도 | even if(though) 비록 …일지라도 |

**If** you see Ann, can you call me?

I can't hear you **unless** you speak loudly.

**Though** I'm sitting in the sun, I still feel cold.

**C** 간접의문문

간접의문문은 다른 문장의 일부인 명사절(주어, 목적어, 보어)로 쓰이는 의문문이다.

**1 의문사가 없는 간접의문문:** 〈if(whether)＋주어＋동사〉의 어순으로 나타낸다.

I don't know **if(whether) she will come** to my birthday party.

Do you know **if(whether) he will visit** Paris next month?

**2 의문사가 있는 간접의문문:** 〈의문사＋주어＋동사〉의 어순으로 나타낸다.

I wonder **when you can show** me the pictures.

Amy doesn't understand **why Jack should leave** Korea.

*cf.* 의문사구 how often, what time, how old 등은 간접의문문에서 분리하지
않고 하나의 의문사처럼 쓴다.

David wants to know **how many legs** an ant has.

**D** 주의해야 할 간접의문문

동사 think, imagine, suppose, guess 등이 쓰인 의문문이, 의문사가 있는 간접
의문문을 목적어로 쓰는 경우, 간접의문문의 의문사는 문장의 맨 앞에 쓴다.

**Where** do you guess **they will go** this Sunday?

**Why** do you think **we have to learn** foreign languages?

···························································· **≫ Expression**

**1 의견 묻고 답하기**

❤ 의견 묻기

- What do you think of(about) ...?
- How do you like ...?
- How do you feel about ...?
- What is your view(opinion)?

❤ 의견 표현하기

- (Well,) I think(feel / believe) ....
- It seems to me (that) ....
- In my view(opinion), ....

❤ 선호 표현하기

- I prefer ... to ....
- I like ... better than ....

**2 허가 여부 묻고 답하기**

❤ 허가 여부 묻기

- May(Can) I ...?
- Is it okay if I ...?
- Do you mind if I ...?
- Would it be possible to ...?

❤ 허가하기

- (Yes,) You may(can) ....
- Sure. / Okay. / All right. / Of course.
- I don't mind (at all).

❤ 불허하기

- (No,) You can't(may not) ....
- (I'm afraid) That's(It's) not possible.
- You're not allowed(supposed) to ....

***Problems are not stop signs,
they are guidelines.***

Robert H. Schuller

# II

# 듣기 실전
# 모의고사

**01** 다음을 듣고, 오늘 오후 날씨로 가장 적절한 것을 고르시오.

**02** 대화를 듣고, 여자가 구입할 가방으로 가장 적절한 것을 고르시오.

**03** 대화를 듣고, 남자의 심정으로 가장 적절한 것을 고르시오.

① happy       ② bored       ③ upset
④ nervous     ⑤ excited

**04** 대화를 듣고, 여자가 어제 한 일로 가장 적절한 것을 고르시오.

① 콘서트 가기       ② 병원 가기
③ 병문안 가기       ④ 그림 그리기
⑤ 미술관 방문하기

**05** 대화를 듣고, 두 사람이 대화하는 장소로 가장 적절한 곳을 고르시오.

① 병원       ② 공원       ③ 쇼핑몰
④ 서점       ⑤ 학교

**06** 대화를 듣고, 여자의 마지막 말의 의도로 가장 적절한 것을 고르시오.

① 충고       ② 축하       ③ 허가
④ 위로       ⑤ 동의

**07** 대화를 듣고, 여자가 직업 선택에 있어서 가장 중요하게 생각하는 것을 고르시오.

① 근무 환경       ② 안정성
③ 봉급           ④ 자신의 흥미
⑤ 평판

**08** 대화를 듣고, 여자가 대화 직후에 할 일로 가장 적절한 것을 고르시오.

① 공부하기       ② 서재 청소하기
③ 미술 숙제하기   ④ 탁자 옮기기
⑤ 방 청소하기

**09** 대화를 듣고, 남자가 교환 학생에 대해 언급하지 않은 것을 고르시오.

① 성별       ② 출신 국가
③ 나이       ④ 외모
⑤ 체류 기간

**10** 다음을 듣고, 여자가 하는 말의 내용으로 가장 적절한 것을 고르시오.

① 감자의 효능
② 감자 심는 방법
③ 정원 용품 소개
④ 정원 관람 안내
⑤ 감자를 이용한 조리법

**11** 다음을 듣고, 여자가 하는 말의 내용과 일치하지 **않는** 것을 고르시오.

① 규칙적인 운동은 몸과 마음에 좋다.
② 준비 운동과 정리 운동은 중요하다.
③ 준비 운동을 많이 하면 부상을 당할 수 있다.
④ 정리 운동의 예로 스트레칭이 있다.
⑤ 정리 운동은 몸과 마음을 편안하게 해준다.

**12** 대화를 듣고, 남자가 전화를 건 목적으로 가장 적절한 것을 고르시오.

① 리포트 주제를 물어보기 위해서
② 리포트 제출 날짜를 미루기 위해서
③ 리포트 작성에 도움을 구하기 위해서
④ 강아지를 돌봐 달라고 부탁하기 위해서
⑤ 강아지를 분양하기 위해서

**13** 대화를 듣고, 집들이에 올 사람의 수를 고르시오.

① 5명 ② 6명 ③ 7명
④ 8명 ⑤ 9명

**14** 대화를 듣고, 두 사람의 관계로 가장 적절한 것을 고르시오.

① 환자 – 의사
② 승객 – 승무원
③ 요리 비평가 – 요리사
④ 손님 – 웨이터
⑤ 식당 주인 – 요리사

**15** 대화를 듣고, 남자가 여자에게 부탁한 일로 가장 적절한 것을 고르시오.

① 아들과 대화하기
② 아들의 준비물 챙겨 주기
③ 아들에게 시계 사 주기
④ 아들을 아침에 깨워 주기
⑤ 아들을 학교에 데려다주기

**16** 대화를 듣고, 여자가 동아리 모임에 참석하지 **못한** 이유로 가장 적절한 것을 고르시오.

① 몸이 아파서
② 장소를 잘못 알아서
③ 자동차를 도난당해서
④ 사고로 인해 부상당해서
⑤ 사고에 대해 진술해야 해서

**17** 다음 그림의 상황에 가장 적절한 대화를 고르시오.

① ② ③ ④ ⑤

**18** 다음을 듣고, 남자가 콘서트에 대해 언급하지 **않은** 것을 고르시오.

① 출연자 ② 공연 날짜
③ 공연 시작 시간 ④ 공연 장소
⑤ 입장권 가격

[19-20] 대화를 듣고, 남자의 마지막 말에 이어질 여자의 말로 가장 적절한 것을 고르시오.

**19** Woman: _____

① I will buy some clothes.
② It opens at 10 o'clock.
③ I've never been there before.
④ Why don't you join us?
⑤ It takes about 20 minutes by car.

**20** Woman: _____

① You can do it.
② Thanks for cheering me up.
③ Did you hurt your finger?
④ Now it's your turn.
⑤ Look at those beautiful butterflies.

**01** 다음을 듣고, 오늘 오후 날씨로 가장 적절한 것을 고르시오.

M Good morning, everyone. It's Friday, March 15th. This is the _____ _____. It's sunny and _____ warm now, but it will be cold and windy in the afternoon. The _____ will go down to zero tonight and it's going to start raining tomorrow morning. The rain will _____ throughout the weekend.

**02** 대화를 듣고, 여자가 구입할 가방으로 가장 적절한 것을 고르시오.

W Wow, there are so many interesting things here.
M Yeah, everything here is made from _____ products.
W Is that so? I love that bag _____ _____ blue jeans.
M You mean the backpack over there?
W No, the _____ bag right next to the clutch bag.
M Oh, I see it. The one with a big star on it.
W That's right. I'll buy it.

**03** 대화를 듣고, 남자의 심정으로 가장 적절한 것을 고르시오.

① happy    ② bored    ③ upset
④ nervous    ⑤ excited

M Mom, I'm home.
W Tom, have a seat here. How did the final exam go today?
M The exam was _____ too easy.
W Did you do well on it, then?
M Not really, Mom. I made a lot of _____.
W Everyone makes mistakes. You will do better next time.
M But I'm so _____ _____ myself.
W Just relax. You have another exam tomorrow. Prepare for it while I make you some hot chocolate.

**04** 대화를 듣고, 여자가 어제 한 일로 가장 적절한 것을 고르시오.

① 콘서트 가기    ② 병원 가기
③ 병문안 가기    ④ 그림 그리기
⑤ 미술관 방문하기

M Did you have a good time at Tina's concert yesterday? You said you were going there with your older sister.
W Yeah, that was my plan. But you know what? The concert was _____ at the last moment.
M What? How come?
W They said the singer got a _____ and was hospitalized.
M Oh, I'm sorry to hear that. So, what did you do?
W I went to an _____ _____ with my sister instead. We saw fine artworks and had a lot of fun.
M I'm happy to hear that.

---

**» WORDS**  **clutch bag** 클러치 백(손잡이나 끈이 없는 소형 핸드백)  **final exam** 기말고사  **at the last moment** 막판에
**hospitalize** 입원시키다  **fine** 질 높은, 멋진  **artwork** 미술품, 예술품

**05** 대화를 듣고, 두 사람이 대화하는 장소로 가장 적절한 곳을 고르시오.

① 병원　　② 공원　　③ 쇼핑몰
④ 서점　　⑤ 학교

M　Excuse me, where are the children's books?
W　Oh, children's books are on the _____ _____.
M　Which floor are we on?
W　We are on the second floor. If you want to _____ _____, use the escalator over there.
M　One more question. Where is the check-out counter?
W　It is between the best-seller section and children's book section. You can't _____ it.
M　Thank you so much.

**06** 대화를 듣고, 여자의 마지막 말의 의도로 가장 적절한 것을 고르시오.

① 충고　　② 축하　　③ 허가
④ 위로　　⑤ 동의

W　What's wrong, Jiho? You look like you're _____.
M　I sprained my ankle playing basketball at lunchtime.
W　Did you visit the _____ _____?
M　No, I didn't. I don't think it's _____.
W　But you can't even walk straight.
M　I guess it's getting _____.
W　I think you should visit her.

**07** 대화를 듣고, 여자가 직업 선택에 있어서 가장 중요하게 생각하는 것을 고르시오.

① 근무 환경　　② 안정성
③ 봉급　　　　④ 자신의 흥미
⑤ 평판

W　Jim, have you _____ on a job you want to do?
M　Well, I have a couple of things in mind, but I can't choose one.
W　What do you think is important in choosing a job?
M　Umm... I think stability is the most important. What if I _____ my job in my middle age?
W　That's right. That's why many teenagers want to work for the government.
M　What about you? What's your _____?
W　Stability is important. But I think that it's more important to do something I'm _____ in. I want to enjoy what I do.

>> WORDS　**check-out counter** 계산대　**sprain** 삐다, 접질리다　**stability** 안정성　**government** 정부

**08** 대화를 듣고, 여자가 대화 직후에 할 일로 가장 적절한 것을 고르시오.

① 공부하기
② 서재 청소하기
③ 미술 숙제하기
④ 탁자 옮기기
⑤ 방 청소하기

M What happened to the table in my _____?

W Oh, I moved it to my room. I needed something _____ than my desk for my art homework.

M Then, can you move it back after you finish it?

W Of course I can. But I need one _____ _____ to finish it. Is it okay, Dad?

M It's okay. And if you need my help, just let me know. It's _____.

W I will. Thanks, Dad.

M You're welcome. You can get back to work now.

**09** 대화를 듣고, 남자가 교환 학생에 대해 언급 하지 <u>않은</u> 것을 고르시오.

① 성별
② 출신 국가
③ 나이
④ 외모
⑤ 체류 기간

M Suji, have you heard about the new exchange student?

W Wait. What is an exchange student?

M A student from another country comes to our school and _____ for a while to study with us.

W For how _____?

M I don't know exactly. But I heard that student is a girl from Canada. She is 15 years old, and pretty!

W You must be thrilled. Oh, she's our age. Then she might be in our _____.

M That's the point. She's going to be our classmate. Isn't it cool?

W Yes. I can't _____ to meet her.

**10** 다음을 듣고, 여자가 하는 말의 내용으로 가장 적절한 것을 고르시오.

① 감자의 효능
② 감자 심는 방법
③ 정원 용품 소개
④ 정원 관람 안내
⑤ 감자를 이용한 조리법

W Listen carefully, everyone. We are here to _____ potatoes today. All of you should have pieces of potatoes, a shovel, and a watering pot. Move to your _____ in the garden and _____ a deep hole in the ground. Then, place a piece of potato and put _____ on it. Water it well, and _____ the same steps over and over again.

>> WORDS   **exchange student** 교환 학생   **thrilled** 아주 신이 난   **shovel** 삽   **watering pot** 물뿌리개

**11** 다음을 듣고, 여자가 하는 말의 내용과 일치하지 **않는** 것을 고르시오.

① 규칙적인 운동은 몸과 마음에 좋다.
② 준비 운동과 정리 운동은 중요하다.
③ 준비 운동을 많이 하면 부상을 당할 수 있다.
④ 정리 운동의 예로 스트레칭이 있다.
⑤ 정리 운동은 몸과 마음을 편안하게 해준다.

W   Do you exercise regularly? It's well-known that _____ _____ is good for your body and mind. But did you know that warm-up and _____ exercises are important as well? Warm-up exercises help your body _____ _____ for the main exercise and reduce the risk of injuries. Cool-down exercises like stretching _____ your body and mind. So, don't forget to warm up and cool down before and after exercising.

**12** 대화를 듣고, 남자가 전화를 건 목적으로 가장 적절한 것을 고르시오.

① 리포트 주제를 물어보기 위해서
② 리포트 제출 날짜를 미루기 위해서
③ 리포트 작성에 도움을 구하기 위해서
④ 강아지를 돌봐 달라고 부탁하기 위해서
⑤ 강아지를 분양하기 위해서

*[Telephone rings.]*

W   Hello?
M   Hello. Ms. White. This is David.
W   Hi, David. What's up?
M   I called you to ask for a _____. Is it okay if I hand in the report the day after tomorrow?
W   But the report is _____ tomorrow.
M   Yes, I know. But something _____ happened. My dog gave birth to puppies. So, I have to take care of them.
W   Oh, congratulations. Okay. I'll give you one more day. But _____ _____ you hand it in first thing in the morning the day after tomorrow.
M   Of course I will. Thank you so much.

**13** 대화를 듣고, 집들이에 올 사람의 수를 고르시오.

① 5명      ② 6명      ③ 7명
④ 8명      ⑤ 9명

W   Did you send the _____ to our housewarming party?
M   Yes. I _____ them _____ at work today.
W   How many people are coming over?
M   Three people said they were coming. How about your friends?
W   Two _____ are coming.
M   Then seven people are coming, right?
W   Oh, wait. Susan's husband is on a business trip, so she will come _____.
M   Okay.

>> **WORDS**   **well-known** 유명한, 잘 알려진   **risk** 위험   **injury** 부상   **hand in** 제출하다   **first thing** 맨 먼저   **housewarming party** 집들이
**come over** 오다   **business trip** 출장

**14** 대화를 듣고, 두 사람의 관계로 가장 적절한 것을 고르시오.

① 환자 – 의사
② 승객 – 승무원
③ 요리 비평가 – 요리사
④ 손님 – 웨이터
⑤ 식당 주인 – 요리사

W  May I have the _____, please?
M  Okay. I will bring it to you right now. *[Pause]* Here it is. Did you enjoy the _____?
W  Yes, everything was so delicious. But I want to _____ just one thing.
M  What is it? Were there any problems?
W  I asked for extra bread before, but I didn't get it.
M  Oh, I'm so sorry about that. I totally _____ about it.
W  That's all right.

**15** 대화를 듣고, 남자가 여자에게 부탁한 일로 가장 적절한 것을 고르시오.

① 아들과 대화하기
② 아들의 준비물 챙겨 주기
③ 아들에게 시계 사 주기
④ 아들을 아침에 깨워 주기
⑤ 아들을 학교에 데려다주기

*[Telephone rings.]*
M  Hello, Ms. Wright. This is John Clark.
W  Hello. Mr. Clark. Is there something _____ with Chris?
M  He was late for school again. This is the _____ time this week.
W  Oh, I'm so sorry. I didn't know that. You know, I leave home _____ _____ him every morning.
M  Could you _____ him _____ before you leave home, Ms. Wright? He says he can't hear the alarm clock ringing.
W  Okay. I'll make sure he is wide awake before I leave home. I'm sorry again.

**16** 대화를 듣고, 여자가 동아리 모임에 참석하지 못한 이유로 가장 적절한 것을 고르시오.

① 몸이 아파서
② 장소를 잘못 알아서
③ 자동차를 도난당해서
④ 사고로 인해 부상당해서
⑤ 사고에 대해 진술해야 해서

M  Hey, Yuna. Where were you yesterday? We were supposed to have the club meeting at the school library.
W  Yeah, I know. But there was a _____ _____ on my way to school.
M  What? Were you hurt?
W  No, I wasn't. I wasn't in the accident. I just _____ it.
M  That's a relief. Then why didn't you come?
W  I was the only one who saw the accident. So I had to tell the _____ about it. It took a longer time than I expected.
M  Oh, I see. Anyway, you were _____.

---

>> **WORDS**  **ring** 울리다  **wide awake** 완전히 깨어 있는, 정신이 말똥말똥한  **be supposed to** …하기로 되어 있다  **relief** 안도, 안심

**17** 다음 그림의 상황에 가장 적절한 대화를 고르시오.

① ② ③ ④ ⑤

① W  Are you ready to _____?

　M  Yes, I'd like a cup of coffee.

② W  Does this bus go to City Hall?

　M  No, the bus to City Hall runs _____ the street.

③ W  How much is it?

　M  It is 2,000 won.

④ W  May I _____ the window?

　M  Sure. Go ahead.

⑤ W  Please show me your driver's license.

　M  Here it is.

**18** 다음을 듣고, 남자가 콘서트에 대해 언급하지 <u>않은</u> 것을 고르시오.

① 출연자　　　　② 공연 날짜
③ 공연 시작 시간　④ 공연 장소
⑤ 입장권 가격

M  Hello, everyone. I'm Peter Park, manager at MJ Record Company. We will _____ a concert called the Fantasy Music Festival. Famous pop singers and musicians will sing at the concert. It will start at 6 p.m. next Saturday. It will _____ _____ at the Olympic Stadium Concert Hall. Tickets are 40 dollars for _____. Those who are under 19 can get 50 percent discount. You can buy tickets _____ at the box office or online.

**[19-20]** 대화를 듣고, 남자의 마지막 말에 이어질 여자의 말로 가장 적절한 것을 고르시오.

**19** ① I will buy some clothes.
② It opens at 10 o'clock.
③ I've never been there before.
④ Why don't you join us?
⑤ It takes about 20 minutes by car.

W  Do you have any _____ _____ for the weekend?

M  I'm thinking of reading some books at home. What about you?

W  I'm going to the new shopping center with my parents.

M  Oh, I've heard about it. What are you going to buy there?

W  I need a _____ of boots, and my parents want a new dinner table.

M  Is it _____ from here? How long does it take to get there?

**20** ① You can do it.
② Thanks for cheering me up.
③ Did you hurt your finger?
④ Now it's your turn.
⑤ Look at those beautiful butterflies.

M  Yuri, are you ready to get on the _____?

W  Almost. I have butterflies in my _____. What if I forget the lyrics?

M  Don't worry. You practiced a lot. Just _____ yourself.

W  Okay. Can I have some water?

M  Sure, here it is. Look at me. You will do great. I'll keep my _____ crossed for you.

---

**>> WORDS**　**driver's license** 운전면허증　**box office** 매표소　**have butterflies** (긴장해서) 가슴이 벌렁거리다　**lyric** (노래의) 가사

**01** 다음을 듣고, 부산의 현재 날씨로 가장 적절한 것을 고르시오.

**02** 대화를 듣고, 남자가 구입할 물건으로 가장 적절한 것을 고르시오.

**03** 대화를 듣고, 여자의 심정 변화로 가장 적절한 것을 고르시오.

① bored → excited
② happy → worried
③ worried → relieved
④ relieved → happy
⑤ excited → disappointed

**04** 대화를 듣고, 여자가 지난 주말에 한 일로 가장 적절한 것을 고르시오.

① 숙제하기
② 동생 돌보기
③ 양로원 방문하기
④ 탁아소 청소하기
⑤ 탁아소 아이들과 놀아 주기

**05** 대화를 듣고, 두 사람이 대화하는 장소로 가장 적절한 곳을 고르시오.

① bank          ② school
③ restaurant     ④ shopping mall
⑤ amusement park

**06** 대화를 듣고, 여자의 마지막 말의 의도로 가장 적절한 것을 고르시오.

① 비난       ② 반대       ③ 격려
④ 간청       ⑤ 부탁

**07** 대화를 듣고, 여자가 가장 좋아하는 과목을 고르시오.

① 수학       ② 국어       ③ 중국어
④ 체육       ⑤ 영어

**08** 대화를 듣고, 여자가 대화 직후에 할 일로 가장 적절한 것을 고르시오.

① 택시 타기              ② 119에 전화하기
③ 병원에 가기            ④ 약국에 가기
⑤ 학교에 전화하기

**09** 대화를 듣고, 여자가 태국에서 할 일이 아닌 것을 고르시오.

① 시내 구경하기          ② 현지 시장 방문하기
③ 마사지 받기            ④ 해변 구경하기
⑤ 해산물 맛보기

**10** 다음을 듣고, 남자가 하는 말의 내용으로 가장 적절한 것을 고르시오.

① 숙면의 중요성
② 불면증의 원인
③ 간단한 스트레칭 방법
④ 잠이 잘 오게 하는 방법
⑤ 규칙적인 운동의 필요성

11 다음을 듣고, 여자가 하는 말의 내용과 일치하지 <u>않는</u> 것을 고르시오.

① 내일 소방 훈련이 있을 것이다.
② 오전 수업이 10분씩 단축될 것이다.
③ 점심시간 후에 훈련을 할 것이다.
④ 훈련은 40분 정도 걸릴 것이다.
⑤ 학생들은 방송에 귀를 기울여야 한다.

12 대화를 듣고, 남자가 전화를 건 목적으로 가장 적절한 것을 고르시오.

① 상품에 대해 문의하기 위해서
② 배송 날짜를 변경하기 위해서
③ 상품에 대해 항의하기 위해서
④ 구매한 상품을 반품하기 위해서
⑤ 인터넷 구매 방법에 대해 문의하기 위해서

13 대화를 듣고, 남자가 지불해야 할 금액으로 가장 적절한 것을 고르시오.

① $54　　② $56　　③ $60
④ $66　　⑤ $70

14 대화를 듣고, 두 사람의 관계로 가장 적절한 것을 고르시오.

① 식당 종업원 – 손님　　② 은행원 – 손님
③ 의사 – 환자　　④ 경찰관 – 운전자
⑤ 가게 점원 – 손님

15 대화를 듣고, 여자가 남자에게 부탁한 일로 가장 적절한 것을 고르시오.

① 일찍 귀가하기
② 함께 쿠키 만들기
③ 간식거리 사다 주기
④ 학교로 데리러 오기
⑤ 식료품점에 데려다주기

16 대화를 듣고, 남자가 잠을 이루지 <u>못하는</u> 이유로 가장 적절한 것을 고르시오.

① 너무 피곤해서
② 시험을 망쳐서
③ 내일 시험이 있어서
④ 중요한 물건을 잃어버려서
⑤ 시험 때문에 스트레스를 받아서

17 다음 그림의 상황에 가장 적절한 대화를 고르시오.

①　　②　　③　　④　　⑤

18 다음을 듣고, 남자가 안내 방송에서 언급하지 <u>않은</u> 것을 고르시오.

① 항공기 번호　　② 현재 시각
③ 목적지　　④ 도착 시간
⑤ 목적지 날씨

[19-20] 대화를 듣고, 남자의 마지막 말에 이어질 여자의 말로 가장 적절한 것을 고르시오.

19 Woman: _____

① It's $10.
② What's your size?
③ How much is this?
④ Show me another one.
⑤ Do you have it in a small size?

20 Woman: _____

① I've been there.
② Why are you going there?
③ I'm still looking for a job.
④ I'm here for sightseeing.
⑤ Congratulations. I'm happy for you.

**01** 다음을 듣고, 부산의 현재 날씨로 가장 적절한 것을 고르시오.

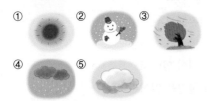

① ② ③ ④ ⑤

W  Hello, everyone. Welcome to the weather channel. Here is today's weather for South Korea. The sun is _____ in Seoul and the temperature is around 19 degrees Celsius. It is sunny and _____ also in Daejeon. In Busan, it's _____ now, and there is a _____ of rain in the late afternoon.

**02** 대화를 듣고, 남자가 구입할 물건으로 가장 적절한 것을 고르시오.

① ② ③ ④ ⑤

W  Minho, what are you doing here?

M  Hi, Jiyeon. I'm _____ _____ a gift for my little brother. His birthday is next week.

W  What about this top? You know, spinning tops are _____ _____ young boys these days.

M  He does like tops but I want to give him something to use at school.

W  I see. Then, how about this pencil case? He can _____ pens and pencils in it.

M  That's a great idea. Thanks a lot.

**03** 대화를 듣고, 여자의 심정 변화로 가장 적절한 것을 고르시오.

① bored → excited
② happy → worried
③ worried → relieved
④ relieved → happy
⑤ excited → disappointed

W  Oh, no!

M  What's wrong?

W  I think I _____ the tickets for the movie. It starts in five minutes. What should I do?

M  Don't worry. You _____ _____ tickets.

W  How come?

M  Just _____ the cinema app on your cell phone. Then you can see the tickets on the app.

W  Wow, is it that simple? I'm _____ now.

**04** 대화를 듣고, 여자가 지난 주말에 한 일로 가장 적절한 것을 고르시오.

① 숙제하기
② 동생 돌보기
③ 양로원 방문하기
④ 탁아소 청소하기
⑤ 탁아소 아이들과 놀아 주기

M  Jina, what did you do last weekend?

W  I did some _____ _____.

M  Where did you volunteer?

W  I visited a day-care center for children.

M  Did you _____ _____ of the children there?

W  Not really. It was my first time doing volunteer work there, so I just _____ the rooms and toys.

M  I see.

---

≫ **WORDS**  **spinning top** 팽이  **app** 애플리케이션, 응용 프로그램  **day-care center** 탁아소

**05** 대화를 듣고, 두 사람이 대화하는 장소로 가장 적절한 곳을 고르시오.

① bank
② school
③ restaurant
④ shopping mall
⑤ amusement park

M  Wow, this place is really _____.
W  Yeah, it will take a day to go on every ride.
M  Let's _____ _____ to ride first.
W  We should ride on the roller coaster first. Look! It looks exciting!
M  But look at that line. It's too long.
W  We can wait. It will take _____ _____ an hour to get on the roller coaster.
M  Okay. Let's wait in line, then.

**06** 대화를 듣고, 여자의 마지막 말의 의도로 가장 적절한 것을 고르시오.

① 비난      ② 반대      ③ 격려
④ 간청      ⑤ 부탁

M  Sora, I'm thinking of _____ for student president.
W  Oh, really? Good for you. I'm sure you will do a good job.
M  But my _____ will be hard to beat. She's smart, pretty, and very popular among students.
W  You are as _____ as her. And even if you lose, you will learn a lot from this.
M  I agree on that.
W  Cheer up! You have my full _____.

**07** 대화를 듣고, 여자가 가장 좋아하는 과목을 고르시오.

① 수학      ② 국어      ③ 중국어
④ 체육      ⑤ 영어

M  Will you tell me about your school?
W  Okay, Dad. I have six classes a day, and the last class _____ at 3 o'clock.
M  Tell me more about your classes.
W  I learn _____ subjects a week, and I like most of them. Oh, _____ _____ one. I hate math.
M  Why is that?
W  It's too difficult for me. But I really like language classes like Korean, English, and Chinese. English is my _____ _____.
M  I'm glad to hear that.

>> WORDS  ride 타다; 놀이 기구  beat 이기다  subject 과목  hate 싫어하다  language 언어

**08** 대화를 듣고, 여자가 대화 직후에 할 일로 가장 적절한 것을 고르시오.

① 택시 타기    ② 119에 전화하기
③ 병원에 가기    ④ 약국에 가기
⑤ 학교에 전화하기

*[Telephone rings.]*

**W** Hi, Tony. What's up?

**M** Mom. Are you busy _____ _____ right now?

**W** No, I'm not that busy right now. Is there any problem?

**M** I'm sick. I have a _____ and I can't move at all.

**W** Since when have you been _____?

**M** I was cold and dizzy at school, but it's getting worse.

**W** Okay. I'll be right there. It will take 20 minutes by taxi. _____ for me.

**09** 대화를 듣고, 여자가 태국에서 할 일이 <u>아닌</u> 것을 고르시오.

① 시내 구경하기
② 현지 시장 방문하기
③ 마사지 받기
④ 해변 구경하기
⑤ 해산물 맛보기

**M** Hajin, what are you going to do this summer vacation?

**W** I'm going on a _____ to Thailand with my family.

**M** What are you going to do there?

**W** Well, we will take a tour of the city and go to the _____ _____.

**M** I heard Thailand is famous for its massage services.

**W** My parents want to get massages, but I don't.

**M** I see. Oh, don't forget to go to the beach and enjoy the _____.

**W** I won't. I'm really _____ _____ to the trip.

**10** 다음을 듣고, 남자가 하는 말의 내용으로 가장 적절한 것을 고르시오.

① 숙면의 중요성
② 불면증의 원인
③ 간단한 스트레칭 방법
④ 잠이 잘 오게 하는 방법
⑤ 규칙적인 운동의 필요성

**M** Do you have _____ going to sleep at night? Here are some _____ for you. First, try to go to sleep at the same time every day. Then your body will be _____ to sleep at that time. Second, take a warm bath before you go to bed. It will help your body and mind relaxed. Another good way is doing some simple _____. Then you will _____ _____ more easily.

>> **WORDS**    **dizzy** 어지러운    **worse** 더 심한, 악화된    **warm bath** 온욕

**11** 다음을 듣고, 여자가 하는 말의 내용과 일치하지 <u>않는</u> 것을 고르시오.

① 내일 소방 훈련이 있을 것이다.
② 오전 수업이 10분씩 단축될 것이다.
③ 점심시간 후에 훈련을 할 것이다.
④ 훈련은 40분 정도 걸릴 것이다.
⑤ 학생들은 방송에 귀를 기울여야 한다.

W  Hello, students. This is your principal. Tomorrow, we are going to have a _____ _____. Morning classes will end ten minutes _____ each. We will have the drill before lunchtime, and it will take about 40 minutes. After the fourth period _____, everyone should stay at their _____ and listen carefully to the _____.

**12** 대화를 듣고, 남자가 전화를 건 목적으로 가장 적절한 것을 고르시오.

① 상품에 대해 문의하기 위해서
② 배송 날짜를 변경하기 위해서
③ 상품에 대해 항의하기 위해서
④ 구매한 상품을 반품하기 위해서
⑤ 인터넷 구매 방법에 대해 문의하기 위해서

*[Telephone rings.]*
W  Hello, Ace Mall customer service.
M  I'd like to _____ a jacket.
W  I'm sorry you were not _____ with our item. When did you buy it?
M  I bought it last Wednesday.
W  Did you buy it online or at the _____?
M  Online.
W  Then you'll have to make a _____ for the return online. I'll tell you how to do it.

**13** 대화를 듣고, 남자가 지불해야 할 금액으로 가장 적절한 것을 고르시오.

① $54    ② $56    ③ $60
④ $66    ⑤ $70

W  Did you enjoy our food, sir?
M  Yes, we are all _____ with the food and service.
W  I'm happy to hear that. So, there were four adults in your _____, right?
M  No, there were only three.
W  Oh, sorry. There's a mistake in the _____. Let me check. *[Pause]* You're right. Three adults.
M  So is the bill 60 dollars?
W  No, it isn't. We are currently offering ten percent _____ for parties of three or more.
M  Really? That's good. Here's my credit card.

>> **WORDS**  **principal** 교장  **drill** 훈련  **period** (학교의 일과를 나눠 놓은) 시간  **customer service** 고객 서비스  **currently** 현재, 지금

02회 듣기 실전 모의고사  **125**

**14** 대화를 듣고, 두 사람의 관계로 가장 적절한 것을 고르시오.

① 식당 종업원 – 손님
② 은행원 – 손님
③ 의사 – 환자
④ 경찰관 – 운전자
⑤ 가게 점원 – 손님

M How can I help you, ma'am?
W I'd like to _____ a bank account.
M What kind of account would you like to open?
W I need a _____ account.
M Would you also like to open a _____ account?
W No, that's fine.
M Please _____ _____ this form and show me your identification card.

**15** 대화를 듣고, 여자가 남자에게 부탁한 일로 가장 적절한 것을 고르시오.

① 일찍 귀가하기
② 함께 쿠키 만들기
③ 간식거리 사다 주기
④ 학교로 데리러 오기
⑤ 식료품점에 데려다주기

[Telephone rings.]
M Hi, Jenny. What's up?
W Dad, when are you _____ _____?
M I'm driving home now. I'll be back in 20 minutes.
W Can I ask you something?
M Of course, sweety. Just tell me.
W Can you _____ _____ the grocery store and get me some cookies and milk?
M Of course I can. Is there _____ else you need?
W That's all. Thanks.

**16** 대화를 듣고, 남자가 잠을 이루지 못하는 이유로 가장 적절한 것을 고르시오.

① 너무 피곤해서
② 시험을 망쳐서
③ 내일 시험이 있어서
④ 중요한 물건을 잃어버려서
⑤ 시험 때문에 스트레스를 받아서

W Why are you still _____, Mike? It's almost 2 a.m.
M I can't sleep _____ of the test.
W But the test is next week.
M I'm _____ out because of it. I really want to do well this time.
W Mike. Just relax. If you have too much _____ on the test, you won't get a good score.
M Is it true, Mom?
W Of course it is. So relax, and get some sleep.

>> **WORDS**  account 계좌  identification card 신분증  grocery store 식료품점

**17** 다음 그림의 상황에 가장 적절한 대화를 고르시오.

① ② ③ ④ ⑤

① W Excuse me, sir. You _____ your wallet.

　M Oh, I didn't know that. Thank you so much.

② W Could you _____ me some money?

　M How much do you need?

③ W What present do you have _____ _____?

　M What about a wallet?

④ W Can you show me the way to the subway station?

　M Sure. Go down two blocks.

⑤ W Do you have _____ _____?

　M It's three thirty right now.

**18** 다음을 듣고, 남자가 안내 방송에서 언급하지 <u>않은</u> 것을 고르시오.

① 항공기 번호　　② 현재 시각
③ 목적지　　　　④ 도착 시간
⑤ 목적지 날씨

M Good afternoon, passengers. This is your captain speaking. First I'd like to welcome everyone on ABC Flight 75A. It is 1:25 p.m. now, and the weather looks good. We are _____ to land in London approximately fifteen minutes _____ of schedule. The weather in London is clear and sunny. I'll talk to you again before we _____ our destination. Enjoy your flight. Thank you.

**[19-20]** 대화를 듣고, 남자의 마지막 말에 이어질 여자의 말로 가장 적절한 것을 고르시오.

**19** ① It's $10.
② What's your size?
③ How much is this?
④ Show me another one.
⑤ Do you have it in a small size?

M Excuse me. Could you help me?

W Certainly. What can I do for you?

M I'm _____ _____ a T-shirt.

W What about this one over here? It sells very well.

M Well. Actually, I want a _____ T-shirt.

W Then, how about this one?

M I really like it. It's so nice.

W Would you like to _____ it _____?

M I'd love to, but it looks a little small for me.

**20** ① I've been there.
② Why are you going there?
③ I'm still looking for a job.
④ I'm here for sightseeing.
⑤ Congratulations. I'm happy for you.

W Hi, Paul. It's a _____ to see you here.

M Hi, Mina. It's been a long time. How have you _____?

W Pretty good. Thanks. How about you?

M I've been great, too. Oh, I'm _____ for China next month.

W Why? To study?

M No. I got a _____ there.

**>> WORDS**　wallet 지갑　**present** 선물　**captain** 기장　**land** 착륙하다　**approximately** 대략　**destination** 목적지

**01** 다음을 듣고, 내일의 날씨로 가장 적절한 것을 고르시오.

**02** 대화를 듣고, 남자가 마음에 들어 하는 머그컵으로 가장 적절한 것을 고르시오.

**03** 대화를 듣고, 여자의 심정으로 가장 적절한 것을 고르시오.

① proud   ② angry   ③ surprised
④ sad   ⑤ happy

**04** 대화를 듣고, 남자가 지난 주말에 한 일로 가장 적절한 것을 고르시오.

① 영화 보기   ② 책 읽기
③ 밭 갈기   ④ 동물 먹이 주기
⑤ 씨앗 심기

**05** 대화를 듣고, 두 사람이 대화하는 장소로 가장 적절한 곳을 고르시오.

① 병원   ② 주유소   ③ 경찰서
④ 공항   ⑤ 자동차 정비소

**06** 대화를 듣고, 여자의 마지막 말의 의도로 가장 적절한 것을 고르시오.

① 거절   ② 칭찬   ③ 부탁
④ 동의   ⑤ 위로

**07** 대화를 듣고, 여자가 지적한 나비정원의 문제점으로 가장 적절한 것을 고르시오.

① 비싼 입장료
② 협소한 주차장
③ 적은 수의 나비
④ 너무 많은 이용객
⑤ 다양하지 않은 야생 식물

**08** 대화를 듣고, 남자가 대화 직후에 할 일로 가장 적절한 것을 고르시오.

① 버터 만들기   ② 샌드위치 먹기
③ 샌드위치 만들기   ④ 은행에서 돈 찾기
⑤ 슈퍼마켓 가기

**09** 대화를 듣고, 여자가 에너지 절약 방법에 대해 언급하지 않은 것을 고르시오.

① 전등 끄기   ② 가전제품 끄기
③ 계단 이용하기   ④ 밤에 커튼 치기
⑤ 충전기 뽑기

**10** 다음을 듣고, 남자가 하는 말의 내용으로 가장 적절한 것을 고르시오.

① 신간 도서 소개   ② 베스트셀러 목록
③ 책 사인회 개최   ④ 영업시간 연장
⑤ 신입 사원 모집

**11** 다음을 듣고, 여자가 하는 말의 내용과 일치하지 <u>않는</u> 것을 고르시오.

① 일반적으로 패스트푸드에는 지방과 소금이 많다.
② 패스트푸드 식당에서 건강한 음식을 제공하고 있다.
③ 저지방, 저염 식단은 건강에 좋지 않다.
④ 패스트푸드 식당에서 샐러드를 먹을 수 있다.
⑤ 자신만의 버거와 샌드위치를 만들 수 있는 패스트푸드 식당이 있다.

**12** 대화를 듣고, 여자가 전화를 건 목적으로 가장 적절한 것을 고르시오.

① 예약을 하기 위해서
② 예약을 변경하기 위해서
③ 예약을 취소하기 위해서
④ 음식에 대해 불평하기 위해서
⑤ 잃어버린 물건을 찾기 위해서

**13** 대화를 듣고, 두 사람이 만날 시각을 고르시오.
① 7:30 a.m.  ② 8:00 a.m.  ③ 8:30 a.m.
④ 9:00 a.m.  ⑤ 9:30 a.m.

**14** 대화를 듣고, 두 사람의 관계로 가장 적절한 것을 고르시오.

① 간호사 – 환자      ② 교사 – 학생
③ 종업원 – 손님      ④ 연출자 – 배우
⑤ 코치 – 운동선수

**15** 대화를 듣고, 여자가 남자에게 부탁한 일로 가장 적절한 것을 고르시오.

① 여행 같이 가기      ② 아침에 깨워 주기
③ 여행 가방 싸 주기    ④ 운전 가르쳐 주기
⑤ 여행지까지 태워다 주기

**16** 대화를 듣고, 남자가 테니스 수업에 가지 않은 이유로 가장 적절한 것을 고르시오.

① 몸이 아파서
② 급한 일이 생겨서
③ 이사를 가게 되어서
④ 다른 운동을 배워서
⑤ 수업 시간을 잘못 알아서

**17** 다음 그림의 상황에 가장 적절한 대화를 고르시오.

①      ②      ③      ④      ⑤

**18** 다음을 듣고, 여자가 재즈 축제에 대해 언급하지 <u>않은</u> 것을 고르시오.

① 연기 사유          ② 개최 날짜
③ 장소 변동 여부      ④ 입장권 가격
⑤ 환불 방법

[19-20] 대화를 듣고, 여자의 마지막 말에 이어질 남자의 말로 가장 적절한 것을 고르시오.

**19** Man: _____

① Let's go there.
② It was too expensive.
③ I didn't like the service.
④ The waiters were so kind.
⑤ Why don't we go to the Korean restaurant?

**20** Man: _____

① No, I am not.
② I agree with you.
③ I've already been there.
④ How about this Saturday?
⑤ I bought a pair of jeans there.

# Dictation Test >> 03회

**01** 다음을 듣고, 내일의 날씨로 가장 적절한 것을 고르시오.

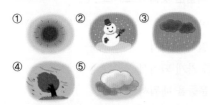

① ② ③ ④ ⑤

M Good morning. I'm Jim Clark from the weather center. Today, it's going to be cloudy and rainy in some _____. The rain will _____ by tonight. Tomorrow it will be _____ all around the country with a _____ of 30 degrees Celsius in the afternoon. Don't forget to wear a hat when you go out.

**02** 대화를 듣고, 남자가 마음에 들어 하는 머그컵으로 가장 적절한 것을 고르시오.

① ② ③ ④ ⑤

M Wow, look at these mugs. Are they all yours?

W No, they're my parents'. They buy mugs every time they _____ _____.

M So they're all from different countries. Fantastic! I really like the one on the top of the _____.

W You mean with stars and the moon on it?

M No, the one right next to it.

W Ah, the one with a _____ on it, right?

M That's it. It's so pretty.

**03** 대화를 듣고, 여자의 심정으로 가장 적절한 것을 고르시오.

① proud ② angry ③ surprised
④ sad ⑤ happy

W Did you _____ your homework, Andy?

M Not yet. I'll do it after watching this program.

W But you said you would do it after _____ games in the morning.

M This program _____ only in 20 minutes, Mom.

W Don't _____ _____ your work. How many times do I have to tell you?

M Okay, Mom. I got it.

W I'm warning you. Turn off the TV and go to your room now.

**04** 대화를 듣고, 남자가 지난 주말에 한 일로 가장 적절한 것을 고르시오.

① 영화 보기 ② 책 읽기
③ 밭 갈기 ④ 동물 먹이 주기
⑤ 씨앗 심기

M What did you do last weekend?

W I _____ _____ watching movies and reading books. What about you?

M I went to my grandmother's to help her with the farm work.

W Farm work? Sounds tough. Did you _____ a field?

M No, nothing like that. I just _____ the farm animals and _____ some fruits.

W That must be exciting.

---

>> WORDS   **mug** 머그컵   **warn** 경고하다   **farm** 농장   **field** 밭

**05** 대화를 듣고, 두 사람이 대화하는 장소로 가장 적절한 곳을 고르시오.

① 병원　　　　② 주유소
③ 경찰서　　　④ 공항
⑤ 자동차 정비소

M   What can I do for you?

W   I think there's a problem with my car. Sometimes it makes a lot of _____ when I start the engine.

M   Umm... there must be something wrong. Let me take a _____ _____.

W   How long will it take?

M   It will take _____ _____ half an hour.

W   Then I will be back in 30 minutes.

M   Okay.

**06** 대화를 듣고, 여자의 마지막 말의 의도로 가장 적절한 것을 고르시오.

① 거절　　② 칭찬　　③ 부탁
④ 동의　　⑤ 위로

W   You look gloomy. What's wrong?

M   Oh, I feel _____.

W   What happened? Tell me about it.

M   I was cleaning my teacher's desk, and I dropped her cell phone _____ _____.

W   Oh, that's too bad. Did the cell phone _____?

M   The cell phone works but the screen is cracked. She says it's okay, but I feel _____ about it.

W   Don't be so _____. It was an accident.

**07** 대화를 듣고, 여자가 지적한 나비정원의 문제점으로 가장 적절한 것을 고르시오.

① 비싼 입장료
② 협소한 주차장
③ 적은 수의 나비
④ 너무 많은 이용객
⑤ 다양하지 않은 야생 식물

M   Did you hear that the Butterfly Garden opened last week?

W   Yeah. Actually, I went there with my family last weekend.

M   Really? How was it? They say they have a lot of _____ _____ there.

W   That's right. There were many I had never seen before. And there were lots of butterflies, too.

M   That's why they _____ it the Butterfly Garden. So, was everything great?

W   Yes, except for one thing. The parking lot was too _____. We had to wait for an hour to park the car.

M   Um. That's a problem.

---

**>> WORDS**　**gloomy** 우울한　**drop** 떨어뜨리다　**crack** 금이 가다　**park** 주차하다

**08** 대화를 듣고, 남자가 대화 직후에 할 일로 가장 적절한 것을 고르시오.

① 버터 만들기　　② 샌드위치 먹기
③ 샌드위치 만들기　④ 은행에서 돈 찾기
⑤ 슈퍼마켓 가기

M Mom. I'm _____.
W Do you want me to _____ you some sandwiches?
M That would be nice.
W Oh, there's no butter in the _____.
M I'll go get some butter at the _____ supermarket.
W Will you? Take the money on the table.
M Okay, Mom.

**09** 대화를 듣고, 여자가 에너지 절약 방법에 대해 언급하지 않은 것을 고르시오.

① 전등 끄기　　② 가전제품 끄기
③ 계단 이용하기　④ 밤에 커튼 치기
⑤ 충전기 뽑기

M I have to write a report about _____ _____ at home. But I don't have any ideas.
W There are many easy _____ you can save energy at home.
M Like what? Give me some _____.
W Well, you can turn off the lights and electrical appliances when they are not _____ _____.
M That's right. Anything else?
W You can also close the curtains at night and _____ battery chargers when the batteries are fully charged.
M Wow! There are a lot of simple ways to save energy.

**10** 다음을 듣고, 남자가 하는 말의 내용으로 가장 적절한 것을 고르시오.

① 신간 도서 소개　② 베스트셀러 목록
③ 책 사인회 개최　④ 영업시간 연장
⑤ 신입 사원 모집

M Hello, this is the manager speaking. Can I have your _____ for one minute, please? For this month's special event, the _____ of the best-seller, Sally Brown will be coming to our bookstore. She will _____ _____ of her books. The event will be at 2 p.m. this Saturday. We would like to _____ you to come and talk with her. Thank you.

>> WORDS　**electrical appliance** 가전제품　**charger** 충전기　**charge** 충전하다

**11** 다음을 듣고, 여자가 하는 말의 내용과 일치하지 <u>않는</u> 것을 고르시오.

① 일반적으로 패스트푸드에는 지방과 소금이 많다.
② 패스트푸드 식당에서 건강한 음식을 제공하고 있다.
③ 저지방, 저염 식단은 건강에 좋지 않다.
④ 패스트푸드 식당에서 샐러드를 먹을 수 있다.
⑤ 자신만의 버거와 샌드위치를 만들 수 있는 패스트푸드 식당이 있다.

W  Many people think fast food is bad for one's health. In general, fast food _____ a lot of fat and salt. These days, however, fast food restaurants are _____. More and more customers are concerned about their _____. Therefore, fast food restaurants are offering healthy food like low-fat, low-salt meals and _____ salads. Customers can even _____ ingredients and make their own burgers and sandwiches.

**12** 대화를 듣고, 여자가 전화를 건 목적으로 가장 적절한 것을 고르시오.

① 예약을 하기 위해서
② 예약을 변경하기 위해서
③ 예약을 취소하기 위해서
④ 음식에 대해 불평하기 위해서
⑤ 잃어버린 물건을 찾기 위해서

[Telephone rings.]

M  Best Dining Restaurant. How can I help you?

W  Hello. I ate brunch at your restaurant this morning and I think I _____ my wallet there.

M  Let me check if anyone _____ _____ a wallet. Just a moment.

W  Okay.

M  Is it a _____ wallet in wine color?

W  That's it. I'm glad someone found it.

M  Drop by here _____ to get it.

**13** 대화를 듣고, 두 사람이 만날 시각을 고르시오.

① 7:30 a.m.       ② 8:00 a.m.
③ 8:30 a.m.       ④ 9:00 a.m.
⑤ 9:30 a.m.

M  How about _____ _____ at the public library tomorrow?

W  Okay. What time shall we meet?

M  Let's meet in front of the library at 9:30 in the morning.

W  But there will be too many students at that time.

M  Then how about an _____ _____?

W  Let's _____ _____ at 8 o'clock. Is it okay?

M  All right, then.

>> WORDS   **in general** 일반적으로   **fat** 지방   **meal** 식사

**14** 대화를 듣고, 두 사람의 관계로 가장 적절한 것을 고르시오.

① 간호사 – 환자  ② 교사 – 학생
③ 종업원 – 손님  ④ 연출자 – 배우
⑤ 코치 – 운동선수

W  Sorry to keep you waiting. Are you _____ to shoot the scene?
M  Of course I am.
W  Good. In this _____, your role is very important.
M  I'll try my _____.
W  I know that you're a good actor. Just don't forget the _____.
M  I won't.
W  Okay. Let's go.

**15** 대화를 듣고, 여자가 남자에게 부탁한 일로 가장 적절한 것을 고르시오.

① 여행 같이 가기
② 아침에 깨워 주기
③ 여행 가방 싸 주기
④ 운전 가르쳐 주기
⑤ 여행지까지 태워다 주기

M  Did you finish _____ your stuff?
W  Almost. I'm so excited.
M  What time do you need to be at the airport?
W  I have to be there by 9 a.m. Dad, can you _____ me to the airport tomorrow?
M  I wish I could. But, you know, my car _____ _____.
W  Oh, I forgot. Then, could you _____ me _____ tomorrow morning?
M  Okay, I will.

**16** 대화를 듣고, 남자가 테니스 수업에 가지 않은 이유로 가장 적절한 것을 고르시오.

① 몸이 아파서
② 급한 일이 생겨서
③ 이사를 가게 되어서
④ 다른 운동을 배워서
⑤ 수업 시간을 잘못 알아서

[Telephone rings.]
W  Hello, Jiho? This is Sujin.
M  Oh, hi. What's up?
W  You didn't come to the _____ lesson yesterday. Were you sick?
M  Not really. Actually, I decided to try _____ sport.
W  Really? What's that?
M  I've _____ learning ice-skating. I'm sorry I didn't tell you earlier.
W  That's okay. See you later.

>> **WORDS**  **shoot** 촬영하다  **scene** 장면  **stuff** 물건  **airport** 공항

**17** 다음 그림의 상황에 가장 적절한 대화를 고르시오.

① ② ③ ④ ⑤

① M How about fish and chips for lunch?

 W Sounds great!

② M What do you usually do in your free time?

 W I like _____ _____ with my father.

③ M Let's go swimming to the lake.

 W I don't think it's a good idea. It's too _____.

④ M Look! I caught a fish.

 W Wow. It's big. _____ tight! It might get away.

⑤ M We should hurry. The boat _____ in ten minutes.

 W Okay. Let's run.

**18** 다음을 듣고, 여자가 재즈 축제에 대해 언급하지 <u>않은</u> 것을 고르시오.

① 연기 사유　　② 개최 날짜
③ 장소 변동 여부　　④ 입장권 가격
⑤ 환불 방법

W We are sorry to tell you that the jazz festival will be postponed. This is _____ _____ the storm that is moving toward this area. The event will be _____ on July 15th instead of July 8th. The venue will be the _____. If you wish to get a _____ for the tickets, you can do so on the website.

[19-20] 대화를 듣고, 여자의 마지막 말에 이어질 남자의 말로 가장 적절한 것을 고르시오.

**19** ① Let's go there.
② It was too expensive.
③ I didn't like the service.
④ The waiters were so kind.
⑤ Why don't we go to the Korean restaurant?

W Let's _____ _____ for dinner.

M That's a good idea. Which restaurant do you want to visit?

W How about the new Italian restaurant we went to last week?

M I don't want to go there _____.

W Why not? You said the food was great.

M Yeah, I liked the food and the price was _____.

W Then, what's the problem?

**20** ① No, I am not.
② I agree with you.
③ I've already been there.
④ How about this Saturday?
⑤ I bought a pair of jeans there.

M A new shopping mall _____ yesterday.

W I know. Have you been there?

M Not yet. But people say it's really _____.

W Yes. My sister went there with her friends, and she said all the _____ were nice.

M Why don't we _____ _____ sometime?

W When?

>> **WORDS**　**tight** 단단히, 꽉　**postpone** 연기하다　**storm** 폭풍

**01** 다음을 듣고, 한국의 현재 날씨로 가장 적절한 것을 고르시오.

**02** 대화를 듣고, 남자가 구입할 스카프로 가장 적절한 것을 고르시오.

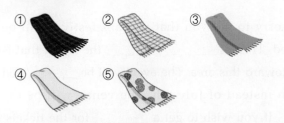

**03** 대화를 듣고, 여자의 심정으로 가장 적절한 것을 고르시오.

① upset      ② proud
③ bored      ④ disappointed
⑤ regretful

**04** 대화를 듣고, 남자가 지난 주말에 한 일로 가장 적절한 것을 고르시오.

① 수영 배우기
② 해변에서 수영하기
③ 해변에서 선탠하기
④ 인명 구조 봉사하기
⑤ 해변에서 쓰레기 줍기

**05** 대화를 듣고, 두 사람이 대화하는 장소로 가장 적절한 곳을 고르시오.

① hospital      ② airport
③ school      ④ movie theater
⑤ shopping mall

**06** 대화를 듣고, 여자의 마지막 말의 의도로 가장 적절한 것을 고르시오.

① 동의      ② 충고      ③ 거절
④ 제안      ⑤ 감사

**07** 대화를 듣고, 내용과 일치하지 않는 것을 고르시오.

① 여자는 전화로 음식을 미리 주문했다.
② 여자를 포함해 총 3명이 식당에 갈 것이다.
③ 여자는 저녁 7시 30분에 도착할 예정이다.
④ 남자는 예약 내용을 확인했다.
⑤ 여자는 음료를 마시지 않을 것이다.

**08** 대화를 듣고, 남자가 대화 직후에 할 일로 가장 적절한 것을 고르시오.

① 초대장 만들기
② 생일 파티 준비하기
③ 친구 생일 파티에 가기
④ 쇼핑몰 가서 선물 사기
⑤ 은행에 돈 인출하러 가기

**09** 대화를 듣고, 두 사람이 전화 통화에서 언급하지 않은 것을 고르시오.

① 전화를 건 사람      ② 전화를 받은 사람
③ 찾는 사람      ④ 전화를 건 목적
⑤ 연락 받을 번호

**10** 다음을 듣고, 여자가 하는 말의 내용으로 가장 적절한 것을 고르시오.

① 시험 공지      ② 특별 강연 공지
③ 담임 교사 소개      ④ 강당 이용 안내
⑤ 수업 시간 변경 공지

**11** 다음을 듣고, 찾고 있는 여자아이에 대한 내용과 일치하지 않는 것을 고르시오.

① 네 살이고, 이름은 Lucy이다.
② 키가 1미터가량이다.
③ 갈색 곱슬머리이다.
④ 노란색 스웨터와 청바지를 입고 있다.
⑤ 발견하면 2층 고객 센터로 데려가야 한다.

**12** 대화를 듣고, 여자가 전화를 건 목적으로 가장 적절한 것을 고르시오.

① 호텔을 예약하기 위해서
② 비행기표를 예매하기 위해서
③ 비행기표를 취소하기 위해서
④ 비행 날짜를 변경하기 위해서
⑤ 체류 기간을 변경하기 위해서

**13** 대화를 듣고, 여자가 거슬러 받을 금액으로 가장 적절한 것을 고르시오.

① 1,000원  ② 2,000원  ③ 3,000원
④ 4,000원  ⑤ 5,000원

**14** 대화를 듣고, 두 사람의 관계로 가장 적절한 것을 고르시오.

① 교장 – 학부모  ② 운동 코치 – 학부모
③ 의사 – 환자  ④ 감독 – 선수
⑤ 점원 – 손님

**15** 대화를 듣고, 남자가 여자에게 부탁한 일로 가장 적절한 것을 고르시오.

① 공항에 마중 나오기
② 친구 송별회 열기
③ 전학 간 친구 방문하기
④ 캐나다 여행 정보 주기
⑤ 친구에게 안부 전해 주기

**16** 대화를 듣고, 남자가 늦은 이유로 가장 적절한 것을 고르시오.

① 늦잠을 자서  ② 차가 막혀서
③ 지하철을 잘못 타서  ④ 약속을 잊어버려서
⑤ 밥을 오랫동안 먹어서

**17** 다음 그림의 상황에 가장 적절한 대화를 고르시오.

①  ②  ③  ④  ⑤

**18** 다음을 듣고, 남자가 박물관 이용에 대해 언급하지 않은 것을 고르시오.

① 개장 시간  ② 입장권 구매처
③ 입장권 가격  ④ 폐장 시간
⑤ 관람 시 유의 사항

[19-20] 대화를 듣고, 여자의 마지막 말에 이어질 남자의 말로 가장 적절한 것을 고르시오.

**19** Man: _____

① I don't like history, either.
② I can teach you history.
③ I take the class twice a week.
④ She is very nice, and teaches well.
⑤ Let's study history together, then.

**20** Man: _____

① Good for you.
② I agree on that.
③ I have to go now.
④ Nice to meet you.
⑤ How long have you been at the graduate school?

**01** 다음을 듣고, 한국의 현재 날씨로 가장 적절한 것을 고르시오.

M Here is the world weather forecast. First, let's look at the Asia-Pacific _____. In China, it's very windy and cold. The temperature is around 1 degree Celsius. In Japan, it's drizzling now, and it's going to rain _____ _____ today. In South Korea, the weather is cloudy, but there will be no rain today. In Australia, the sun is shining and it's a perfect weather to go to the _____.

**02** 대화를 듣고, 남자가 구입할 스카프로 가장 적절한 것을 고르시오.

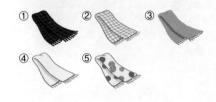

M Excuse me. Can I get some help?
W Sure. What do you need?
M Today is my wife's birthday, so I need a present for her.
W How about this scarf? It's _____ very well.
M Do you mean the black one over there? It looks good, but she _____ a bright color.
W Then how about this one with ivory color?
M It's nice. I _____ like the pink rose pattern.

**03** 대화를 듣고, 여자의 심정으로 가장 적절한 것을 고르시오.

① upset          ② proud
③ bored          ④ disappointed
⑤ regretful

W How did the science fair _____, Chris?
M It was great, Mom. There were so many good science projects.
W How did your robot do?
M Everyone there really liked it. Actually, I have good news for you.
W What is it? I'm really _____.
M I got _____ _____ with my robot!
W Amazing! That's my boy!

**04** 대화를 듣고, 남자가 지난 주말에 한 일로 가장 적절한 것을 고르시오.

① 수영 배우기
② 해변에서 수영하기
③ 해변에서 선탠하기
④ 인명 구조 봉사하기
⑤ 해변에서 쓰레기 줍기

W Minho, you look _____. Did you go to the beach last weekend?
M Yeah, but I didn't go swimming there.
W Then why did you go to the beach?
M You know I am a good swimmer. I started doing volunteer work as a _____.
W Really? It sounds like fun.
M It's not only fun but it is also _____.

>> **WORDS**  **drizzle** 이슬비가 내리다  **bright** 밝은  **pattern** 무늬  **fair** 박람회, 전시회  **volunteer work** 자원봉사

**05** 대화를 듣고, 두 사람이 대화하는 장소로 가장 적절한 곳을 고르시오.

① hospital
② airport
③ school
④ movie theater
⑤ shopping mall

M Hi, I'd like two tickets for *Spiderman*, please.

W Would you prefer to sit at the _____, middle or the back?

M The _____ please. Oh, do you offer a student _____?

W Yes, we do. Are you _____ students?

M Yes, here are our student cards.

W Okay, that'll be 14,000 won.

M Here you are.

**06** 대화를 듣고, 여자의 마지막 말의 의도로 가장 적절한 것을 고르시오.

① 동의
② 충고
③ 거절
④ 제안
⑤ 감사

M Are you busy tonight?

W Not really. What's up?

M Let's go to the movies. There's a new movie just _____ today.

W Well, I'm not in the _____ for a movie today.

M Come on. It's a _____. You'll love it.

W Today is not the day. Maybe _____ _____.

**07** 대화를 듣고, 내용과 일치하지 <u>않는</u> 것을 고르시오.

① 여자는 전화로 음식을 미리 주문했다.
② 여자를 포함해 총 3명이 식당에 갈 것이다.
③ 여자는 저녁 7시 30분에 도착할 예정이다.
④ 남자는 예약 내용을 확인했다.
⑤ 여자는 음료를 마시지 않을 것이다.

*[Telephone rings.]*

M Hello. Fine View Restaurant. May I help you?

W Yes, can I _____ an order before we arrive for dinner today?

M Sure, ma'am. If you order now, we can have your order _____ when you arrive.

W That's nice. We are just three people and we will arrive at 7:30 this evening. We would like to have roasted chicken, shrimp cream spaghetti, and fresh salad.

M Just a minute. Let me _____ your order. Roasted chicken, shrimp cream spaghetti, and fresh salad for three people. Is that right?

W Correct. I want to order drinks _____ at the restaurant.

M Okay. See you this evening.

>> **WORDS**　**student card** 학생증　**arrive** 도착하다　**roasted** 구운　**correct** 정확한

**08** 대화를 듣고, 남자가 대화 직후에 할 일로 가장 적절한 것을 고르시오.

① 초대장 만들기
② 생일 파티 준비하기
③ 친구 생일 파티에 가기
④ 쇼핑몰 가서 선물 사기
⑤ 은행에 돈 인출하러 가기

W Are you going to come to Sora's birthday party?
M Yes, I am.
W I'm thinking of buying her a necklace. She really likes _____. What are you going to buy?
M I haven't decided yet.
W Then why don't we buy the necklace together? In fact, it's a little _____ my budget.
M Okay. But I need to go to the bank first to _____ some money.
W Let's hurry, then.

**09** 대화를 듣고, 두 사람이 전화 통화에서 언급하지 <u>않은</u> 것을 고르시오.

① 전화를 건 사람      ② 전화를 받은 사람
③ 찾는 사람          ④ 전화를 건 목적
⑤ 연락 받을 번호

[Telephone rings.]
M Hello, this is John speaking.
W Hello, can I speak to Mary?
M Sorry, but she's not _____.
W Can I _____ a _____?
M Sure.
W This is Susan. Please tell her to _____ _____ to me. My number is 555-1234.
M Okay. I'll tell her.
W Thanks a lot.

**10** 다음을 듣고, 여자가 하는 말의 내용으로 가장 적절한 것을 고르시오.

① 시험 공지
② 특별 강연 공지
③ 담임 교사 소개
④ 강당 이용 안내
⑤ 수업 시간 변경 공지

W Listen carefully, students. Tomorrow, we are going to have a special event. A world-famous _____, Chanwoo Kim is going to visit our school. He's going to speak about his job and how he _____ his dream. Then, you can ask him _____ about his life as a magician. There will be no class, so please come to the _____. Thank you.

---

**>> WORDS**  necklace 목걸이  **budget** 예산  **world-famous** 세계적으로 유명한

Answer p. 31

**11** 다음을 듣고, 찾고 있는 여자아이에 대한 내용과 일치하지 <u>않는</u> 것을 고르시오.

① 네 살이고, 이름은 Lucy이다.
② 키가 1미터가량이다.
③ 갈색 곱슬머리이다.
④ 노란색 스웨터와 청바지를 입고 있다.
⑤ 발견하면 2층 고객 센터로 데려가야 한다.

W Ladies and gentlemen, may I have your attention, please? We are _____ _____ a four-year-old girl named Lucy. She's about 100 centimeters tall and has _____ brown hair. She is wearing a yellow _____ and blue jeans. If you see her, please bring her to the _____ center on the _____ floor. Thank you.

**12** 대화를 듣고, 여자가 전화를 건 목적으로 가장 적절한 것을 고르시오.

① 호텔을 예약하기 위해서
② 비행기표를 예매하기 위해서
③ 비행기표를 취소하기 위해서
④ 비행 날짜를 변경하기 위해서
⑤ 체류 기간을 변경하기 위해서

[Telephone rings.]
M Hello, Cloud Travel Agency.
W Hello. This is Linda Marcus. I _____ a flight to Washington D.C. with you.
M Yes, Ms. Marcus. I remember you. How may I help you?
W I want to _____ a hotel room. Can you help me with that?
M Of course I can. _____ _____ are you going to stay?
W I'm going to _____ for two nights. And I prefer a hotel near the subway station.
M I found the perfect one for you.

**13** 대화를 듣고, 여자가 거슬러 받을 금액으로 가장 적절한 것을 고르시오.

① 1,000원   ② 2,000원   ③ 3,000원
④ 4,000원   ⑤ 5,000원

W Wow, these hairpins are so pretty! How much are they?
M They're 1,000 won _____, but if you buy seven, you can get one _____.
W Seven hairpins? I don't need that _____.
M You can give them to your friends. Christmas is next week.
W That's a great idea. Then I will buy seven, and get one free. Here is 10,000 won.
M Okay, here's your _____.

>> WORDS   **attention** 주의, 주목   **travel agency** 여행사   **free** 무료로

**14** 대화를 듣고, 두 사람의 관계로 가장 적절한 것을 고르시오.

① 교장 – 학부모  ② 운동 코치 – 학부모
③ 의사 – 환자  ④ 감독 – 선수
⑤ 점원 – 손님

*[Telephone rings.]*

M  Hello, Richard Rogers speaking.

W  Hello, Mr. Rogers. This is Tom's mother.

M  Hello. Ms. Parker. What's the matter?

W  I'm sorry to say this, but Tom can't go to the soccer _____ today.

M  Is he sick?

W  No, he's not. But his grandfather is _____. I have to take Tom to the hospital to visit him.

M  Oh, I see. Do you think he will be _____ _____ be at practice tomorrow? We have an important _____ next week.

W  Of course he will.

**15** 대화를 듣고, 남자가 여자에게 부탁한 일로 가장 적절한 것을 고르시오.

① 공항에 마중 나오기
② 친구 송별회 열기
③ 전학 간 친구 방문하기
④ 캐나다 여행 정보 주기
⑤ 친구에게 안부 전해 주기

W  Have you heard that they are going to hold a _____ party for Yumi this Saturday?

M  Yes, I have. I'm sorry to hear that she's _____ to another school. But I can't come to the party.

W  Why not?

M  My cousins from Canada are visiting Korea. I have to _____ them _____ at the airport.

W  Oh, I see.

M  Please _____ _____ to her for me.

W  Of course I will.

**16** 대화를 듣고, 남자가 늦은 이유로 가장 적절한 것을 고르시오.

① 늦잠을 자서
② 차가 막혀서
③ 지하철을 잘못 타서
④ 약속을 잊어버려서
⑤ 밥을 오랫동안 먹어서

W  You're late again. Did you get up late?

M  I'm so sorry. But I woke up on time.

W  Then what took you _____ _____?

M  I took the subway on the _____ side. I realized my mistake when it was too late.

W  Oh, come on. This isn't the first time you took the _____ subway.

M  You're right. I keep making the same mistakes.

W  Let's go get something to eat. I'm starving.

---

**>> WORDS**  cousin 사촌  **realize** 깨닫다  **starve** 몹시 배고프다, 굶주리다

**17** 다음 그림의 상황에 가장 적절한 대화를 고르시오.

① ② ③ ④ ⑤

① W  Do you have a pet?
   M  Yes, I'm _____ a dog.
② W  Do you prefer cats or dogs?
   M  I like cats _____ than dogs.
③ W  Have you _____ this dog?
   M  No, I'm sorry.
④ W  Can you take care of my dog for a _____?
   M  Okay.
⑤ W  I'm _____ to dog hair.
   M  Really? I didn't know that.

**18** 다음을 듣고, 남자가 박물관 이용에 대해 언급하지 않은 것을 고르시오.

① 개장 시간        ② 입장권 구매처
③ 입장권 가격      ④ 폐장 시간
⑤ 관람 시 유의 사항

M  Attention, please. We are going to open at 10 a.m. It is _____ _____ ten now. You can buy tickets by the _____. Tickets _____ ten dollars for adults and five dollars for children. You can't take any food or drinks _____ the museum. You may take pictures, but please do not _____ any exhibits. We hope you enjoy the exhibition.

[19-20] 대화를 듣고, 여자의 마지막 말에 이어질 남자의 말로 가장 적절한 것을 고르시오.

**19** ① I don't like history, either.
② I can teach you history.
③ I take the class twice a week.
④ She is very nice, and teaches well.
⑤ Let's study history together, then.

W  You know what? History is too _____ for me.
M  Who is your history teacher at school?
W  Mr. Park teaches me history.
M  I heard that he knows a lot about history.
W  Yeah. But _____ is one thing, and _____ is another. Who's your history teacher?
M  Ms. Lee, the new teacher.
W  What's she _____?

**20** ① Good for you.
② I agree on that.
③ I have to go now.
④ Nice to meet you.
⑤ How long have you been at the graduate school?

M  Wow, Claire! It's been a long time since I've seen you.
W  It really has.
M  You haven't _____ a bit.
W  _____ have you. What do you do these days?
M  I'm still studying at the _____ _____. What about you?
W  I'm a lawyer now.

>> **WORDS**  **prefer** 선호하다  **museum** 박물관, 미술관  **exhibit** 전시품  **lawyer** 변호사

# 05회 » 듣기 실전 모의고사

**01** 다음을 듣고, 목요일의 날씨로 가장 적절한 것을 고르시오.

① ② ③ ④ ⑤

**02** 대화를 듣고, 여자가 구입할 물병으로 가장 적절한 것을 고르시오.

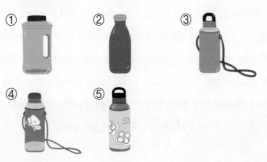

① ② ③ ④ ⑤

**03** 대화를 듣고, 남자의 심정으로 가장 적절한 것을 고르시오.

① happy      ② bored      ③ proud
④ excited      ⑤ discouraged

**04** 대화를 듣고, 여자가 어제 한 일로 가장 적절한 것을 고르시오.

① 기차 여행하기        ② 할머니 배웅하기
③ 아버지 찾아뵙기      ④ 할머니 댁 방문하기
⑤ 봉사활동 하기

**05** 대화를 듣고, 두 사람이 대화하는 장소로 가장 적절한 곳을 고르시오.

① clinic              ② park
③ grocery store      ④ fitness center
⑤ restaurant

**06** 대화를 듣고, 남자의 마지막 말의 의도로 가장 적절한 것을 고르시오.

① 감사        ② 충고        ③ 허가
④ 비난        ⑤ 동의

**07** 대화를 듣고, 남자가 수학여행에 가져갈 물건이 아닌 것을 고르시오.

① underwear        ② socks
③ toothbrush        ④ toothpaste
⑤ flashlight

**08** 대화를 듣고, 여자가 대화 직후에 할 일로 가장 적절한 것을 고르시오.

① 방 청소하기          ② 미술 숙제하기
③ 준비물 사러 가기      ④ 친구 집 방문하기
⑤ 미술 숙제 알아보기

**09** 대화를 듣고, 남자가 새로 오신 선생님에 대해 언급하지 않은 것을 고르시오.

① 이름        ② 나이        ③ 전공
④ 출신지      ⑤ 결혼 여부

**10** 다음을 듣고, 남자가 설명하는 운동 종목으로 가장 적절한 것을 고르시오.

① soccer              ② volleyball
③ basketball        ④ baseball
⑤ ping-pong

**11** 다음을 듣고, 여자가 소개하는 책에 대한 내용과 일치하지 <u>않는</u> 것을 고르시오.

① 작가는 Katherine Paterson이다.
② 아동 문학상을 받았다.
③ 10대 소녀가 주인공이다.
④ 우정, 용기, 희망에 대한 내용이다.
⑤ 영화로도 만들어졌다.

**12** 대화를 듣고, 남자가 전화를 건 목적으로 가장 적절한 것을 고르시오.

① 책을 빌리기 위해서
② 책을 주문하기 위해서
③ 청소를 부탁하기 위해서
④ 휴관일을 알아보기 위해서
⑤ 봉사활동을 알아보기 위해서

**13** 대화를 듣고, 두 사람이 만날 시각을 고르시오.

① 6:30      ② 6:50      ③ 7:00
④ 7:10      ⑤ 7:30

**14** 대화를 듣고, 두 사람의 관계로 가장 적절한 것을 고르시오.

① 환자 – 의사        ② 아들 – 엄마
③ 범인 – 경찰관      ④ 손님 – 점원
⑤ 손님 – 마사지사

**15** 대화를 듣고, 여자가 남자에게 부탁한 일로 가장 적절한 것을 고르시오.

① 딸기잼 만들기
② 딸기 사다 주기
③ 공원에 같이 가기
④ 농구 가르쳐 주기
⑤ 할머니께 음식 가져다드리기

**16** 대화를 듣고, 남자가 학교에 가야 하는 이유로 가장 적절한 것을 고르시오.

① 수업이 있어서
② 공부를 더 해야 해서
③ 공연 연습이 있어서
④ 축제 준비를 도와야 해서
⑤ 축제를 구경하고 싶어서

**17** 다음 그림의 상황에 가장 적절한 대화를 고르시오.

①      ②      ③      ④      ⑤

**18** 다음을 듣고, 여자가 안내 방송에서 언급하지 <u>않은</u> 것을 고르시오.

① 현재 시각      ② 목적지        ③ 소요 시간
④ 화장실 위치    ⑤ 음료 가격

[19-20] 대화를 듣고, 남자의 마지막 말에 이어질 여자의 말로 가장 적절한 것을 고르시오.

**19** Woman: _____

① That is my fault.
② I also bought some pens.
③ I've never been there before.
④ Let's go there someday.
⑤ They cost more than 30,000 won.

**20** Woman: _____

① It's on Main Street.
② I didn't check it yet.
③ It's jessy@email.com.
④ I'll send it right away.
⑤ I read the books already.

# Dictation Test » 05회

**01** 다음을 듣고, 목요일의 날씨로 가장 적절한 것을 고르시오.

① ② ③ ④ ⑤

M  It's Monday morning, and here's the weather report for this week. It's raining now and the rain will continue _____ Wednesday. On Wednesday, a typhoon is expected to hit the city so please take precautions for it. On Thursday, the sky will _____ _____ and the sun will be shining _____ the weekend.

**02** 대화를 듣고, 여자가 구입할 물병으로 가장 적절한 것을 고르시오.

① ② ③ ④ ⑤

M  Do you need help?
W  Yes, I'm looking for a water bottle.
M  Okay. What about this one? It can _____ a lot of water.
W  It looks nice. But I need one with a strap. I _____ _____ my stuff.
M  I see. What about this one? It has a strap, and a handle as well.
W  I like it. But I don't want any _____ on it.
M  Then this is what you're looking for.
W  I love it. I'll take it.

**03** 대화를 듣고, 남자의 심정으로 가장 적절한 것을 고르시오.

① happy     ② bored
③ proud     ④ excited
⑤ discouraged

M  Sora, did you read my novel?
W  Yeah, I've just _____ reading it.
M  What do you think of it? Please talk _____ to me.
W  Well. To be _____, there are some parts that I didn't understand. Maybe you should make some changes.
M  Thanks for being frank. But you know, I've read and rewrote the novel _____ _____ three times. Maybe I'm not good enough to be a writer.
W  No way! You're good enough.
M  No, I'm not. I think I should _____.

---

**» WORDS**  **typhoon** 태풍  **precaution** 예방 조치  **strap** 끈  **handle** 손잡이  **maybe** 어쩌면, 아마  **frank** 솔직한

**04** 대화를 듣고, 여자가 어제 한 일로 가장 적절한 것을 고르시오.

① 기차 여행하기　② 할머니 배웅하기
③ 아버지 찾아뵙기　④ 할머니 댁 방문하기
⑤ 봉사활동 하기

M　Where were you going yesterday? I saw you at the train station.
W　Did you?
M　Yes. I _____ out your name, but you didn't hear me.
W　I didn't go anywhere. I went there to _____ my grandmother _____. She stayed at my house for a week.
M　I see.
W　What were you _____ at the train station?
M　I went there to see my father. He _____ there.
W　Really? I didn't know that.

**05** 대화를 듣고, 두 사람이 대화하는 장소로 가장 적절한 곳을 고르시오.

① clinic　② park
③ grocery store　④ fitness center
⑤ restaurant

M　Susan. What a _____ to see you here!
W　Jason. It's you. Long time no see.
M　Is it your _____ _____ here?
W　Yes, it is.
M　I've been _____ out here for more than a year.
W　I can see that. You look to be in _____.
M　Thanks. I'm going to run on the treadmill now. See you later.

**06** 대화를 듣고, 남자의 마지막 말의 의도로 가장 적절한 것을 고르시오.

① 감사　② 충고　③ 허가
④ 비난　⑤ 동의

M　Are you all right, Mina? You look depressed.
W　I got into a _____ with my younger sister this morning.
M　Why did you have a fight with her?
W　She asked me to _____ her my new jacket but I said no.
M　Come on, what are sisters for? You wear her clothes sometimes.
W　You're right. Now I feel so _____ about it.
M　I think you should give her a call and _____ to her right now.

>> WORDS　**train station** 기차역　**treadmill** 트레드밀(걷기나 달리기용 운동 기구)　**depressed** 우울한

**07** 대화를 듣고, 남자가 수학여행에 가져갈 물건이 아닌 것을 고르시오.

① underwear    ② socks
③ toothbrush    ④ toothpaste
⑤ flashlight

W   Jim, are you ready to go on the school field trip tomorrow?

M   Yes, I am. I finished packing my bag. I also _____ on what to wear tomorrow.

W   Did you pack your _____? Last time, you didn't bring any.

M   Yes, I did. I put my underwear, socks, _____, toothpaste, and everything I need in my bag.

W   Are you going to take a _____? It's in the garage.

M   The teacher said we don't need it. We're not going to _____ _____ at night this time.

W   That's a relief.

**08** 대화를 듣고, 여자가 대화 직후에 할 일로 가장 적절한 것을 고르시오.

① 방 청소하기    ② 미술 숙제하기
③ 준비물 사러 가기    ④ 친구 집 방문하기
⑤ 미술 숙제 알아보기

[Telephone rings.]

M   Hello, Jina? This is Minho.

W   Hello, Minho. What's up?

M   Did you finish the art homework?

W   No, I didn't _____ start.

M   Why don't we do it _____? You can come to my house or I can go there.

W   Well, then can you come to my house? I was in the _____ of cleaning my room. I have to finish it first.

M   Okay. I'll be there in 30 minutes.

**09** 대화를 듣고, 남자가 새로 오신 선생님에 대해 언급하지 않은 것을 고르시오.

① 이름    ② 나이    ③ 전공
④ 출신지    ⑤ 결혼 여부

W   Hey, did you hear about the new teacher?

M   Yes, she's our new _____ teacher. She's from New York, and she went to a college in Austria.

W   Awesome! Do you know _____ she's married or not?

M   She's _____. She's only 28 years old. Oh! She majored in piano.

W   Really?

M   Yeah. You want to be a _____. I bet you'll love her.

W   I can't wait to see her.

---

**》 WORDS**   **field trip** 수학여행   **bring** 가져오다   **awesome** 굉장한   **married** 결혼을 한, 기혼의   **major in** …을 전공하다
          **bet** …이 틀림없다

**10** 다음을 듣고, 남자가 설명하는 운동 종목으로 가장 적절한 것을 고르시오.

① soccer        ② volleyball
③ basketball    ④ baseball
⑤ ping-pong

M This is a sport that two teams play _____. Each team has one or two members. To play the sport, the players need a table with a net, a _____, and a light-weight ball. Players should pass the ball _____ the net to the other side of the table. The ball should not get out of the table or fall to the _____.

**11** 다음을 듣고, 여자가 소개하는 책에 대한 내용과 일치하지 <u>않는</u> 것을 고르시오.

① 작가는 Katherine Paterson이다.
② 아동 문학상을 받았다.
③ 10대 소녀가 주인공이다.
④ 우정, 용기, 희망에 대한 내용이다.
⑤ 영화로도 만들어졌다.

W Hello, everyone. Today, I want to _____ you to a popular novel, *Bridge to Terabithia*. It was written by Katherine Paterson, and won a medal for children's best novel. A _____ boy is the main character, and the writer talks about friendship, _____, and hope through his story. It was also made into a _____ with the same title. I highly recommend this novel.

**12** 대화를 듣고, 남자가 전화를 건 목적으로 가장 적절한 것을 고르시오.

① 책을 빌리기 위해서
② 책을 주문하기 위해서
③ 청소를 부탁하기 위해서
④ 휴관일을 알아보기 위해서
⑤ 봉사활동을 알아보기 위해서

*[Telephone rings.]*

W Hello. Namsan Public Library. How may I help you?
M Hello. I called you to _____ something.
W Yes, what is it?
M Is it possible to _____ at your library?
W Of course. There are a lot of different types of volunteer jobs like cleaning or _____ bookshelves.
M Nice. So how do I apply?
W First, can I have your name? Then tell me when you can begin.

**13** 대화를 듣고, 두 사람이 만날 시각을 고르시오.

① 6:30    ② 6:50    ③ 7:00
④ 7:10    ⑤ 7:30

M When are you coming back today?
W The bus will arrive at the express bus terminal at 6:50 p.m. Could you _____ me _____, Dad?
M Of course. I can pick you up if you don't mind _____ for me for a while.
W How long?
M The meeting will finish around 6:40 but it will take about _____ an hour to get to the bus terminal. Is it okay?
W That's fine with me.

>> **WORDS**  **each** 각각의   **light-weight** 가벼운   **novel** 소설   **main character** 주인공   **title** 제목   **recommend** 추천하다
**bookshelf** 책꽂이   **express bus** 고속버스

**14** 대화를 듣고, 두 사람의 관계로 가장 적절한 것을 고르시오.

① 환자 – 의사　　② 아들 – 엄마
③ 범인 – 경찰관　④ 손님 – 점원
⑤ 손님 – 마사지사

M　Ouch! It _____.
W　Don't be nervous. Tension will make your muscles stiff, and it will cause more _____.
M　All right. I'll try to be relaxed.
W　If I _____ you too hard, just tell me.
M　It's okay now.
W　Now I'll massage your back. Please _____ _____.

**15** 대화를 듣고, 여자가 남자에게 부탁한 일로 가장 적절한 것을 고르시오.

① 딸기잼 만들기
② 딸기 사다 주기
③ 공원에 같이 가기
④ 농구 가르쳐 주기
⑤ 할머니께 음식 가져다드리기

W　Where are you going, Minjun?
M　I'm going to the park to play basketball with my friends.
W　Okay. Can you do me a _____?
M　What is it, Mom?
W　I made strawberry jam for your grandmother. Can you _____ it to her on your _____ to the park?
M　No problem. Grandma will love it.
W　Thanks.

**16** 대화를 듣고, 남자가 학교에 가야 하는 이유로 가장 적절한 것을 고르시오.

① 수업이 있어서
② 공부를 더 해야 해서
③ 공연 연습이 있어서
④ 축제 준비를 도와야 해서
⑤ 축제를 구경하고 싶어서

M　Mom, I'm going to school.
W　School? But it's Saturday. Are you going to study?
M　No. The school festival is next week.
W　Oh, are you _____ _____ in the festival?
M　Yeah, I'm _____ _____ as a staff member.
W　I see. You're playing an important _____.
M　Thank you for telling me.

---

≫ **WORDS**　**tension** 긴장(감)　**stiff** 뻣뻣한　**back** (등)허리

**17** 다음 그림의 상황에 가장 적절한 대화를 고르시오.

① ② ③ ④ ⑤

① M  What do you usually do in your free time?

W  I usually take pictures.

② M  Who took this picture?

W  It _____ _____ by my father.

③ M  Could you take a picture of me in front of the statue?

W  No problem. Go _____.

④ M  What do you want to be in the future?

W  I want to be a _____.

⑤ M  Do you know who built the statue?

W  I have _____ _____.

**18** 다음을 듣고, 여자가 안내 방송에서 언급하지 <u>않은</u> 것을 고르시오.

① 현재 시각          ② 목적지
③ 소요 시간          ④ 화장실 위치
⑤ 음료 가격

W  Welcome _____ Blue Star Ferry. The time is now 10:15 a.m. and it will take about 30 minutes to get to Salt Spring Island. The _____ are on the first and the second floor, and the snack bar is on the _____ floor. You can enjoy hot and cold _____ there as well. We hope you have a wonderful trip. Thank you.

[19-20] 대화를 듣고, 남자의 마지막 말에 이어질 여자의 말로 가장 적절한 것을 고르시오.

**19** ① That is my fault.
② I also bought some pens.
③ I've never been there before.
④ Let's go there someday.
⑤ They cost more than 30,000 won.

M  How was it like shopping at the new shopping center?

W  It was great. There were a lot of _____ restaurants, so I had wonderful lunch with my friends.

M  Didn't you buy _____?

W  Of course I did. I bought a shirt, a _____ _____ jeans, and a cap.

M  Is that all?

**20** ① It's on Main Street.
② I didn't check it yet.
③ It's jessy@email.com.
④ I'll send it right away.
⑤ I read the books already.

[Telephone rings.]

W  Hi, John. This is Jessy.

M  Hi, Jessy. What's up?

W  You _____ it, didn't you?

M  What are you talking about?

W  You were supposed to _____ me the book list by e-mail.

M  Oh, I'm so sorry. What was the _____?

**>> WORDS**  **statue** 동상  **ferry** 연락선, 여객선  **book list** 서적 일람표

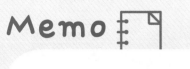

VISANG

중학 영어의 모든 것

All
that

중학 영어 2-2

Answers

책 속의 가접 별책 (특허 제 0557442호)
'Answers'는 본책에서 쉽게 분리할 수 있도록 제작되었으므로
유통 과정에서 분리될 수 있으나 파본이 아닌 정상제품입니다.

**ABOVE IMAGINATION**

우리는 남다른 상상과 혁신으로
교육 문화의 새로운 전형을 만들어
모든 이의 행복한 경험과 성장에 기여한다

# 실력 다지기

## Lesson 01 현재완료시제

>> **Grammar Practice**      pp. 12~15

**A1** (1) I have not(haven't) finished cooking dinner.

(2) Jason has not(hasn't) met her before.

(3) Has he just arrived at the class?

(4) I have not(haven't) eaten Thai food before.

(5) Has she broken my favorite vase?

**A2** (1) hasn't  (2) have  (3) haven't

**A3** (1) has rained  (2) have used  (3) Have, seen

**B1** (1) bought  (2) Did you go  (3) stopped  (4) arrived

(5) did you move  (6) did you go

**B2** (1) I began to study English two years ago.

(2) He bought a new car last week.

(3) Sam taught me Korean last month.

(4) I finished reading the novel an hour ago.

(5) I ran into an old friend of mine yesterday.

**C1** (1) D  (2) S  (3) D

**C2** (1) have, done  (2) has been  (3) has, bought

(4) has, read

**C3** (1) 엄마는 슈퍼마켓에서 막 집으로 돌아오셨다.

(2) 그녀는 이미 오늘 신문을 읽었다.

(3) 나는 그에게서 아직 편지를 받지 못했다.

**D1** (1) ⓑ  (2) ⓐ  (3) ⓐ

**D2** (1) since  (2) for

**D3** (1) has gone  (2) has grown  (3) have lost  (4) has had

>> **Grammar Test**      pp. 16~17

**01** ④  **02** ③  **03** ④  **04** Have, seen  **05** ⑤  **06** No, she hasn't  **07** (1) Has Jina broken  (2) has not(hasn't) fixed  **08** gone, been  **09** ⑤  **10** ②  **11** (1) has lost  (2) has studied, for  **12** I have lived in Seoul since last year.  **13** She has been to Paris to attend a design school. → She has gone to Paris to attend a design school.  **14** ③

**01** '유리는 일주일 동안 감기에 걸렸다'는 계속의 의미를 나타 내야 하므로 현재완료시제를 쓴다.

**02** 현재완료시제의 형태는 〈have+과거분사〉이며, 의문문은 〈Have+주어+과거분사 ...?〉의 형태이다.

**03** •'2015년 이후로 계속'의 의미이므로 현재완료시제가 알맞 다. / •'1952년에 헤밍웨이가 썼다'라는 과거의 일이므로 과거시제가 알맞다.

**04** 현재완료시제의 의문문은 〈Have(Has)+주어+과거분사 ...?〉의 형태이다.

**05** have lived라는 현재완료시제가 온 것으로 보아 특정한 과거를 나타내는 부사구 last year는 알맞지 않다.

**06** 빈칸 뒤의 말로 보아 부정의 응답이 알맞다.

**07** (1) 현재완료시제의 의문문은 〈Have(Has)+주어+과거 분사 ...?〉의 형태이다. (2) 현재완료시제의 부정문은 〈have (has)+not+과거분사〉의 형태이다.

**08** •디즈니랜드에 가고 없다: has gone to Disneyland / •디 즈니랜드에 가 본 적이 있다: has been to Disneyland

**09** ⑤ 과거의 특정 시점을 나타내는 two hours ago가 있으 므로 과거시제로 써야 한다. (has finished → finished)

**10** 〈보기〉와 ②는 계속의 의미를 나타내는 현재완료이다. ① 완 료 ③, ⑤ 경험 ④ 결과

**11** 과거에 일어난 일이 현재까지 영향을 미치므로 현재완료시제 로 나타낸다.

**12** '작년 이래로 계속 서울에 살았다'는 계속의 의미를 나타내야 하므로 현재완료시제를 쓴다.

**13** Jane은 파리에 가서 지금 여기에 없기 때문에 결과를 나타 내는 현재완료 has gone to로 써야 알맞다.

**14** ③은 '그들은 막 새 냉장고를 샀다'는 완료를 나타내고, 나머 지는 모두 경험을 나타낸다.

>> **Reading**      pp. 18~19

**1** ④  **2** ⑤  **3** ④  **4** ④

**[1~2]**

우리 마음의 소리

　오늘 Bella는 기분이 안 좋아 보입니다. Bella의 감정에 귀 기울여 봅시다.

Day 1

Anger　학교 연극이 끝난 후에 Jenny가 Bella에게 소리 를 지르다니 믿을 수가 없어.

Sadness 글쎄, 그건 Bella가 무대에서 자신의 대사를 잊어 버렸기 때문이잖아.

Joy　난 Jenny가 Bella에게 상처를 주려고 했던 건 아니었다고 확신해. 그들은 초등학교 때부터 가장 친한 친구였잖아.

| | |
|---|---|
| Fear | 난 그들이 더 이상 친구로 지내지 않을까 봐 걱정<br>돼. |
| Day 2 | |
| Joy | 휴! 난 그 애들이 다시 이야기하게 되어서 무척<br>기뻐. |
| Anger | 그래, Bella가 Jenny에게 먼저 말을 걸었지.<br>Jenny는 사과하는 방법을 몰랐던 거야. |
| Fear | 난 Bella에게 이번과 같은 문제가 더 이상 없기를<br>바라. |
| Joy | 이번과 마찬가지로, Bella는 문제들에 직면하게<br>될 거고, 그것들을 해결하고, 결국 더 현명해질<br>거야. |

**1** ⓓ Bella와 Jenny가 다시 이야기하게 되어서 기쁘다는 내용이 되어야 하므로 depressed(우울한)를 happy(기쁜)로 써야 한다.

**2** ⑤ Bella와 Jenny가 초등학교 때부터 지금까지 쭉 가장 친한 친구였다는 현재완료의 계속적 의미를 나타내는 문장으로, 빈칸에는 '… 이후로'라는 뜻의 since가 알맞다.

**3**
> 미국에서 푸드 트럭은 매우 인기를 끌어 왔는데, 이는 사람들이 적은 예산으로 자신의 사업을 쉽게 시작할 수 있기 때문이다. 푸드 트럭은 돌아다니며 다양한 음식을 판다. 가장 인기 있는 푸드 트럭들 중 하나인 Kogi는 한국식 바비큐와 멕시코 음식을 조합한 음식을 판다. Kogi는 누리소통망을 활발히 이용해 그들의 음식과 위치에 관한 정보를 퍼뜨린다. Kogi는 몇몇 음식 관련 상을 타며 명성을 얻어 왔다.

④ Kogi는 누리소통망을 이용해 메뉴와 위치에 대한 정보를 제공한다고 했다.

**4**
> 여러분은 스트레스를 받을 때 무엇을 하나요? 모든 사람에게는 자신만의 스트레스 해소법이 있습니다. 저에게는 독서가 휴식을 취하는 가장 효과적인 방법입니다. 어렸을 때부터, 재미있는 책을 읽는 것은 스트레스를 줄이는 데 도움이 되어 왔습니다. 그것은 제가 편안함과 안정감을 느끼게 해 줄 뿐만 아니라 저에게 많은 유용한 정보를 제공합니다. 그래서 저는 스트레스 해소를 위해 독서를 추천합니다. 단 10분간의 독서로도 충분합니다. 무슨 책을 읽을지에 대해 걱정하지 마세요. 어떤 책이든 좋습니다. 그러니, 스트레스를 줄일 좋은 방법을 찾고 있다면 책을 한번 읽어보세요.

④ 자신의 경험을 예로 들며, 독서가 스트레스 해소에 도움이 된다고 말하고 있다.

**› Expression Test**  pp. 20~21

**1** Have  **2** ⑤  **3** ⑤  **4** going(planning) to do  **5** ②
**6** ③

**1** 경험을 물을 때는 Have you (ever)+과거분사 …?로 표현한다.

**2** I'm going to ….는 '나는 …할 것이다'라는 뜻으로 계획을 말하는 표현이므로 I'm planning to ….로 바꿔 쓸 수 있다.

**3** 싱가포르에 가 본 적이 있는지 묻는 A의 말에 아직 결정하지 못했다는 ⑤는 알맞지 않다.

**4** 계획을 물을 때는 What are you going(planning) to do?를 쓴다.

**5** ②는 〈be going to+장소 명사〉의 형태로 '…에 가고 있는 중이다'라는 뜻이고, 나머지는 〈be going to+동사원형〉의 형태로 '…할 예정이다'라는 뜻이다.

**6** (A) 스페인에 가 본 적 있니? – (D) 아니, 없어. 가 봤니? – (C) 응, 가 봤어. 나는 작년에 그곳에 갔어. 라 토마티나 축제에 참가했어. (B) 재미있겠다. 언젠가 그곳에 가고 싶다.

**›› 서술형 평가**  p. 22

**1** (1) Have you ever traveled to another country? (2) I'm planning to go to Hong Kong with my sister  **2** (1) has studied (2) she hasn't  **3** (1) has skipped → skipped (2) have finished → finished  **4** (1) has broken (2) has written  **5** (1) have raised (2) has grown (3) has never been

**1** 경험을 물을 때는 Have you (ever)+과거분사 …?를 써서 묻고, 답할 때는 Yes, I have. 또는 No, I haven't.로 할 수 있다. 계획을 말할 때는 I'm planning(going) to ….를 쓴다.

**2** (1) 과거에 일어난 일이 현재까지 영향을 미치고 있을 때 현재완료시제(have(has)+과거분사)를 쓴다. (2) 현재완료시제의 의문문에 대한 부정의 대답은 〈No, 주어+haven't (hasn't).〉로 한다.

**3** 현재완료시제는 yesterday, last weekend 등 명백한 과거 시점을 나타내는 어구와 함께 쓸 수 없다.

**4** 과거에 일어난 일이 현재까지 영향을 미치고 있을 때 〈have (has)+과거분사〉 형태의 현재완료시제를 쓴다.

**5** (1) 강아지 Lucy를 한 살 때부터 계속 키워 오고 있다는 의미를 나타내도록 have raised로 쓴다. (2) Lucy가 자랐다는 완료의 의미를 나타내도록 has grown을 쓴다. grow up 은 '성장하다'를 뜻한다. (3) Lucy가 아픈 적이 없었다는 의미를 나타내도록 has never been을 쓴다.

**01** ③   **02** (1) hurt (2) forgive (3) avoid   **03** ③   **04** ④
**05** Have you ever eaten   **06** planning to make
*gimchi*   **07** ③   **08** (C) → (B) → (A)   **09** (1) ⓒ (2) ⓑ
(3) ⓐ   **10** (1) have known (2) read   **11** bought   **12** ①
**13** ⑤   **14** ④   **15** ④   **16** has been making   **17** ⑤
**18** ③   **19** ②   **20** ⑤   **21** (1) S (2) D   **22** be → been
**23** yet → already   **24** ③   **25** ⑤   **26** ①   **27** ④   **28** ④
**29** ⑤   **30** ④

**01** '연극이나 공연에서 외워서 말해야 하는 것'은 line(대사)
이다.

**02** (1) hurt는 '다치게 하다' (2) forgive는 '용서하다' (3) avoid
는 '피하다'라는 뜻이다.

**03** ③ 뮤지컬을 본 적이 있는지 묻는 A의 질문에 대해 아니라고
하며 가장 좋아하는 것이라고 하는 것은 어색하다.

**04** 〈오만과 편견〉을 읽어 본 적이 있는지 묻는 질문에 대한 응답
으로 그것을 잘하지 못한다는 ④는 알맞지 않다.

**05** 경험을 묻는 표현이 되도록 Have you ever+과거분사 ...?
로 문장을 완성한다. 경험 말하기는 Yes, I have. 또는 No,
I haven't. 등으로 할 수 있다.

**06** 그림은 김장 자원봉사를 하는 모습이고, A가 다음 주말에 무
엇을 할 계획인지 물어보고 있으므로, B의 답으로는 도움이 필
요한 사람들을 위해 김치를 만들 것이라는 내용이 적절하다.

**07** What are you planning to ...?는 계획에 대해 묻는 질문
이므로 앞으로의 계획을 말해야 한다. ③은 '...하는 중이다'라
는 뜻의 현재진행시제이다.

**08** A: 너는 전에 뮤지컬을 본 적이 있니? – (C) 응, 있어. 나는
뮤지컬을 아주 좋아해. – (B) 나에게 뮤지컬 표가 두 장 있어.
나와 함께 갈래? – (A) 물론, 그러고 싶어.

**09** (1) '...해 본 적이 없다'는 경험을 나타낸다. (2) '...동안 ...해
왔다'는 계속의 의미를 나타낸다. (3) '이미 ...했다'의 뜻으로
현재까지의 동작의 완료를 나타낸다.

**10** (1) '작년 이후로 계속'이라는 의미이므로 현재완료시제로 나
타낸다. (2) 특정한 과거 시점을 나타내는 부사 yesterday가
있으므로 과거형 동사 read가 알맞다.

**11** last weekend라는 특정한 과거를 나타내는 부사구가 있으
므로 과거형 동사를 써야 한다.

**12** 동작의 결과가 현재까지 영향을 미치므로 현재완료시제로
나타낸다.

**13** ⑤ '4일 동안'의 의미로 '기간'을 나타내는 말이 올 때는 since
가 아니라 for를 쓴다.

**14** ④는 '13년 동안 선생님이었다'는 '계속'의 의미를 나타내고,
나머지는 모두 '경험'을 나타내는 현재완료이다.

**15** ④ 현재완료시제(has owned)가 쓰였으므로, 특정한 과거
를 나타내는 부사구 two years ago는 알맞지 않다.

**16** 과거에 시작한 동작이 현재까지 '계속'되는 것을 강조할 때는
현재완료진행형(have(has)+been+-ing)으로 나타낸다.

**17** ⑤ 과거를 나타내는 부사구(several years ago)는 현재완
료시제와 함께 쓸 수 없다.

**18** • 과거를 나타내는 부사구 Last night로 보아 과거형 동사
가 알맞다.
• '금요일 이후로'라는 계속의 의미를 나타내므로 현재완료
시제가 알맞다.

**19** 〈보기〉는 '막 스웨터를 샀다'는 완료를 나타낸다. ① 결과
② 완료 ③ 계속 ④, ⑤ 경험

**20** ⑤ '작년 이후로 좋아해 왔다'는 계속의 의미이므로 현재완료
시제로 나타내고, '... 이후로'는 since를 쓴다.

**21** (1) ⓐ, ⓑ 계속 (2) ⓐ 완료 ⓑ 경험

**22** 과거에 시작된 일이 현재에도 계속되고 있는 것을 강조할 때
는 현재완료진행형(have(has)+been+-ing)을 쓴다.

**23** 긍정문에서의 '이미, 벌써'라는 의미는 already로 나타낸다.
yet은 '아직'이라는 뜻으로 부정문에 쓰이거나 '이미, 벌써'라
는 뜻으로 의문문에서 쓰인다. already는 주로 have(has)
와 과거분사 사이에, yet은 문장의 끝에 쓴다.

**24** ③ have gone to(...에 가 버렸다)는 1인칭 주어와 함께 쓸
수 없다.

**25** 예전에 영화와 장난감은 서로 관련이 없었다. (C) 하지만
1977년에 〈스타워즈〉가 나온 이후로 상황은 달라졌다. (B)
〈스타워즈〉 시리즈의 제작자인 George Lucas는 회사들과
특별한 계약을 맺고 영화 관련 장난감, 의류, 그 외의 제품들
을 제작했다. (A) 그 결과, 〈스타워즈〉는 영화 관련 제품을
팔아 90억 달러의 수익을 올렸다.

예전에는 영화와 장난감은 서로 관련이 없었지만 (C) 1977
년에 영화 〈스타워즈〉가 나온 이후로 상황이 달라졌는데,
(B) 〈스타워즈〉 시리즈의 제작자인 George Lucas는 회사
들과 계약을 맺고 영화 관련 제품들을 제작했고, (A) 그 결
과, 〈스타워즈〉는 영화 관련 제품을 팔아 90억 달러의 수익
을 올렸다는 흐름이 자연스럽다.

**26** 나는 현재 Habitat for All이라고 불리는 프로젝트에서 자
원봉사를 하고 있다. 나는 3년 동안 그 프로젝트를 해 왔다.
우리는 도움이 필요한 사람들에게 집을 지어 준다. 우리 팀의
일은 땅을 파고 안전 점검을 하는 것이다. 육체적 활동은 가
끔 힘들 수 있다. 하지만 새롭게 지어진 집을 보고 너무 좋아
하는 사람들을 보는 것은 정말 즐겁다.

① 육체적 활동은 힘들지만, 새롭게 지어진 집을 보고 좋아하
는 사람들을 보면 즐겁다는 내용이므로 빈칸에는 pleasure
가 알맞다.

수년간 의사들은 사람들에게 규칙적으로 운동을 하는 것이 건강에 좋다고 말해 왔다. 하지만 운동을 하는 것이 건강에 해로울 수도 있다는 생각을 해 본 적이 있는가? 최근 한 의학 보고서에서는 과도한 운동이 신체에 악영향을 줄 수 있다는 증거를 찾아냈다. 우리가 운동을 할 때 엔도르핀이라고 불리는 화학 물질이 뇌로 분비된다. 이 엔도르핀은 몸에 활력을 주고, 우리에게 '황홀감'을 준다. 운동을 과하게 하는 사람들은 이 '황홀감'에 중독될 수 있다. 의사들은 그들에게 너무 자주 운동하는 것을 삼가라고 조언한다. 오랜 속담이 말해 주듯, "지나친 것은 모자람만 못하다."

**27** ④ 운동을 너무 많이 하는 것은 몸에 좋지 못한 영향을 준다고 했으므로 '지나친 것은 모자람만 못하다.' 즉, 과유불급에 해당하는 속담이 알맞다.

**28** 밑줄 친 have thought와 ④는 '…해 본 적이 있다'는 경험을 나타내는 현재완료시제이다. ①, ⑤는 결과, ②는 계속, ③은 완료의 용법으로 쓰였다.

[29~30]

여러분은 어떤 제품을 단지 그것의 브랜드명 때문에 사고자 결심한 적이 있는가? 그렇다면 여러분은 후광 효과(halo effect)에 영향을 받았을지 모른다. 후광 효과란 어떤 것에 대한 한 가지 긍정적인 인상이 한 번도 그것을 시도해 보지 않았을지라도 그것의 전체적인 특성에 관한 여러분의 생각에 영향을 미칠 수 있다는 것을 의미한다. 예를 들어, 여러분이 자신의 노트북 컴퓨터에 만족하고 있다면 다른 회사의 것보다는 같은 회사에서 나온 휴대전화를 살 가능성이 더 높다. 이 개념은 사람에게도 역시 적용될 수 있다.

**29** ⑤ 잘생긴 얼굴이 그 사람의 지능과 신뢰도에 대해서도 긍정적인 판단을 내리는 데 영향을 미쳤으므로 후광 효과(halo effect)에 해당하는 내용이라고 볼 수 있다.

**30** ④ 문맥상 경험을 나타내는 현재완료시제로 쓰는 것이 적절하므로 have never tried로 써야 한다.

---

# Lesson 02 관계대명사

## ▶▶ Grammar Practice
pp. 32~35

**A1** (2) whose  (4) who  (5) which  (6) which

**B1** (1) ○  (2) who  (3) ○

**B2** (1) whose  (2) who  (3) whom(who)  (4) whose  (5) whom(who)

**C1** (1) which  (2) which  (3) whose  (4) which  (5) which  (6) whose

**C2** (1) which(that)  (2) which(that)  (3) whose  (4) whose

**D1** (1) that  (2) whose  (3) that  (4) that  (5) that

**D2** (1) that  (2) that  (3) that(which)

**D3** (1) that  (2) that(who)  (3) that(which)

**E1** (1) what you saw  (2) what I wished  (3) What he said  (4) What our country needs  (5) what he wrote  (6) the things which you can do

**E2** (1) S  (2) S  (3) S  (4) D  (5) D  (6) S

## ▶▶ Grammar Test
pp. 36~37

**01** ③  **02** ④  **03** (1) which I want to buy  (2) that she said yesterday  (3) whom he respects  **04** which → whose  **05** the thing(s) which(that)  **06** ③  **07** (1) whose name  (2) which(that)  **08** ③  **09** that  **10** of which  **11** ④  **12** ⑤  **13** I don't believe what my brother said yesterday.

**01** '…하는(한) 것'이라는 뜻으로 선행사를 포함하는 관계대명사는 what이다.

**02** • 선행사가 사람이고 빈칸은 관계대명사절의 목적어 자리이므로 목적격 whom이 알맞다.
• 관계대명사절에서 소유격(the tree's)을 나타내므로 whose가 알맞다.

**03** 선행사(the shoes, the words, The person)를 꾸미는 목적격 관계대명사절이 들어가야 한다.

**04** He turned off the radio.와 Its volume was too high.를 연결한 문장으로 소유격 Its를 대신하는 whose가 필요하다.

**05** 관계대명사 what은 the thing(s) which(that)로 바꿔 쓸 수 있다.

**06** ③의 that은 문장에서 보어 역할을 하는 명사절을 이끄는 접속사로 쓰였고, 〈보기〉와 나머지는 관계대명사 that으로 쓰였다.

**07** (1) '…의 이름'이라는 소유의 의미를 나타내므로 whose를 이용하여 연결한다. (2) 선행사가 The dog이고 주어 역할을 하므로 which(that)를 이용하여 연결한다.

**08** 첫 번째 빈칸에는 선행사가 사람이므로 who(that)가 알맞고, 두 번째에는 선행사가 사물이므로 which(that)가 들어가야 하며, 세 번째에는 선행사에 the last가 있으므로 that이 알맞다.

**09** • 목적절을 이끄는 접속사 that이 필요하다.
　　• 선행사에 only가 포함되어 있으므로 관계대명사 that이 필요하다.

**10** 선행사가 사물일 때 쓸 수 있는 소유격 관계대명사로 whose와 of which가 있다.

**11** ④ 빈칸에는 '…의'라는 뜻의 소유격 관계대명사인 whose가 필요하며, that은 소유격 대신 쓸 수 없다. ①, ③, ⑤에는 which 또는 that이 적절하고 ②는 선행사에 최상급이 포함되어 있으므로 that이 들어가야 한다.

**12** ⑤ 관계대명사 앞에 선행사가 없으므로 선행사를 포함하는 관계대명사 what을 써야 한다.

**13** what은 선행사를 포함한 관계대명사이므로 the thing을 생략하고 문장을 연결한다.

---

>> **Reading**　　　　　　　　pp. 38~39

**1** that　**2** ⑤　**3** ④　**4** ⑤

**[1~2]**

> 돌멩이
> 　어느 날, Maibon은 Doli라는 난쟁이가 통나무 아래에 깔린 자신의 다리를 빼내려고 하고 있는 것을 봤습니다. Maibon은 그 난쟁이를 풀어 주었습니다. "너는 보상을 받게 될 거야. 원하는 게 뭐니?" "나는 네가 사람의 젊음을 유지해주는 마법의 돌을 가지고 있다고 들었어. 나는 그것을 원해." Doli는 그에게 마법의 돌을 건네고 가 버렸습니다. Maibon은 그의 수염이 자라지 않아서 행복해졌지만, 그의 아내는 화가 났습니다. "달걀이 닭이 되지 않아요!" Maibon은 그녀에게 그 돌에 대해 이야기했고, 그녀는 그에게 그것을 버리라고 말했습니다. 그는 창밖으로 돌을 던졌습니다. 그러나 다음 날

아침, 그는 창가에 그 돌이 있는 것을 발견했습니다. 그리고 나서 그는 그의 아기가 이가 나지 않는 것을 발견했습니다. Maibon은 걱정이 되기 시작했습니다. "기대할 것이 아무것도 없어." Maibon은 그 돌을 없애려고 노력했지만, 돌은 계속 되돌아왔습니다. Maibon은 난쟁이를 다시 봤습니다. "너는 왜 내게 그 돌에 대해 경고하지 않았어? 나는 그것을 더 이상 원하지 않아!" Doli는 그 돌을 없애는 방법을 설명했습니다. Maibon은 Doli가 말한 대로 했습니다. 그가 집에 도착했을 때, Maibon은 그의 아기의 입에 이가 난 것을 봤습니다. 달걀은 닭이 되었습니다. Maibon은 그의 하얗고 긴 수염을 자랑스러워했습니다.

**1** (A)에는 목적절을 이끄는 접속사 that이 알맞고, (B)에는 선행사 magic stones를 꾸미는 관계대명사절을 이끄는 관계대명사 that이 알맞다.

**2** Maibon은 젊음을 유지하게 해주는 마법의 돌을 얻고 처음에는 좋아했지만, 그로 인해 어떤 것도 변하지 않으며 앞으로 기대할 것이 아무것도 없다는 것을 알게 되고, 늙어가는 것이 자연스러운 과정임을 깨닫게 된다. 그러므로 하얀 긴 수염을 자랑스러워했다는 흐름이 적절하므로 ⑤가 알맞다.

**3**
> 　코알라는 먹는 데 많은 시간을 보낸다. 그들은 유칼립투스 나뭇잎만 먹는다. 그러나 그들이 모든 종류의 유칼립투스 잎을 먹을 수 있는 것은 아니다. 어떤 나뭇잎들은 독성이 있고, 어떤 것들은 불쾌한 맛을 지닌다. 코알라의 크고 예민한 코는 최상의 잎을 골라내는 데 도움이 된다. 유칼립투스 잎은 코알라가 필요로 하는 모든 수분을 제공한다. 실제로, 오스트레일리아 원주민 언어 중 하나에서 유래된 코알라라는 이름은 '마시지 않는다'라는 의미이다.

④ 코알라는 크고 예민한 후각으로 최상의 잎을 골라낼 수 있다고 했다.

**4**
> 　1968년에 시작된 유명한 실험에서, 아이들은 자신이 원할 때마다 마시멜로를 하나씩 먹는 것과 연구원이 두 개의 마시멜로를 가지고 돌아올 때까지 기다리는 것 중에서 고르는 선택권이 주어졌다. 기다리는 인내심을 가지고 있던 참가자들이 실패와 동반되는 좌절감을 더 잘 견뎌낼 수 있었다. 그들은 더 좋은 대학에 입학했고 더 보람 있는 직장을 가지게 되었다. 여기서의 교훈은 좋은 일은 기다리는 사람에게 일어난다는 것이다. 빠르고, 쉬운 해결책이 항상 가장 좋은 것은 아니다. 약간의 인내심이 문제를 해결하고 장기적인 성공을 이루는 데 많은 도움이 된다.

⑤ 마시멜로 두 개를 받을 때까지 인내심을 가지고 기다렸던 아이들은 좌절이 와도 잘 견뎌내고 더 좋은 결과를 얻었다는 실험 결과를 통해 장기적인 문제 해결을 위해서는 인내심이 필요하다고 말하고 있다.

1 ④   **2** had better   3 ④   4 ③   5 ④   6 (C) → (A) →
(B) → (D)

**1** 금지의 표현으로 shouldn't(…해서는 안 된다)를 써야
한다.

**2** You had better ….는 '너는 …하는 게 좋겠다.'라는 뜻으로
상대방에게 충고를 하는 표현이다.

**3** I agree with you.와 I couldn't agree more.는 모두 동
의하는 표현이다.

**4** ③은 '왜 일찍 자러 가니?'의 뜻으로 이유를 묻는 말이고, 나
머지는 모두 충고하는 말이다.

**5** 뒤에 나오는 말로 보아 빈칸에는 A의 말에 동의하는 표현이
들어가야 하는데 ④는 '너는 틀렸어.'라는 뜻으로 동의하는 표
현이 아니다.

**6** (C) 여기에 우산을 놓아 주시겠어요? – (A) 네? – (B) 박물관
안에 우산을 가지고 가면 안 됩니다. – (D) 오, 알겠습니다.

>> **서술형 평가**

p. 42

**1** am not with you on that   **2** (1) I'll take my camera
which(that) I bought yesterday.   (2) I saw a man whose
costume was very unique.   **3** (1) who(that) invented
the light bulb   (2) which(that) brightens the darkness
**4** (1) making cookies that are   (2) who draws beautiful
scenery   **5** ② that you should do → what you should
do   ④ who you can do → which(that) you can do

**1** A의 의견에 반대하는 내용이 뒤에 나오므로 동의하지 않을
때 쓰는 표현인 I am not with you on that.을 쓴다.

**2** (1) 선행사가 사물이고 목적격이므로 which(that)를 이용
하여 문장을 연결한다. (2) 소유 관계를 표현할 때는 whose
를 쓴다.

**3** (1) 선행사 the inventor는 사람이므로 주격 관계대명사
who(that)를 이용하여 문장을 완성한다. (2) 선행사 the
light bulb는 사물이므로 주격 관계대명사 which(that)를
이용한다.

**4** (1) 주격 관계대명사 that이 이끄는 절이 선행사 cookies를
꾸민다. (2) 주격 관계대명사 who가 이끄는 절이 선행사 an
artist를 꾸민다.

**5** ② that 앞에 선행사가 없으므로, 선행사를 포함하며 '…하는
(한) 것'의 의미인 관계대명사 what으로 고쳐야 한다. ④ 관
계대명사 who는 사람을 선행사로 취하므로, 사물 선행사
things를 꾸미는 목적격 관계대명사 which나 that이 필요
하다.

>> **Final Test**

pp. 43~47

01 ④   **02** hand   03 ⑤   04 ③   05 ③   **06** should not
take photos   **07** agree   08 ⑤   09 ④   10 ②   **11** that
12 ①   **13** that you know   **14** is → are   **15** Which
(which)   16 ①   17 ①   18 ③   19 ②   20 ④   21 ③
22 ①   23 ②   24 ②   25 ⑤   26 ③   27 ⑤   28 ②
29 ③   30 ④

**01** '어떤 것을 심각하게 훼손하여 더 이상 존재하거나 쓸 수 없
게 하다'는 destroy(파괴하다)의 영영풀이이다. ① 보여 주
다 ② 건네주다 ③ 바꾸다 ⑤ 던지다

**02** '손, 조력, 건네주다'의 뜻을 모두 나타내는 단어는 hand
이다.

**03** ⑤는 반대하는 표현이고, 나머지는 모두 동의하는 표현이다.

**04** ③ A가 Mike의 책을 잃어버렸다고 하며 어떻게 해야 할지
물어보고 있으므로 사과를 해야 할 것 같다며 충고하는 표현
이 알맞다.

**05** ③ '생일 선물로 무엇을 사야 할지 모르겠다.'는 말에 '생일 파
티에 같이 갈까?'라고 제안하는 것은 어색하다.

**06** 그림에서 여자가 촬영 금지 표지판을 가리키며 말하고 있으
므로 should not을 이용하여 금지하는 표현을 쓰는 것이
적절하다.

**07** 빈칸 뒤에 이어지는 내용으로 보아 동의하는 표현이 들어가
야 한다.

**08** '…은 허용되지 않는다'는 금지의 표현은 You're not allowed
to …. / … is not allowed. 등으로 나타낼 수 있다.

**09** '…의 책'이라는 소유의 의미이므로 소유격 관계대명사가 알
맞다.

**10** 문장에서 명사절을 이끌어 주어 역할을 하고 있으므로 선행
사를 포함하는 관계대명사 what이 필요하다.

**11** 선행사가 〈사람+동물〉인 경우에는 관계대명사 that을 쓴다.

**12** 선행사가 사람, 사물, 동물인 경우에 모두 쓸 수 있는 관계대명사는 that이다.

**13** -thing으로 끝나는 선행사이므로 관계대명사 that을 넣어 문장을 완성한다.

**14** 주격 관계대명사 다음에 오는 동사는 선행사와 수일치를 해야 한다. 선행사 people이 복수이므로 is를 are로 써야 한다.

**15** '어느 것'이라는 의미의 의문사 which와 사물을 선행사로 하는 주격 관계대명사 which가 필요하다.

**16** ①은 의문대명사 who이고 나머지는 모두 관계대명사 who이다.

**17** The cat이 선행사이고 뒤에 〈주어+동사〉의 절이 있으므로 목적격 관계대명사로서 ①에 위치한다.

**18** a company가 선행사이고 뒤에 동사가 있으므로 주격 관계대명사로서 ③에 위치한다.

**19** ② 선행사가 없고 보어 역할을 하는 명사절이 필요하므로 that은 선행사를 포함하는 관계대명사 what이 되어야 한다.

**20** ④ 관계대명사 뒤에 동사가 있으므로 주격 관계대명사인 who 또는 that이 와야 한다.

**21** 〈보기〉와 ③은 관계대명사 that, ①은 지시형용사, ②, ⑤는 접속사, ④는 진주어를 나타낸다.

**22** ① I 앞에 목적격 관계대명사 which 또는 that이 생략된 문장으로 어법상 옳다. ② 선행사 the bag이 있으므로 what은 올 수 없고 which 또는 that이 알맞다. ③ 주격 관계대명사가 필요하므로 who 또는 that이 알맞다. ④ 주격 관계대명사 which가 이끄는 절 안에 주어인 it이 없어야 한다. ⑤ 선행사가 the news이므로 which 또는 that이 알맞다.

**23** 선행사를 포함하며, '…하는 것'이라는 뜻으로 명사절을 이끄는 관계대명사 what을 이용한다.

**24** ② the last가 선행사를 꾸미므로 관계대명사 that이 와야 한다.

**25**

> 풍력 에너지가 지닌 장점이 많이 있다. 우선, 화석 연료와 달리, 바람은 무한하고, 돈이 들지 않으며, 재생이 가능한 자원이다. 풍력은 또한 대기 오염을 유발하는 가스를 생성하지 않으므로 깨끗한 에너지 형태이다. 게다가, 풍력 에너지는 제조, 설치, 유지에 있어 일자리를 만들어 낸다. (풍력 에너지는 야생 동물들에게 위협이 되어 왔는데, 새들이 회전하는 풍력 발전용 터빈으로 날아들어 종종 죽음을 당하기 때문이다.)

ⓐ-ⓓ는 풍력 에너지의 장점에 대해 설명하고 있으나, ⓔ는 단점에 해당하는 내용이다.

**26**

> 오늘날 로봇은 다양한 일을 한다. 진공청소기 로봇은 집안 구석구석을 청소한다. 어떤 로봇들은 전자 부품을 연결한다. 다른 로봇들은 사람들이 하기에 매우 어렵거나 위험한 일을 하는 데 쓰인다. 예를 들어, 그들은 화성 탐사, 이집트의 거대한 피라미드 내부 관찰, 뉴욕의 월드 트레이드 센터의 잔해를 살펴보는 데 이용되었다.

빈칸 앞에서 사람들이 하기 어렵거나 위험한 일을 하는 로봇이 있다고 언급한 후, 그것에 대한 예들이 나오고 있으므로 For example(예를 들어)이 알맞다.

**[27~28]**

> 오늘날 많은 아이들은 두 살이 되기 전부터 교육용 비디오를 시청하기 시작한다. 하지만 연구에 따르면, 아기들은 다른 사람들과 상호 작용을 하면서 가장 잘 배운다. 비디오는 아기들에게 이러한 종류의 상호 작용을 제공하지 못한다. 또한, 교육용 비디오에 전형적으로 나타나는 빠른 장면 전환이나 선명한 색감은 아기들의 주의력 발달에 부정적으로 영향을 미칠지도 모른다. 게다가, 어린 나이에 폭력적인 비디오를 시청한 아이들은 나이가 들면서 집중하는 데 어려움을 겪을 가능성이 크다.

**27** ⑤ 비디오가 유아에게 미치는 부정적인 영향에 대해 설명하고 있다.

**28** (A) 선행사가 사물(rapid scene changes and bright colors)이고 뒤에 동사가 있으므로 주격 관계대명사 which [that] (B) 선행사가 사람(children)이고 뒤에 동사가 있으므로 주격 관계대명사 who[that]가 알맞다.

**[29~30]**

> 갈라파고스 제도 내와 주변에만 존재하는 멋진 동물들이 있다. 황충은 메뚜기와 비슷한데 이는 이들 모두 훌륭한 점프력을 갖추고 있기 때문이다. 하지만 갈라파고스 황충은 3미터 가까이 뛰어오를 수 있는데, 이 능력은 포식자로부터 탈출할 때 도움이 될 수 있다. 갈라파고스 펭귄은 북반구에 서식하는 유일한 펭귄이다. 갈라파고스 펭귄은 그들의 고립된 서식지에 적응하기 위한 독창적인 방법을 찾아냈다. 그들은 화산암으로 둥지를 만든다!

**29** ③ 갈라파고스 펭귄은 북반구에 서식하는 유일한 펭귄이라고 했다.

**30** ④ 선행사가 animals와 penguins로 동물이므로 관계대명사 which와 that이 가능하겠지만, the only가 penguins를 꾸미고 있으므로 that만 가능하다.

>> **Grammar Practice**                    pp. 52~55

Ⓐ1 (1) shoes (2) beauty (3) water (4) much (5) little
Ⓐ2 (1) bottles of (2) pieces of paper (3) pairs of
Ⓑ1 (1) the (2) the (3) an (4) a (5) the (6) The (7) a
Ⓑ2 (1) a (2) an (3) The (4) a (5) The (6) an, a (7) the
    (8) the
Ⓒ1 (1) train (2) lunch (3) her (4) school (5) soccer
Ⓒ2 (1) × (2) a (3) × (4) × (5) × (6) × (7) ×
Ⓓ1 (1) D (2) S (3) D
Ⓓ2 (1) himself (2) herself (3) myself (4) ourselves
    (5) yourself
Ⓓ3 (1) by herself (2) for myself
Ⓔ1 (1) All (2) the others (3) every (4) the other (5) one
    (6) the others
Ⓔ2 (1) others (2) Each (3) another, the other

>> **Grammar Test**                    pp. 56~57

01 ④    02 myself    03 ③    04 ④, ⑤    05 ①    06 ③
07 (1) few → little   (2) other → the other   08 ④   09 ①
10 ①   11 ②   12 Please show me bigger ones.   13 ③
14 ③

01 water는 물질명사로 a를 붙이거나 복수형으로 쓸 수 없으며, 복수형으로 나타낼 때는 단위를 나타내는 a glass of에서 glass를 복수형으로 쓴다.
02 강조 용법으로 쓰인 재귀대명사는 생략할 수 있다.
03 a pair of 뒤에는 짝을 이루는 복수명사만 들어갈 수 있다.
04 ④ Washington은 지역 이름으로 관사와 함께 쓰이지 않으며, ⑤ go to school은 '공부하러 학교에 가다'라는 의미로 건물이 본래의 목적으로 쓰인 경우 school 앞에 관사를 쓰지 않는다.
05 a lot of(많은)는 셀 수 있는 명사와 셀 수 없는 명사에 모두 쓰는데, novels는 셀 수 있는 명사의 복수형이므로 a lot of는 many와 바꿔 쓸 수 있다.
06 each는 '각각의'의 뜻으로, 단수명사와 함께 쓰이며, 단수 취급하므로 동사는 has가 알맞다.
07 (1) 셀 수 없는 명사가 '거의 없는'이라고 할 때는 little을 쓴다. (2) '나머지 하나'를 나타낼 때는 the other를 쓴다.
08 ④ 두 개가 하나의 쌍을 이루는 명사는 a pair of로 수량을 나타낸다. ① advice는 추상명사로 복수형으로 쓸 수 없다. ② many 다음에는 복수명사가 온다. ③ pizza는 물질명사

로 a piece of로 수량을 나타낸다. ⑤ 앞에 나온 명사 (newspaper)와 같은 종류의 불특정한 것을 가리킬 때 단수형이면 one을 쓴다.
09 ① 강조 역할을 하는 재귀대명사로 생략할 수 있다. ②, ③, ④, ⑤ 목적어 역할을 하며 생략할 수 없다.
10 ① 수식어구가 명사를 꾸밀 때는 정관사 the를 써야 한다.
11 ② apples는 셀 수 있는 명사이므로 그 앞에 a little이 아니라 a few를 써야 한다.
12 앞에 나온 명사 pants와 같은 종류를 나타내는 대명사가 되어야 하므로 복수형인 ones를 써야 한다.
13 ⓐ each 뒤에는 단수명사가 오고 단수 취급한다. (girls → girl) ⓓ the people이 복수명사이므로 복수 취급한다. (has → have)
14 ③ 정해진 수에서 나머지 전부를 가리킬 때는 the others를 쓴다. (others → the others)

>> **Reading**                    pp. 58~59

1 ⑤   2 work   3 ②   4 ⑤

**[1~2]**

가능한가, 불가능한가?
　만화영화에서는 놀라운 일들이 가능하다. 하지만 그것이 실제로 실생활에서 가능할까?
높이, 높이 그리고 멀리!
　만화영화에서는 집이 수천 개의 풍선에 의해 들려 올라가고 날아간다. 그게 실제로 가능할까? 집 한 채의 무게가 5만 킬로그램 정도라고 가정해 보자. 놀이공원에 있는 보통의 풍선은 약 14그램을 들어 올릴 수 있다. 그래서 우리는 집을 들어 올리기 위해 약 3,570,000개의 풍선이 필요하다. 우리는 또한 풍선 자체의 무게와 줄의 무게도 생각해야 한다. 그렇게 되면 우리는 수천 개의 풍선을 더 더해야 한다. 이제 가장 큰 어려움은 그 모든 풍선에 바람을 넣는 일이다!

1 앞에 나온 the balloons를 강조하는 강조 용법으로 쓰인 재귀대명사가 들어가야 하므로 themselves가 알맞다.
2 '효과가 있거나 성공하다'는 work에 해당하는 영영풀이이다.
3
　모두가 어떤 것에서 최고가 되고 싶어 한다. 하지만, 하루 아침에 기술을 완전히 익히는 것은 불가능하다. 예를 들어, 만약 당신이 골프를 잘 치기를 원한다면, 당신은 숙련된 선수들을 지켜보고 기본 기술을 익혀야 한다. 하지만 이것은 훌륭한 골프 선수가 되기에는 충분하지 않다. 당신은 매일 연습을 해야 한다. 당신이 그저 골프채를 잡고 공을 치며 일주일 혹은 이주일 안에 세계 챔피언이 되기를 바랄 수는 없다. 당신은 훌륭한 선수가 되기 위해 많은 시간과 노력을 들여야 한다.

하루아침에 어떤 분야의 최고가 되기는 불가능하며 매일매일 연습을 해야 한다는 내용이므로 ② '연습이 최고를 만든다.'가 알맞다.

**4**

> 중앙아메리카의 마야 문명은 세계에서 가장 잘 알려진 고대 문명들 중 하나이다. 유럽과 멀리 있음에도 불구하고, 마야 문명은 고대 그리스, 이집트 문명과 공통점이 많이 있었다. 그리스인들처럼, 마야인들은 석조 건물을 지었고 신을 숭배했다. 또한 그들에게는 고대 그리스와 비슷한 독립된 도시 국가들이 많이 있었다. 이집트인들과 마찬가지로, 마야인들은 아주 높은 피라미드를 지었다. 마야식 피라미드는 꼭대기에 사원이 있었지만, 이집트의 피라미드들과 같은 가파른 측면과 계단이 있었다.

⑤ 마야 문명과 이집트의 피라미드 둘 다 가파른 측면과 계단이 있지만, 마야식 피라미드에는 꼭대기에 사원이 있다고 했다.

---

## ≫ Expression Test

pp. 60~61

**1** What time  **2** ③  **3** ②  **4** I'm curious about Paulo Coelho.  **5** ③  **6** ④

**1** 대화의 흐름상 '몇 시에 만나기로 할까?'라는 뜻이 되어야 하므로 What time이 알맞다.

**2** 나머지는 궁금증을 나타내는 표현이고, ③은 걱정을 나타내는 표현이다.

**3** 상대방에게 어떤 것이나 사실에 대해 알고 있는지 물어볼 때는 Have you heard about(of) ...? / Do you know about ...? 등을 쓸 수 있다.

**4** I'm curious about ....은 '나는 …에 대해 궁금해.'라는 뜻으로 궁금증을 표현할 때 쓴다.

**5** When do you want to meet?은 시간을 정하는 표현이므로 ③이 알맞다.

**6** (D) 내일 우리 학교 축제에 올래? – (C) 물론이야. 몇 시에 만날까? – (A) 우리 학교 앞에서 6시 어때? – (B) 좋아. 내일 봐.

---

## ≫ 서술형 평가

p. 62

**1** (1) Have you heard about  (2) I'm curious about how
**2** (1) is looking at herself  (2) my homework by myself
**3** (1) We don't have much snow in winter.  (2) Love is actually all around.  **4** (1) a  (2) an  (3) a  (4) a  (5) the
**5** (1) Some  (2) One, other  (3) others

---

**1** 들어 본 적이 있는지 물을 때는 Have you heard about ...? 을 써서 나타내고, 궁금증을 표현할 때는 I'm curious about ....을 쓴다.

**2** (1) 주어와 전치사의 목적어가 같으므로 재귀대명사 herself가 쓰였다. (2) by oneself: 혼자서

**3** (1) snow는 셀 수 없는 명사이므로 much로 꾸민다. (2) Love는 셀 수 없는 명사이므로 단수 취급한다.

**4** a는 셀 수 있는 명사의 단수형 앞에 쓴다. 단어의 첫 발음이 모음일 때는 an을 쓴다. the는 특정한 것을 가리키는 명사 앞에 온다.

**5** (1), (3) 부정대명사 some은 전체의 일부를 가리키고 others는 또 다른 일부를 나타낸다. the others는 나머지 전체를 나타낸다. (2) 둘 중 하나는 one으로, 나머지 하나는 the other로 나타낸다.

---

## ≫ Final Test

pp. 63~67

**01** ③  **02** ③  **03** ④  **04** curious about the bird  **05** ④
**06** (B) → (C) → (A)  **07** ⑤  **08** wonder how high Mt. Everest is  **09** ④  **10** (1) one  (2) ones  **11** (1) a loaf of  (2) a glass of  (3) a pair of  **12** ④  **13** (a) themselves (b) herself  **14** All  **15** ④  **16** One, the other  **17** ②
**18** another  **19** (1) many(lots of)  (2) few  **20** ①  **21** two slices(pieces) of, a slice(piece) of  **22** ②  **23** ⑤  **24** ④
**25** ①  **26** ②  **27** ④  **28** ④  **29** ②  **30** ⑤

**01** '보통의, 전형적인, 예상되는'은 normal(보통의)에 해당하는 영영풀이이다.

**02** lift는 '들어 올리다'라는 뜻으로 '어떤 것을 공기 중에 위로 옮기다'의 의미가 되도록 빈칸에는 move가 적절하다.

**03** ④ 새로 나온 전화기에 대해 들어 봤는지 묻는 질문에 대해 아니라고 하며 이미 그것을 샀다는 대답은 어색하다.

**04** I'm curious about ....으로 궁금증을 표현할 수 있다.

**05** 쇼핑 가자는 말에 수락의 대답을 했고, 바로 뒤에 A가 시간을 제안하는 것으로 보아 빈칸에는 '몇 시에 만날까?'라는 질문이 이어져야 한다.

**06** (B) 뭐 하고 있니? – (C) 책을 읽고 있어. 인상주의미술에 대해 들어 봤니? – (A) 응, 하지만 그것에 대해서 많이 알고 있지는 않아.

**07** 언제 만날지를 묻고 있으므로 약속 시간을 정하는 내용이 이어져야 한다.

**08** '…이 궁금하다'는 I wonder ....로 표현한다. wonder 다음에는 ⟨의문사＋주어＋동사⟩의 어순이 이어진다.

**09** ④ 셀 수 있는 명사 앞에 little은 올 수 없다.

**10** 앞에 나온 명사와 같은 종류의 불특정한 것을 가리킬 때 단수이면 one, 복수이면 ones를 쓴다.

**11** ⑴ 빵 한 덩어리: a loaf of bread ⑵ 주스 한 컵: a glass of juice ⑶ 바지 한 벌: a pair of pants

**12** ④ 사람의 이름 앞에는 관사가 오지 않으므로 an을 없애야 한다.

**13** 주어와 일치하는 목적어 대상을 나타내기 위해 각각 재귀대명사를 써야 한다.

**14** all은 '모두'의 뜻을 나타내는 부정대명사이다.

**15** ④ 건물, 장소가 본래의 목적으로 쓰인 경우 관사를 붙이지 않는다.

**16** '(둘 중에서) 하나는 …, 다른 하나는 …'을 나타낼 때는 〈one …, the other …〉로 쓴다.

**17** 첫 번째는 주어(The professor)와 일치하는 목적어이므로 재귀대명사가 적절하고, 두 번째는 '우리에 대해'라는 의미로 목적격 형태가 오는 것이 적절하다.

**18** '(셋 중) 하나는 …, 또 하나는 …, 나머지 하나는 …'을 나타내는 〈one …, another …, the other …〉에서 쓰이고, '또 다른 것'을 의미하는 말은 another이다.

**19** ⑴ 뒤에 셀 수 있는 명사인 books가 있으므로 a lot of는 many나 lots of로 바꿔 쓸 수 있다. ⑵ '약간의'의 의미로 쓰일 때 some은 셀 수 있는 명사 앞에서 a few로 바꿔 쓸 수 있다.

**20** ① 교통수단 앞에는 관사가 오지 않는다. ② 유일한 것 앞 ③ 뒤에 수식어구가 있을 때 ④ 상황으로 보아 서로가 알고 있는 명사 앞 ⑤ 앞에서 언급한 명사 앞에는 the가 붙는다.

**21** 빵과 치즈는 얇게 썬 조각이므로 a slice of(한 장의)나 a piece of(한 조각 의) 모두 쓸 수 있다. 복수형으로 나타낼 때는 단위만 복수형으로 쓴다.

**22** ② All 뒤에 단수명사(my money)가 왔으므로 단수 취급한다. ① looks → look ③ are → is ④ students → student ⑤ learn → learns

**23** '(정해지지 않은 수에서) 어떤 사람들은 …하고, 또 어떤 사람들은 …하다'는 〈Some …, others …〉로 나타내고, 정해진 수에서 하나는 one, 나머지 전부를 가리킬 때는 the others를 쓴다.

**24** ④ 주어 Sue를 강조하는 역할이므로 생략할 수 있다. 나머지는 모두 목적어 역할을 하므로 생략할 수 없다.

**25**

> 행복을 돈으로 살 수 있는가? 음, 자신에게 물어보라. 여러분의 친구와 하는 대화가 비싼 옷을 입었을 때 더 즐겁다고 생각하는가? 텔레비전 쇼가 32인치보다 60인치 텔레비전으로 볼 때 더 재미있는가? 답은 '아니요'이다. 행복한 순간은 돈으로 살 수 있는 것에서 기인하는 것이 아니다. 다시 말해, 행복은 당신이 돈을 얼마나 가지고 있는지에 달려있지 않다.

행복은 돈으로 살 수 있는 것에서 비롯되는 것이 아니라고 했으므로, 빈칸에는 ① '당신이 돈을 얼마나 가지고 있는지'가 알맞다.

**26**

> 지난 일요일에 나는 Amazing Show를 보러 갔다. 쇼는 줄타기로 시작되었다. 한 남자가 공중에서 가느다란 줄 위를 따라 걸었다. 그 남자는 한 번은 줄에서 거의 떨어질 뻔 했지만 균형을 유지할 수 있었다. 재미있는 다른 공연들도 많았다. 하지만 내가 가장 좋아했던 것은 스케이트보드 묘기였다. 나는 열 명의 소년들이 스케이트보드를 타고 공중으로 점프했을 때 매우 놀랐다.

② 공연을 보고 아주 신이 난 상태이다.

**[27~28]**

> Miranda Smith라는 선생님이 학생들을 위해 피아노를 치고 기타를 연주한다. 음, 이는 선생님이 아무것도 볼 수 없다는 점을 제외하면 평범한 음악 수업처럼 보인다. Miranda는 태어날 때부터 눈이 안 보였지만, 그녀의 부모님은 그녀를 특수학교에 보내고 싶지 않았다. 그래서 그녀는 지역의 고등학교에 다녔다. 그녀는 훌륭한 학생이었고, 대학에 갔다. 대학을 졸업한 후, Miranda는 시각 장애인을 위한 학교에서 숙련된 교사로서 20년 동안 근무해 왔다.

**27** ④ Miranda Smith는 눈이 안 보였지만 학교를 성공적으로 마치고 시각 장애인을 위한 학교의 선생님이 되었다는 내용이므로 빈칸에는 blind(눈이 먼)가 알맞다.

**28** (A) 악기 이름 앞에는 정관사 the가 알맞다. (B) 동격의 명사절을 이끄는 접속사 that이 알맞다. (C) for와 during은 '…동안'이라는 뜻의 전치사로, for 뒤에는 숫자가, during 뒤에는 구체적인 기간이 나온다.

**[29~30]**

> 태양계의 모든 행성들 중 화성은 (인간이) 살 수 있는 새로운 행성으로서 가장 인기 있는 선택이었다. 화성은 지구와 매우 비슷한데, 이것이 인간이 화성에서 사는 것이 다른 행성들보다 더 쉬울 것이라 여기는 이유이다. 하지만 화성과 지구의 차이점은 화성에서 사는 것을 어렵게 한다. 화성은 대기를 지니고 있음에도 불구하고, 그것이 아주 미약하고 대부분 이산화탄소이다. 인간이 숨을 쉴 산소가 충분하지 않다! 화성에는 물이 거의 없고 찾기 매우 어려울 수 있다. 또한, 화성은 아주 춥고 중력이 약하다.

**29** ②의 앞부분은 화성이 지구를 대체할 행성으로 주목받는다는 내용이고, 뒷부분에는 화성과 지구의 차이점에 대한 내용이 나오므로, 주어진 문장은 ②에 들어가는 것이 자연스럽다.

**30** ⓔ water는 셀 수 없는 명사이므로 little을 써야 한다.

## Lesson 04 형용사, 부사, 비교

**>> Grammar Practice** pp. 72~75

**A1** (1) cute (2) angry (3) great (4) everything possible (5) sick (6) happy (7) something strange (8) the weak

**A2** (1) a Chinese restaurant (2) on the sofa are alike (3) something comfortable

**A3** (1) looks cute (2) something hot to drink (3) The injured

**B1** (1) hardly (2) late (3) highly (4) fast (5) high

**B2** (1) late (2) carefully (3) hardly (4) perfectly (5) highly

**B3** (1) D (2) S

**C1** (1) as (2) much (3) as (4) the richest (5) the most important (6) of (7) better

**C2** (1) bigger than (2) as fast as (3) as(so) comfortable as

**C3** (1) more useful than that one (2) the same watch as hers (3) the richest man in

**D1** (1) bigger and bigger (2) as soon as possible (3) twice (4) the more

**D2** (1) Our world is getting smaller and smaller.
(2) The bee is one of the busiest insects.
(3) My book is three times thicker than yours.

**D3** bigger, bigger, any other

**>> Grammar Test** pp. 76~77

**01** ① **02** more interesting than **03** ④ **04** ④ **05** (1) nothing important (2) highly (3) complicated **06** ② **07** more difficult than **08** ③ **09** ④ **10** ② **11** ③, ⑤ **12** Would you like to have something cold? **13** ⑤

**01** 원급 비교일 때, 긍정문은 〈as＋형용사(부사) 원급＋as〉의 형태로 쓰고, 부정문은 〈not as(so)＋형용사(부사) 원급＋as〉의 형태로 쓴다.

**02** '…보다 더 …한'이라는 뜻은 〈비교급＋than〉의 형태로 쓰는데 interesting은 3음절 이상의 단어이므로 비교급은 more interesting이다.

**03** 동사를 꾸미는 부사 자리이다. ④ friendly는 형용사이다.

**04** '최근에'라는 뜻의 부사 lately가 알맞다.

**05** (1) -thing으로 끝나는 대명사는 형용사가 뒤에서 꾸민다. (2) '매우 성공한'의 뜻이 되어야 하므로 highly가 알맞다. (3) 감각동사는 형용사를 보어로 취하므로 complicated가 알맞다.

**06** 비교급을 강조할 때는 much, even, still, far 등으로 한다. very는 비교급을 강조할 수 없다.

**07** 수학 성적이 영어 성적보다 좋지 않으므로 민준이에게는 수학이 영어보다 더 어렵다. 따라서 〈비교급＋than〉의 형식을 이용하여 써야 하는데, difficult는 3음절 이상의 단어이므로 비교급은 more difficult이다.

**08** ③ '매우 비싼'의 뜻이 되어야 하므로 highly로 써야 한다.

**09** 가격의 정도는 a sofa > a table = a chair이므로 ④ '소파가 모두 중에서 가장 비싸다'라는 설명이 알맞다.

**10** ① '가장 …한 것들 중 하나'는 〈one of the＋최상급＋복수명사〉의 형태로 쓴다. (actor → actors) ③ '…보다 몇 배 …한'은 〈배수사＋as＋원급＋as …〉를 쓴다. (larger → large) ④ sooner → soon ⑤ '점점 더 많은'은 more and more의 형태로 쓴다. (most → more)

**11** '현명한 사람들'은 the wise(= wise people)로 나타낸다.

**12** -thing으로 끝나는 대명사는 형용사가 뒤에서 꾸민다.

**13** ⑤ 비교급으로 최상의 의미를 나타낼 때는 〈비교급＋than any other＋단수명사〉의 형태이다. (girls → girl)

**>> Reading** pp. 78~79

**1** ④ **2** (A) bright (B) warmly **3** ③ **4** ②

**[1~2]**

아기 코끼리의 발자국
날짜/시간: 7월 8일, 오후 2시 35분
오늘은 내가 아프리카에 온 첫 날이었다. 오늘 아침에 나는 작은 물웅덩이 옆에 있는 한 코끼리 무리를 발견했다. 나는 아기 코끼리 한 마리가 엄마 옆에서 물을 마시고 있는 것을 보았다. 그 코끼리의 눈이 별처럼 밝았다. 나는 그 코끼리에게 Stella라는 이름을 붙여 주었다.
날짜/시간: 7월 12일, 오후 7시 20분
해 질 녘에 나는 Stella가 자신의 엄마 옆에서 울고 있는 것을 발견했다. 엄마 코끼리는 죽어서 누워 있었다. 나는 코끼리 보호소에 전화를 해서 도움을 요청했다. 나는 구조대가 올 때까지 Stella 곁에 머물기로 결정했다.
날짜/시간: 7월 13일, 오전 6시
새로운 코끼리 무리가 나타났고 Stella는 그 무리에 다가갔다. 아마도 가장 나이가 많은 암컷인 듯한 코끼리 한 마리가 Stella가 그 무리의 일원이 되도록 허락했다. 믿을 수 없게도, 암컷 코끼리 중 한 마리가 Stella의 엄마만큼 따뜻하게 Stella를 보살폈다. 이것은 너무나 놀라운 순간이었다!

**1** ⓓ는 Stella's mom을 가리키고, 나머지는 모두 Stella를 가리킨다.

**2** 원급 비교는 〈as + 형용사(부사) 원급 + as〉의 형태로 쓴다.

**3**
> Angela는 Octopus Friend이다. 그녀는 가까이 있고 싶은 Vanessa라는 친구가 있다. 문어처럼 Angela는 Vanessa를 아주 꽉 붙잡으려고 한다. 하지만 Vanessa는 이런 상황을 좋아하지 않을 것이다. 누구도 갇힌 느낌을 좋아하지 않는다. Angela가 계속해서 Vanessa를 통제하려 한다면, Vanessa는 도망치기를 원할 것이다. Angela는 Vanessa를 친구로서 잃는 것을 두려워하지만, 그녀가 행동하는 방식은 결국 Vanessa를 밀어낼 수 있다. 친구가 꼭 한 명이어야 할 필요가 없다는 것을 명심하라. 가지각색의 친구들을 사귐으로써 여러분의 학교생활이 분명히 즐겁고 흥미로워질 것이다.

글에서 Octopus Friend란 한 친구에게만 집착하여 그 친구를 옭아매고 통제하려는 친구를 가리킨다.

**4**
> 사람들은 종종 더 큰 것을 사려고 하는 데 많은 시간을 보낸다. 그들은 더 큰 집, 더 큰 차, 그리고 때로는 더 큰 침대를 원한다. 하지만 때때로 더 큰 것이 항상 더 좋은 것은 아니다. 컴퓨터를 예로 들어 보자. 최초의 컴퓨터는 너무 크고 무거워서 방을 몇 개씩 차지했다. 지금은 어떤 컴퓨터는 책보다 작고 완전히 무선이다. 자동차들 역시 점점 작아지고 있다. 작은 자동차는 복잡한 교통 속에서 운전하기 쉽고 주차하기 훨씬 더 쉽다. 작은 차는 큰 차보다 기름도 훨씬 덜 먹는데, 이는 작은 차를 소유하는 것을 더 경제적으로 만들어 준다.

주어진 문장은 But으로 시작하며 더 큰 것이 항상 더 좋은 것은 아니라는 내용이므로 그에 대한 예시 앞인 ②에 들어가야 한다.

## Expression Test
pp. 80~81

**1** ③  **2** ②  **3** ⑤  **4** easier than  **5** I can't  **6** ②

**1** ③은 '도와주겠다'는 뜻이고, 나머지는 모두 '도와 달라'는 요청의 표현이다.

**2** 빈칸 앞에 as로 보아 as small as(…만큼 작은)가 적절하다.

**3** 흐름상 도움을 요청하는 말에 승낙하는 표현이 와야 알맞다. ⑤는 요청에 거절하는 표현이다.

**4** '…보다 더 …한'의 뜻은 〈비교급 + than〉으로 표현한다.

**5** 요청에 거절하는 표현이 와야 한다.

**6** (C) 부탁 하나 해도 될까? – (A) 물론이야. 뭔데? – (D) 과학 프로젝트 좀 도와줄 수 있어? – (B) 문제없어.

## 서술형 평가
p. 82

**1** that tree is as old as me  **2** (1) He is usually at his office.  (2) She will never come.  **3** (1) much younger  (2) far more difficult than  (3) even better than  **4** (1) the healthier I become  (2) the earlier I can go home  **5** (1) not as(so) old as Louis  (2) as fast as Louis  (3) not as(so) tall as Louis

**1** '…만큼 …한'의 뜻으로 동등한 것을 비교할 때는 〈as + 형용사(부사) 원급 + as〉로 표현한다.

**2** 빈도를 나타내는 부사를 빈도부사라고 하며 usually, always, never, often 등이 있다. 빈도부사는 be동사와 조동사 뒤, 일반동사 앞에 쓴다.

**3** 비교급 문장은 〈비교급 + than〉으로 나타내고, 비교급 앞에 much, a lot, far, even 등을 붙여 강조할 수 있다.

**4** 〈The + 비교급 …, the + 비교급 …〉: …하면 할수록 더 …하다

**5** 〈as + 형용사(부사) 원급 + as〉는 '…만큼 …한'의 뜻으로 동등한 것을 비교할 때 쓴다. 부정문은 〈not as(so) + 형용사(부사) 원급 + as〉로 쓴다.

## Final Test
pp. 83~87

**01** ④  **02** (1) beside (2) care (3) lying  **03** ③  **04** ④  **05** sold as well as  **06** you help me (to) hang  **07** ⑤  **08** ④  **09** ④  **10** hard  **11** (1) bigger than the earth (2) one of the most interesting books  **12** ⑤  **13** ②  **14** The house looks so beautiful.  **15** ②  **16** ④  **17** Nothing  **18** ②  **19** ②  **20** ③  **21** ②  **22** successful → successfully  **23** wrong anything → anything wrong  **24** (1) He wanted much more than he needed. (2) This box is four times as heavy as that one.  **25** ⑤  **26** ③  **27** ③  **28** ⑤  **29** ③  **30** ⑤

**01** '떠나기 보다는 그 자리에 머물다'는 stay(머물다)의 영영풀이에 해당한다.

**02** (1) beside: …옆에 (2) care for: …을 돌보다 (3) lie: (어떤 상태로) 있다

**03** ③ 요청하는 A의 말에 B가 늦어서 미안하다고 하는 것은 어색하다.

**04** 요청하는 표현으로 Can(May) I ask you a favor? / Would you do me a favor? 등을 쓸 수 있다.

**05** 〈as + 형용사(부사) 원급 + as〉를 이용하여 '…만큼 …한(하게)'의 비교의 뜻을 나타낼 수 있다.

**06** 부탁을 하며 대화를 시작하고 있고 주어진 단어와 그림을 볼 때, '그림을 벽에 거는 것을 도와 달라'는 요청의 표현이 와야 한다.

**07** 집에 놀러 오라는 권유에 내일 시험이 있다고 말하고 있으므로 빈칸에는 거절하는 표현이 와야 한다.

**08** ④ 내용상 중고책이 새 책보다 더 싸다는 흐름이 적절하므로 more expensive를 cheaper로 써야 한다.

**09** hardly: 거의 … 않는

**10** hard는 형용사로 '딱딱한, 어려운', 부사로 '열심히'의 뜻을 나타낸다.

**11** (1) 비교급 비교는 〈비교급＋than〉으로 쓴다. (2) '가장 …한 것들 중 하나'는 〈one of the＋최상급＋복수명사〉의 어순으로 쓴다.

**12** '…보다 몇 배 …한'은 〈배수사＋as＋원급＋as …〉의 형태로 쓴다.

**13** ② long의 비교급은 longer이고 비교급을 강조할 때는 much, far, a lot 등을 쓴다.

**14** 감각동사는 형용사를 보어로 취한다. 부사 so가 앞에서 beautiful을 꾸민다.

**15** 〈one of the＋최상급＋복수명사〉는 '가장 …한 것들 중 하나'라는 뜻으로 writer는 복수형 writers로 고쳐야 한다.

**16** • 〈비교급＋and＋비교급〉: 점점 더 …하다
  • 〈The＋비교급 …, the＋비교급 …〉: …하면 할수록 더 …하다

**17** 〈부정 주어＋비교급＋than〉을 이용하여 최상급의 뜻을 나타낼 수 있다.

**18** 〈비교급＋than any other＋단수명사〉: 다른 어떤 것보다 더 …한

**19** ② 〈as＋원급＋as＋주어＋can[could]〉: 가능한 한 …한 [하게] (so → as)

**20** • lately: 최근에 • high: 높게 • nearly: 거의

**21** ① happily → happy  ③ special anything → anything special  ④ a book interesting → an interesting book  ⑤ is → are

**22** 동사 passed를 꾸며야 하므로 부사가 필요하다.

**23** -thing으로 끝나는 대명사는 형용사가 뒤에서 꾸민다.

**24** (1) more가 온 것으로 보아 비교 대상 앞에 than이 와야 한다. (2) 〈배수사＋as＋원급＋as …〉의 형태로 써야 하므로 four times로 고친다.

**25** 　어떤 사람들은 화려한 그래픽과 효과음 때문에 컴퓨터 게임을 좋아한다. 하지만 나는 컴퓨터 게임보다 보드게임을 더 좋아한다. 주된 이유는 가족과 함께 보드게임을 하는 것을 좋아하기 때문이다. 우리 가족이 가장 좋아하는 보드게임은 모노폴리이다. 그것은 실제 부동산을 사고, 팔고, 빌리는 것과 비슷하다. 보드게임을 하는 것은 가족과 유대감을 형성하는

훌륭한 방법이다. 아는가? 이는 정확히 컴퓨터가 제공하지 못하는 것이다.

⑤ 컴퓨터 게임보다 보드게임을 좋아하는 이유에 대해 말하고 있다.

**26** 　지구에서 가장 높은 산은 무엇인가? 에베레스트산인가? 놀랍게도, 그것은 하와이에 있는 활화산인 마우나로아이다. 꼭대기에서 가장 아래까지 56,000피트로, 마우나로아는 에베레스트산의 29,035피트보다 거의 두 배 높다. 그렇다면 왜 그렇게 보이지 않는 것일까? 그것은 마우나로아의 4분의 1만이 수면 위로 나와 있기 때문이다! 그것의 아랫부분은 해저 26,200피트에 가라앉아 있다.

마우나로아의 아랫부분이 해저에 가라앉아 있기 때문에 실제 높이만큼 커 보이지 않는다고 했다.

**[27~28]**

　코끼리는 세상에서 가장 똑똑한 동물들 중 하나로 알려져 있다. 하지만 태국의 Hong이라 불리는 한 암컷 코끼리는 코끼리가 인간만큼 예술적일 수 있다는 것을 보여 주었다. 2001년 태국에서 태어난 Hong은 네 살 때 그림 그리는 것을 배우기 시작했다. 그녀는 코끼리가 걸어가거나 코로 꽃을 물고 있는 그림을 그릴 수 있었다. 이 코끼리는 코끝에 붓을 들고 자화상과 태국 국기를 아름답게 그려 관광객들을 즐겁게 해 주었다.

**27** ③ Hong이 그림 그리는 것을 누구에게 배웠는지에 대한 언급은 없다.

**28** (A) 〈one of the＋최상급＋복수명사〉의 형태로 smartest가 알맞다. (B) 〈as＋형용사 원급＋as〉의 원급 비교로 as가 알맞다.

**[29~30]**

　사람들이 특히 뭔가를 처음으로 할 때 실수를 하는 것은 자연스러운 일이다. 당신은 아마 당신이 행했던 어리석은 일 때문에 자책해 봤을지도 모른다. 실수를 만회하기 위해서는 단지 가능한 한 빨리 간단한 사과를 하라. 그저 "죄송합니다. 제가 그것을 잘 처리하지 못했어요." 또는 "제가 한 일에 대해 사과하고 싶어요."라고 말하라. 당신이 실수를 인지한 후 더 빨리 이렇게 할수록, 더 좋다. 당신이 사과하기를 오래 기다린다면 그것은 상황을 더 악화시킨다.

**29** 실수를 했을 때 늦게 사과하면 상황이 악화되므로 되도록 빨리 사과를 하라고 했다.

**30** (A) 주어와 목적어가 동일하므로 yourself가 알맞다. (B) 부사적 용법의 to부정사가 알맞다. (C) 〈the＋비교급 …, the＋비교급 …〉이 되어야 하므로 better가 알맞다.

## Lesson 05  접속사

### ▶▶ Grammar Practice    pp. 92~95

**A1** (1) ⓐ (2) ⓒ (3) ⓑ (4) ⓑ (5) ⓒ

**A2** (1) It (2) whether

**A3** (1) that (2) Whether (3) that

**B1** (1) when (2) until (3) before (4) after (5) because

**B2** (1) If (2) Though(Although) (3) Though(Although) (4) unless

**C1** (1) if I can park here (2) when the party begins (3) how they go to the park (4) how the machine works (5) whether he likes the story

**C2** (1) if(whether) he bought (2) why the baby is crying (3) what your name is (4) if(whether) Jane rides

**C3** (1) the weather is (2) ○ (3) Jack won (4) how long you stayed (5) ○

**D1** (1) Where do you suppose (2) Who do you think made (3) Who do you guess will be (4) What do you think the book (5) When do you think Sam went

### ▶▶ Grammar Test    pp. 96~97

**01** ⑤　　**02** ④　　**03** (1) Though (2) because (3) If
**04** (1) that (2) when　　**05** ③　　**06** ⑤　　**07** ②　　**08** ②
**09** (1) so (2) Though(Although)　　**10** ⑤　　**11** ③　　**12** ⑤
**13** (1) if → whether (2) whether → that

**01** 의문사가 없으므로 〈if(whether)＋주어＋동사〉의 어순으로 연결한다.

**02** • '만약 …라면'의 뜻으로 조건의 if가 들어가야 한다.
• '…하지 않으면'의 뜻으로 부정의 조건을 나타내는 unless가 알맞다.

**03** (1) '웃고 있지만 걱정한다'는 양보의 의미를 나타낸다. (2) it was a nice day가 We went for a walk에 대한 이유이다. (3) '누르면'의 뜻으로 조건의 의미를 나타낸다.

**04** (1) 진주어절을 이끄는 접속사 that이 알맞다. (2) '영화가 언제 시작하는지'라는 의미가 되어야 하므로 의문사 when이 알맞다.

**05** looked both ways가 먼저 한 행동이고, crossed the road가 나중에 한 행동이므로 after를 이용하여 나타낼 수 있다.

**06** ⑤ '비록 …일지라도'의 뜻으로 양보를 나타내는 (al)though가 들어가는 것이 적절하다.

**07** ② 의문사가 있는 간접의문문은 〈의문사＋주어＋동사〉 어순이다. (where does Bill live → where Bill lives)

**08** • It은 가주어이고 진주어 역할을 하는 that절이 필요하다.
• '…인지 아닌지'의 뜻으로 절을 이끌어 문장에서 목적어 역할을 하는 것은 if이다.

**09** (1) 〈결과＋because＋원인〉은 〈원인, so＋결과〉로 바꿔 나타낼 수 있다. (2) '코트를 입었지만'의 뜻으로 양보의 의미를 나타낸다.

**10** ⑤ 시간이나 조건의 부사절에서는 현재시제가 미래시제를 대신한다. will leave를 leaves로 써야 한다.

**11** ③ creature를 꾸미는 주격 관계대명사로 쓰였다. ① 진주어 ②, ⑤ 목적어 ④ 보어 역할을 하는 접속사로 쓰였다.

**12** ⑤ 동사가 think이므로 의문사를 문장의 맨 앞에 써서 간접의문문을 만든다. (→ Why do you think she bought the backpack?)

**13** (1) or not은 whether 바로 다음에는 붙일 수 있지만, if 바로 다음에는 붙일 수 없다. (2) 가주어 It에 대한 진주어절을 이끌 때에는 that을 써야 한다.

### ▶▶ Reading    pp. 98~99

**1** see where Icarus is　**2** ④　**3** ⑤　**4** ③

**[1~2]**

> 보면 볼수록 더 많이 알아요
> 　세계 미술관 투어에 오신 것을 환영합니다. 먼저 이 그림을 보세요. 바닷가 풍경이 매우 평화롭고 아름답죠, 그렇지 않나요? 이 그림의 제목은 〈추락하는 이카루스가 있는 풍경〉입니다. 그러면 여러분은 이카루스가 어디에 있는지 보이나요? 배 근처에 물 밖으로 나와 있는 두 다리가 보이나요? 이것이 그리스의 유명한 신화에 나오는 이카루스입니다. 그 신화에서 이카루스의 아버지는 그를 위해 깃털과 밀랍으로 날개를 만들어 주고 그에게 태양에서 멀리 떨어지라고 말했습니다. 하지만 이카루스는 듣지 않았습니다. 그는 태양에 너무 가깝게 날았습니다. 그래서 밀랍이 녹았고 그는 물에 빠졌습니다. 이제 다시 그림 전체를 보세요. 이카루스의 비극에도 불구하고, 사람들은 일상의 행동을 계속하고 있습니다. 그림이 여전히 평화로워 보이나요? 화가가 우리에게 무엇을 말하려 한다고 생각하나요?

**1** 간접의문문은 〈의문사＋주어＋동사〉의 어순으로 쓴다.

**2** 아버지가 이카루스에게 깃털과 밀랍으로 날개를 만들어 주었다. 이카루스는 태양에 가까이 가지 말라는 아버지의 말을 듣지 않고 태양에 가까이 가서 밀랍이 녹아 물에 빠졌다.

**3**

> 지난주는 내게 끔찍한 한 주였다. 월요일 아침에 늦잠을 자서 학교에 지각했다. 나는 선생님께서 수요일 시험을 위해 무엇을 공부해야 하는지 설명해 주시는 것을 놓쳤다. (C) 당연하게도, 나는 무엇을 공부해야 하는지 몰라서 아주 낮은 점수를 받았다. (B) 다음 날, 엄마가 내 시험 성적을 보셨을 때, 엄마는 아주 화가 났다. 나는 주말 동안 친구들과 밖에 나갈 수 없었다. (A) 오늘, 나는 친구들이 주말 동안 얼마나 재미있게 보냈는지 이야기하는 것을 들었을 때 슬펐다.

월요일에 지각해서 수요일 시험에 대한 설명을 놓쳤고, (C) 시험에서 낮은 점수를 받았으며, (B) 엄마가 성적을 보고 화가 나서 주말에 나가지 못하게 해서, (A) 주말을 재미있게 보낸 친구들의 이야기를 듣고 슬펐다는 내용이다.

**4**

> 공부를 할 때, 여러분은 주로 손으로 노트에 적는가 아니면 컴퓨터 키보드로 타이핑하는가? 한 연구에서, 한 집단은 모르는 알파벳 문자들을 손으로 쓰면서 외우도록 하고, 반면에 다른 집단은 키보드를 이용하도록 했다. 6주 후, 그 학생들이 여전히 이 철자들을 기억하는지 알아보기 위해 테스트를 했다. 연구는 손으로 썼던 학생들이 타이핑했던 학생들보다 더 잘했다는 것을 알아냈다. 연구자들은 종이에 펜을 두는 것이 키보드를 이용하는 것보다 뇌로 하여금 어떤 것을 기억하는 데 더 효과적일 수 있다는 결론을 내렸다.

타이핑하는 것보다 손으로 쓰는 것이 학습에 더 효율적이라는 내용이다.

---

> **Expression Test**   pp. 100~101

1 ②  2 like  3 ④  4 ④  5 ③  6 ④

**1** B가 불허하고 있으므로 허락을 구하는 표현이 들어가야 한다. Will you ...?는 '…해 주겠니?'라고 부탁하는 표현이다.

**2** How do you like ...?는 '…은 어떠니?'라는 뜻으로 의견을 묻는 표현이다.

**3** You can't .... / You're not allowed to .... 등은 상대방의 허락을 구하는 말에 대한 불허의 표현이다.

**4** 의견을 묻고 답하는 대화이므로 opinion(의견)이 알맞다.

**5** like better는 '더 좋아하다'라는 뜻이므로 prefer(선호하다)로 바꿔 쓸 수 있다.

**6** (D) 이 책에 대해 어떻게 생각하니? – (A) 그건 아주 재미있어. – (B) 너는 그게 왜 재미있다고 생각하니? – (C) 그것은 모든 사람을 웃게 해.

---

> **서술형 평가**   p. 102

**1** (1) How did you feel about (2) liked the movie better than  **2** (1) that he likes her (2) that she was in hospital  **3** (1) where it is (2) how big they are  **4** (1) While (2) Though (3) because  **5** (1) if the robot can clean the house (2) whether he will like my present

**1** 의견을 물을 때는 How do(did) you feel about ...? 등을 쓰고, 선호를 표현할 때는 I like ... better than .... 등을 쓴다.

**2** 접속사 that은 문장에서 주어, 목적어, 보어 역할을 하는 명사절을 이끈다.

**3** (1) 간접의문문은 〈의문사＋주어＋동사〉의 어순으로 쓴다. (2) 의문사구는 간접의문문에서 분리하지 않고 하나의 의문사처럼 쓴다.

**4** while은 시간을, though는 양보를, because는 이유를 나타내는 접속사이다.

**5** if와 whether는 '…인지 아닌지'의 의미로 명사절을 이끄는 접속사이며, 의문사가 없는 간접의문문에 쓰인다.

---

> **Final Test**   pp. 103~107

**01** ④  **02** (1) close (2) Listen (3) Look  **03** ②  **04** ④  **05** Do you mind if I  **06** ②  **07** you can't  **08** ⑤  **09** ③  **10** ①  **11** ④  **12** ②  **13** ①  **14** ③  **15** ①, ⑤  **16** ①  **17** (1) D (2) S  **18** ③  **19** ⑤  **20** (1) although (2) since (3) before  **21** how much money you spent  **22** ③  **23** Unless  **24** ②  **25** ①  **26** ⑤  **27** ④  **28** ②  **29** ④  **30** (C) → (A) → (B) → (D)

**01** ④는 '예술' – '예술가'의 뜻으로 둘 다 명사이고, 나머지는 명사와 형용사의 관계이다.

**02** (1) live close to: 근처에 살다 (2) listen to: …을 듣다 (3) look at: …을 보다

**03** ② '여기서 수영을 해도 될까요?'라고 허락 여부를 묻는 말에 '진정해. 그들은 단지 어린 아이들이야.'라고 대답하는 것은 어색하다.

**04** Which do you prefer, A or B?, I prefer A to B.는 선호하는 것에 대해 묻고 답하는 표현이다.

**05** Do you mind if I ...?로 허가 여부를 물을 수 있다.

**06** What do you think of ...?와 How do you like ...?는 의견을 묻는 표현이다.

**07** 컴퓨터를 쓸 수 없다고 불허하는 표현은 I'm afraid you can't.로 할 수 있다.

**08** 수영을 더 좋아한다고 대답하고 있으므로 빈칸에는 수영하기와 달리기 중 어느 것을 더 좋아하는지 선호를 묻는 질문이 들어가야 한다.

**09** even though는 '비록 …일지라도'의 뜻을 나타내는 부사절 접속사로 although와 바꿔 쓸 수 있다.

**10** '…할 때'의 뜻으로 시간을 나타내는 부사절 접속사는 when과 as이다.

**11** 간접의문문의 의문사가 문장 맨 앞에 있으므로 동사 know는 들어갈 수 없다.

**12** 의문사 what이 있으므로 〈의문사＋주어＋동사〉 어순으로 연결한다.

**13** We are tired가 결과, we walked so long이 원인으로 because와 so를 이용하여 문장을 완성한다.

**14** 목적절을 이끄는 접속사 that은 생략할 수 있다.

**15** '…인지 아닌지'의 뜻으로 명사절을 이끄는 접속사 if와 whether가 알맞다.

**16** '날씨가 좋으면'의 뜻으로 조건을 나타내는 말은 if이며, 조건 절에서는 현재시제가 미래시제를 대신하므로 현재시제로 나타낸다.

**17** 〈보기〉와 ②는 '…할 때'의 뜻으로 시간을 나타내는 접속사이다. ①은 '언제'의 의미를 나타내는 의문사로 쓰였다.

**18** ③ 시간이나 조건을 나타내는 부사절에서는 미래시제 대신 현재시제를 쓴다. (I'll finish → I finish)

**19** ①, ②, ③, ④에는 접속사 that이 필요하다. ⑤는 뒤에 or not으로 보아 whether가 들어가야 한다.

**20** (1) 날씨가 추웠지만 달리기를 하러 갔다는 흐름이므로 although (2) 녹차를 처음 맛본 이래로 그것을 즐겨왔다는 흐름이므로 since (3) 엄마가 오기 전에 숙제를 끝내야 한다는 흐름이므로 before가 알맞다.

**21** 의문사 how가 있으므로 〈의문사＋주어＋동사〉의 어순으로 연결한다. 의문사 다음에 오는 형용사(much)는 분리해서 쓰지 않고, how와 붙여서 쓴다.

**22** • '…인지 아닌지'의 뜻으로 명사절을 이끄는 접속사 if가 알맞다.
• '만약 …라면'의 뜻으로 조건의 부사절을 이끄는 접속사 if가 알맞다.

**23** if … not은 '만약 …하지 않으면'의 뜻으로 unless로 바꿔 쓸 수 있다.

**24** ② 의문사 다음에 오는 형용사는 분리해서 쓰지 않으므로 how old your brother is가 되어야 한다.

**25**
> 우리가 왜 역사를 배워야 한다고 생각하는가? 어떤 학생들은 역사가 지루한 과목이라고 불평을 한다. 하지만 그들은 오늘날 세상에서 일어나는 모든 일들이 과거에 이미 일어났던 것에 기반을 두고 있다는 것을 알아야 한다. 우리는 과거에 관해 배움으로써 현재를 진정으로 이해할 수 있다. 아무도 미래에 무슨 일이 일어날지 모르지만, 역사적 사실은 우리를 미래로 안내하는 데 도움을 줄 것이다.

① 역사 공부를 하는 것이 왜 필요한지에 대해 설명하고 있다.

**26**
> 제 이름은 Jaden입니다. 저는 런던에 있는 초콜릿 공장에서 아르바이트를 합니다. 제가 여기서 무엇을 하냐고요? 저는 다양한 맛의 초콜릿을 시식해 보고 어떤 것이 10대들에게 인기가 있을지 예측합니다. 회의에서 새로운 초콜릿을 만드는 것에 대한 저의 의견을 종종 나누기도 합니다. 건강하지 못한 직업처럼 들릴 수 있지만, 저는 제 달콤한 직업을 사랑한답니다!

⑤ 건강하지 못한 직업처럼 들릴지 모르지만 자신의 직업을 정말 좋아한다고 했다.

**[27~28]**
> 아기들이 울 때, 대부분의 부모들은 급히 그들에게 달려가 무슨 일인지 확인한다. 하지만 부모가 청각 장애가 있어서 들을 수 없다면 어떨까? 그들이 아기가 우는 것을 인지하지 못할 가능성이 있다. 그래서 그들은 아기에게 즉각적인 반응을 하지 못할 수 있다. 그때가 바로 신호견이 도움을 줄 수 있는 때이다. 아기에게 무슨 문제가 있다면, 개는 자신의 주인을 재빨리 깨운다. 주인이 깨어나면, 개는 아기에게 달려간다. 그러나 만약 주인이 따라오지 않는다면, 개는 주인이 아기에게 갈 때까지 이것을 반복한다.

**27** 아기에게 무슨 일이 생겼을 때 신호견이 청각 장애가 있는 부모들을 도울 수 있다는 내용이므로 빈칸에는 help(돕다)가 알맞다.

**28** (A) 〈가주어 – 진주어〉 문장에서 진주어절을 이끄는 접속사 that이 알맞다. (B) '주인이 깨어났을 때'를 의미해야 하므로 When이 알맞다. Unless는 '만약 …하지 않으면'의 뜻이다. (C) '주인이 아기에게 갈 때까지'를 의미해야 하므로 until이 알맞다. after는 '…한 후에'의 뜻이다.

**[29~30]**
> Daniel은 종종 잘 잊어버린다. 예를 들어, 그는 모자나 책과 같은 것을 자신이 갔던 곳에 자주 두고 와서 잃어버린다. 어느 날, 그는 모자를 쓰고 있었다. 버스에 타고 있는 동안 그는 잠이 들었다. 눈을 떴을 때, 그는 내려야 한다는 것을 깨달았다. 그는 일어나서 문으로 달려갔다. 버스에서 내린 후에, 그는 자신이 버스에 모자를 두고 내렸다고 생각했다. 그래서 그는 그것을 되찾기 위해 버스를 쫓아갔다. 그때 무언가가 그의 머리 위에서 떨어졌다. 그것은 그의 모자였다.

**29** ④ 버스에서 내린 후에, 버스에 모자를 두고 내렸다고 생각했다는 내용이 되어야 하므로, After가 알맞다.

**30** (C) 모자를 쓴 채 버스에서 잠이 들었는데, (A) 일어나자마자 서둘러 버스에서 내렸고, (B) 버스에 모자를 두고 내렸다고 생각해서 버스를 쫓아갔는데, (D) 모자가 머리 위에 있었음을 깨달았다는 순서가 되어야 한다.

─ Dictation Test ─

**01** weather report, pleasantly, temperature, continue
**02** used, made from, shoulder    **03** way, mistakes, angry at    **04** canceled, flu, art gallery    **05** first floor, go down, miss    **06** hurt, school nurse, serious, worse    **07** decided, lose, priority, interested **08** study, bigger, more hour, heavy    **09** stays, long, class, wait    **10** plant, spot, dig, dirt, follow    **11** regular exercise, cool-down, get ready, relax    **12** favor, due, unexpected, make sure    **13** invitations, gave, out, couples, alone    **14** bill, meal, mention, forgot **15** wrong, third, earlier than, wake, up    **16** car accident, saw, police, lucky    **17** order, across, open **18** hold, be held, adults, either    **19** special plans, pair, far    **20** stage, stomach, trust, fingers

## 01 ④

M Good morning, everyone. It's Friday, March 15th. This is the weather report. It's sunny and pleasantly warm now, but it will be cold and windy in the afternoon. The temperature will go down to zero tonight and it's going to start raining tomorrow morning. The rain will continue throughout the weekend.

남 안녕하세요, 여러분. 오늘은 3월 15일 금요일입니다. 오늘의 일기 예보입니다. 지금은 화창하고 기분 좋게 따뜻합니다만, 오후에는 춥고 바람이 불겠습니다. 오늘 밤에는 기온이 0도까지 내려가겠고 내일 아침에는 비가 내리기 시작하겠습니다. 비는 주말 내내 계속되겠습니다.

## 02 ④

W Wow, there are so many interesting things here.
M Yeah, everything here is made from used products.
W Is that so? I love that bag made from blue jeans.

M You mean the backpack over there?
W No, the shoulder bag right next to the clutch bag.
M Oh, I see it. The one with a big star on it.
W That's right. I'll buy it.

여 와, 이곳에는 재미있는 것들이 정말 많다.
남 응, 여기 있는 모든 것들은 중고 제품으로 만든 거야.
여 그러니? 나는 청바지로 만든 저 가방이 마음에 들어.
남 저기 있는 배낭을 말하는 거니?
여 아니, 클러치 백 바로 옆에 있는 숄더백 말이야.
남 아, 보인다. 큰 별무늬가 있는 거지.
여 맞아. 나는 그것을 살 거야.

## 03 ③

M Mom, I'm home.
W Tom, have a seat here. How did the final exam go today?
M The exam was way too easy.
W Did you do well on it, then?
M Not really, Mom. I made a lot of mistakes.
W Everyone makes mistakes. You will do better next time.
M But I'm so angry at myself.
W Just relax. You have another exam tomorrow. Prepare for it while I make you some hot chocolate.

남 엄마, 저 왔어요.
여 Tom, 여기 앉으렴. 오늘 기말 시험은 어땠니?
남 시험은 너무 쉬웠어요.
여 그러면, 시험을 잘 봤니?
남 그렇지 않아요, 엄마. 실수를 많이 했어요.
여 모두가 실수를 한단다. 다음에는 더 잘할 거야.
남 하지만 제 자신에게 너무 화가 나요.
여 편하게 생각하렴. 내일도 시험이 있잖니. 코코아를 만들어 줄테니, 시험 준비를 하렴.

## 04 ⑤

M Did you have a good time at Tina's concert yesterday? You said you were going there with your older sister.
W Yeah, that was my plan. But you know what? The concert was canceled at the last moment.
M What? How come?
W They said the singer got a flu and was hospitalized.
M Oh, I'm sorry to hear that. So, what did you do?

W I went to an art gallery with my sister instead. We saw fine artworks and had a lot of fun.

M I'm happy to hear that.

---

남 어제 Tina의 콘서트에서 좋은 시간을 보냈니? 언니와 함께 그곳에 간다고 했잖아.

여 응, 그게 내 계획이었지. 그런데 있잖아? 콘서트가 막판에 취소됐어.

남 뭐라고? 어째서?

여 가수가 독감에 걸려서 병원에 입원했다더라고.

남 아, 정말 안됐구나. 그래서 넌 무엇을 했니?

여 그 대신 언니와 함께 미술관에 갔어. 멋진 작품들을 보고 무척 재미있었어.

남 그랬다니 다행이구나.

## 05 ④

M Excuse me, where are the children's books?

W Oh, children's books are on the first floor.

M Which floor are we on?

W We are on the second floor. If you want to go down, use the escalator over there.

M One more question. Where is the check-out counter?

W It is between the best-seller section and children's book section. You can't miss it.

M Thank you so much.

---

남 실례합니다, 아동 도서는 어디에 있나요?

여 오, 아동 도서는 1층에 있어요.

남 저희가 지금 몇 층에 있죠?

여 저희는 2층에 있어요. 내려가시려면 저쪽에 있는 에스컬레이터를 이용하세요.

남 한 가지 더 여쭤볼게요. 계산대는 어디에 있나요?

여 베스트셀러 코너와 아동 도서 코너 사이에 있어요. 쉽게 찾으실 거예요.

남 정말 감사합니다.

## 06 ①

W What's wrong, Jiho? You look like you're hurt.

M I sprained my ankle playing basketball at lunchtime.

W Did you visit the school nurse?

M No, I didn't. I don't think it's serious.

W But you can't even walk straight.

M I guess it's getting worse.

W I think you should visit her.

---

여 무슨 일 있니, 지호야? 너 다친 것 같아 보인다.

남 점심시간에 농구를 하다가 발목을 삐었어.

여 보건실에 가 봤니?

남 아니, 안 갔어. 심각하지 않은 것 같아서.

여 하지만 너 똑바로 걷지도 못하잖아.

남 점점 악화되는 것 같아.

여 너 보건실에 가야 할 것 같아.

## 07 ④

W Jim, have you decided on a job you want to do?

M Well, I have a couple of things in mind, but I can't choose one.

W What do you think is important in choosing a job?

M Umm... I think stability is the most important. What if I lose my job in my middle age?

W That's right. That's why many teenagers want to work for the government.

M What about you? What's your priority?

W Stability is important. But I think that it's more important to do something I'm interested in. I want to enjoy what I do.

---

여 Jim, 너 하고 싶은 일을 정했니?

남 음, 마음속에 몇 가지가 있긴 한데, 하나를 정할 수가 없어.

여 너는 직업을 선택하는 데 있어서 뭐가 중요하다고 생각하니?

남 음… 나는 안정성이 가장 중요하다고 생각해. 내가 중년에 직업을 잃으면 어떡해?

여 맞아. 그래서 많은 10대들이 공무원이 되고 싶어 하지.

남 너는 어때? 네가 가장 중요하게 생각하는 것은 뭐야?

여 안정성이 중요하지. 하지만 나는 내가 흥미를 느끼는 일을 하는 것이 더 중요하다고 생각해. 나는 내가 하는 일을 즐기고 싶거든.

## 08 ③

M What happened to the table in my study?

W Oh, I moved it to my room. I needed something bigger than my desk for my art homework.

M Then, can you move it back after you finish it?

W Of course I can. But I need one more hour to finish it. Is it okay, Dad?

M It's okay. And if you need my help, just let me know. It's heavy.

W I will. Thanks, Dad.

M You're welcome. You can get back to work now.

---

남 내 서재에 있던 탁자가 어떻게 된 거지?

**여** 아, 제가 제 방으로 옮겼어요. 미술 숙제 때문에 제 책상보다 더 큰 것이 필요했거든요.

**남** 그러면, 숙제를 끝낸 후에 다시 옮겨 줄 수 있니?

**여** 물론이죠. 하지만 숙제를 끝내려면 한 시간이 더 필요해요. 괜찮으세요, 아빠?

**남** 괜찮다. 그리고 내 도움이 필요하면, 알려 주렴. 탁자가 무겁거든.

**여** 그럴게요. 고마워요, 아빠.

**남** 천만에. 이제 다시 숙제를 하렴.

## 09 ⑤

**M** Suji, have you heard about the new exchange student?

**W** Wait. What is an exchange student?

**M** A student from another country comes to our school and stays for a while to study with us.

**W** For how long?

**M** I don't know exactly. But I heard that student is a girl from Canada. She is 15 years old, and pretty!

**W** You must be thrilled. Oh, she's our age. Then she might be in our class.

**M** That's the point. She's going to be our classmate. Isn't it cool?

**W** Yes. I can't wait to meet her.

---

**남** 수지야, 너 새로운 교환 학생에 대해서 들었니?

**여** 잠깐만. 교환 학생이 뭐야?

**남** 다른 나라의 학생이 우리 학교에 와서 잠시 머물며 우리와 함께 공부하는 거야.

**여** 얼마 동안?

**남** 정확히 모르겠어. 하지만 그 학생이 캐나다 출신의 여학생이라고 들었어. 그녀는 열다섯 살이고, 예쁘대!

**여** 정말 신나겠구나. 오, 그녀는 우리랑 같은 나이네. 그러면 우리 반이 될 수 있겠는걸.

**남** 바로 그거야. 그녀는 우리 반 친구가 될 거야. 멋지지 않니?

**여** 그래. 빨리 그녀를 만나고 싶다.

## 10 ②

**W** Listen carefully, everyone. We are here to plant potatoes today. All of you should have pieces of potatoes, a shovel, and a watering pot. Move to your spot in the garden and dig a deep hole in the ground. Then, place a piece of potato and put dirt on it. Water it well, and follow the same steps over and over again.

---

**여** 잘 들으세요, 여러분. 우리는 오늘 감자를 심으러 이곳에 왔습니다. 여러분 모두는 감자 조각들, 삽, 그리고 물뿌리개를 가지고 있어야 합니다. 정원에서 정해진 장소로 이동해서 땅에 깊은 구멍을 파세요. 그리고 나서, 감자 조각 하나를 넣고 그 위에 흙을 덮으세요. 물을 잘 주고, 같은 단계를 반복해서 하시면 됩니다.

## 11 ③

**W** Do you exercise regularly? It's well-known that regular exercise is good for your body and mind. But did you know that warm-up and cool-down exercises are important as well? Warm-up exercises help your body get ready for the main exercise and reduce the risk of injuries. Cool-down exercises like stretching relax your body and mind. So, don't forget to warm up and cool down before and after exercising.

---

**여** 여러분은 규칙적으로 운동을 하나요? 규칙적인 운동이 몸과 마음에 좋다는 것은 잘 알려져 있습니다. 하지만 준비 운동과 정리 운동 역시 중요하다는 것을 알고 있었나요? 준비 운동은 몸을 본 운동을 하도록 준비시키고 부상의 위험을 줄여 줍니다. 스트레칭과 같은 정리 운동은 몸과 마음을 편안하게 해 줍니다. 그러므로, 운동하기 전과 후에 준비 운동과 정리 운동을 하는 것을 잊지 마세요.

## 12 ②

*[Telephone rings.]*

**W** Hello?

**M** Hello. Ms. White. This is David.

**W** Hi, David. What's up?

**M** I called you to ask for a favor. Is it okay if I hand in the report the day after tomorrow?

**W** But the report is due tomorrow.

**M** Yes, I know. But something unexpected happened. My dog gave birth to puppies. So, I have to take care of them.

**W** Oh, congratulations. Okay. I'll give you one more day. But make sure you hand it in first thing in the morning the day after tomorrow.

**M** Of course I will. Thank you so much.

---

*[전화 벨소리가 울린다.]*

**여** 여보세요?

**남** 여보세요. White 선생님. 저는 David입니다.

**여** 안녕, David. 무슨 일이니?

**남** 부탁을 하나 드리려고 전화드렸어요. 제가 리포트를 모레 제출해도 될까요?

**여** 하지만 리포트는 내일까지잖니.

**남** 네, 알아요. 하지만 예상치 못한 일이 생겼어요. 제 애완견이 새끼들을 낳았어요. 그래서 강아지들을 돌봐 줘야 해요.

**여** 오, 축하한다. 좋아. 하루를 더 줄게. 하지만 모레 아침 일찍 리포트를 제출해야 한다.

**남** 물론 그렇게 할게요. 정말 감사합니다.

---

## 13 ②

**W** Did you send the invitations to our housewarming party?

**M** Yes. I gave them out at work today.

**W** How many people are coming over?

**M** Three people said they were coming. How about your friends?

**W** Two couples are coming.

**M** Then seven people are coming, right?

**W** Oh, wait. Susan's husband is on a business trip, so she will come alone.

**M** Okay.

- - - - - - - - - - - - - - - - - - - - - - - -

**여** 우리 집들이 초대장을 보냈어요?

**남** 네. 오늘 직장에서 나눠줬어요.

**여** 몇 명이 오나요?

**남** 세 명이 올 거라고 말했어요. 당신 친구들은요?

**여** 두 부부가 올 거예요.

**남** 그러면 7명이 오는 군요, 그렇죠?

**여** 오, 잠깐만요. Susan의 남편이 출장 중이라, 그녀는 혼자 올 거예요.

**남** 알겠어요.

---

## 14 ④

**W** May I have the bill, please?

**M** Okay. I will bring it to you right now. *[Pause]* Here it is. Did you enjoy the meal?

**W** Yes, everything was so delicious. But I want to mention just one thing.

**M** What is it? Were there any problems?

**W** I asked for extra bread before, but I didn't get it.

**M** Oh, I'm so sorry about that. I totally forgot about it.

**W** That's all right.

- - - - - - - - - - - - - - - - - - - - - - - -

**여** 계산서를 주시겠어요?

**남** 네. 금방 가지고 오겠습니다. *[잠시 후]* 여기 있습니다. 식사는 맛있으셨는지요?

**여** 네, 모든 게 너무 맛있었습니다. 하지만 딱 한 가지를 말씀드리고 싶네요.

**남** 뭔가요? 무슨 문제라도 있었나요?

**여** 아까 추가 빵을 요구했는데, 받지를 못했어요.

**남** 오, 정말 죄송합니다. 완전히 잊어 버렸네요.

**여** 괜찮습니다.

---

## 15 ④

*[Telephone rings.]*

**M** Hello, Ms. Wright. This is John Clark.

**W** Hello. Mr. Clark. Is there something wrong with Chris?

**M** He was late for school again. This is the third time this week.

**W** Oh, I'm so sorry. I didn't know that. You know, I leave home earlier than him every morning.

**M** Could you wake him up before you leave home, Ms. Wright? He says he can't hear the alarm clock ringing.

**W** Okay. I'll make sure he is wide awake before I leave home. I'm sorry again.

- - - - - - - - - - - - - - - - - - - - - - - -

*[전화 벨소리가 울린다.]*

**남** 안녕하세요, Wright 부인. 저는 John Clark입니다.

**여** 안녕하세요. Clark 선생님. Chris에게 무슨 일이 있어요?

**남** Chris가 학교에 또 지각을 했습니다. 이번 주에 세 번째입니다.

**여** 오, 정말 죄송해요. 몰랐어요. 아시다시피, 매일 아침 제가 그 아이보다 먼저 집을 나서거든요.

**남** 집을 나서기 전에 Chris를 깨워 줄 수 있으실까요? Chris가 자명종이 울리는 것을 듣지 못한다고 하네요.

**여** 네. 제가 집을 나오기 전에 그 아이가 완전히 깨어 있는 것을 꼭 확인하겠습니다. 다시 한 번 죄송합니다.

---

## 16 ⑤

**M** Hey, Yuna. Where were you yesterday? We were supposed to have the club meeting at the school library.

**W** Yeah, I know. But there was a car accident on my way to school.

**M** What? Were you hurt?

**W** No, I wasn't. I wasn't in the accident. I just saw it.

**M** That's a relief. Then why didn't you come?

**W** I was the only one who saw the accident. So I had to tell the police about it. It took a longer time than I expected.

M  Oh, I see. Anyway, you were lucky.

남  얘, 유나야. 너 어제 어디에 있었니? 우리는 학교 도서관에서 동아리 모임을 갖기로 되어 있었잖아.

여  응, 알아. 그런데 학교에 가는 길에 자동차 사고가 있었어.

남  뭐라고? 다쳤니?

여  아니, 안 다쳤어. 나는 사고를 당한 게 아니었어. 단지 그 사고를 목격했어.

남  다행이다. 그러면 왜 오지 않은 거야?

여  내가 사고를 목격한 유일한 사람이었거든. 그래서 경찰에게 그것에 대해 말해야 했어. 그게 예상보다 시간이 오래 걸렸어.

남  오, 알겠어. 어쨌든, 너 운이 좋았네.

## 17 ②

① W  Are you ready to order?
　 M  Yes, I'd like a cup of coffee.
② W  Does this bus go to City Hall?
　 M  No, the bus to City Hall runs across the street.
③ W  How much is it?
　 M  It is 2,000 won.
④ W  May I open the window?
　 M  Sure. Go ahead.
⑤ W  Please show me your driver's license.
　 M  Here it is.

- - - - - - - - - - - - - - - - - - - - - - - - - - - -

① 여  주문하시겠습니까?
　 남  네, 커피 한 잔 주세요.
② 여  이 버스가 시청에 가나요?
　 남  아니요, 시청에 가는 버스는 길 건너편에 있습니다.
③ 여  이것은 얼마죠?
　 남  2,000원입니다.
④ 여  창문을 열어도 될까요?
　 남  물론입니다. 그렇게 하세요.
⑤ 여  운전면허증 좀 보여 주세요.
　 남  여기 있습니다.

## 18 ②

M  Hello, everyone. I'm Peter Park, manager at MJ Record Company. We will hold a concert called the Fantasy Music Festival. Famous pop singers and musicians will sing at the concert. It will start at 6 p.m. next Saturday. It will be held at the Olympic Stadium Concert Hall. Tickets are 40 dollars for adults. Those who are under 19 can get 50 percent discount. You can buy tickets either at the box office or online.

- - - - - - - - - - - - - - - - - - - - - - - - - - - -

남  안녕하세요, 여러분. 저는 MJ 음반 회사의 매니저인 Peter Park입니다. 저희는 판타지 음악 축제라는 콘서트를 개최할 것입니다. 유명한 팝 가수와 음악가들이 콘서트에서 노래를 부를 것입니다. 콘서트는 다음 주 토요일 오후 6시에 시작됩니다. 올림픽 경기장 콘서트홀에서 개최될 것입니다. 입장권은 성인은 40달러입니다. 19세 미만인 분들에게는 50퍼센트 할인을 해 드립니다. 입장권은 매표소나 인터넷에서 구입하실 수 있습니다.

## 19 ⑤

W  Do you have any special plans for the weekend?
M  I'm thinking of reading some books at home. What about you?
W  I'm going to the new shopping center with my parents.
M  Oh, I've heard about it. What are you going to buy there?
W  I need a pair of boots, and my parents want a new dinner table.
M  Is it far from here? How long does it take to get there?

- - - - - - - - - - - - - - - - - - - - - - - - - - - -

여  주말에 특별한 계획이 있니?
남  집에서 책을 좀 읽으려고 생각 중이야. 너는 어때?
여  나는 부모님과 함께 새로운 쇼핑센터에 갈 거야.
남  아, 그곳에 대해 들어 봤어. 거기서 무엇을 살 거니?
여  나는 부츠 한 켤레가 필요하고, 부모님께서는 새로운 식탁을 원하셔.
남  여기에서 머니? 그곳에 가는 데 얼마나 걸려?

## 20 ②

M  Yuri, are you ready to get on the stage?
W  Almost. I have butterflies in my stomach. What if I forget the lyrics?
M  Don't worry. You practiced a lot. Just trust yourself.
W  Okay. Can I have some water?
M  Sure, here it is. Look at me. You will do great. I'll keep my fingers crossed for you.

- - - - - - - - - - - - - - - - - - - - - - - - - - - -

남  유리야, 무대에 설 준비가 됐니?
여  거의. 나 마음이 조마조마해. 가사를 잊어버리면 어쩌지?
남  걱정 마. 너는 연습을 많이 했잖아. 그냥 너 자신을 믿어.
여  그래. 물 좀 마실 수 있을까?
남  물론이지, 여기 있어. 나를 봐. 너는 잘할 거야. 행운을 빌게.

## >> 02회 듣기 실전 모의고사　　　　pp. 120~127

| | | | | | | | |
|---|---|---|---|---|---|---|---|
| 01 ⑤ | 02 ④ | 03 ③ | 04 ④ | 05 ⑤ | 06 ③ | 07 ⑤ | 08 ① |
| 09 ③ | 10 ④ | 11 ③ | 12 ④ | 13 ① | 14 ② | 15 ③ | 16 ⑤ |
| 17 ① | 18 ④ | 19 ② | 20 ⑤ | | | | |

─ Dictation Test ─

**01** shining, warm, cloudy, chance　**02** looking for, popular among, keep　**03** lost, don't need, download, relieved　**04** volunteer work, take care, cleaned　**05** huge, decide what, less than　**06** running, rival, great, support　**07** finishes, twelve, except for, favorite subject　**08** at work, fever, sick, Wait　**09** trip, local market, seafood, looking forward　**10** trouble, tips, ready, stretching, fall asleep　**11** fire drill, earlier, ends, seats, announcement　**12** return, happy, store, request　**13** satisfied, party, bill, discount　**14** open, checking, savings, fill out　**15** coming back, drop by, anything　**16** awake, because, stressed, pressure　**17** dropped, lend, in mind, the time　**18** expecting, ahead, reach　**19** looking for, striped, try, on　**20** surprise, been, leaving, job

---

### 01　⑤

W　Hello, everyone. Welcome to the weather channel. Here is today's weather for South Korea. The sun is shining in Seoul and the temperature is around 19 degrees Celsius. It is sunny and warm also in Daejeon. In Busan, it's cloudy now, and there is a chance of rain in the late afternoon.

여　여러분, 안녕하세요. 날씨 채널에 오신 것을 환영합니다. 오늘 한국의 날씨입니다. 서울에는 햇살이 비치고 있고 기온은 약 섭씨 19도입니다. 대전 역시 화창하고 따뜻합니다. 부산은 현재 흐리고 늦은 오후에는 비가 올 가능성이 있습니다.

---

### 02　④

W　Minho, what are you doing here?

M　Hi, Jiyeon. I'm looking for a gift for my little brother. His birthday is next week.

W　What about this top? You know, spinning tops are popular among young boys these days.

M　He does like tops but I want to give him something to use at school.

W　I see. Then, how about this pencil case? He can keep pens and pencils in it.

M　That's a great idea. Thanks a lot.

여　민호야, 여기서 뭐 하고 있니?

남　안녕, 지연아. 내 남동생을 위한 선물을 찾고 있어. 그 아이의 생일이 다음 주거든.

여　이 팽이는 어때? 너도 알다시피, 요즘 팽이가 어린 남자아이들 사이에서 인기잖아.

남　동생이 정말로 팽이를 좋아하지만 나는 그 아이에게 학교에서 쓸 뭔가를 주고 싶어.

여　그렇구나. 그러면 이 필통은 어때? 그 안에 펜과 연필을 넣을 수 있어.

남　그거 좋은 생각이다. 정말 고마워.

---

### 03　③

W　Oh, no!

M　What's wrong?

W　I think I lost the tickets for the movie. It starts in five minutes. What should I do?

M　Don't worry. You don't need tickets.

W　How come?

M　Just download the cinema app on your cell phone. Then you can see the tickets on the app.

W　Wow, is it that simple? I'm relieved now.

여　오, 이런!

남　무슨 일이야?

여　영화표를 잃어버린 것 같아. 5분 뒤에 영화가 시작하는데. 어떡하지?

남　걱정 마. 표는 필요 없어.

여　어째서?

남　네 휴대전화에 극장 앱을 내려받기만 해. 그러면 그 앱에서 표를 볼 수 있어.

여　와, 그렇게 간단해? 이제 안심이 된다.

---

### 04　④

M　Jina, what did you do last weekend?

W　I did some volunteer work.

M　Where did you volunteer?

W　I visited a day-care center for children.

M　Did you take care of the children there?

W　Not really. It was my first time doing volunteer work there, so I just cleaned the rooms and toys.

M　I see.

남　지나야, 지난 주말에 뭐 했어?

여　봉사활동을 했어.

남　어디에서 봉사활동을 했니?

여    탁아소를 방문했어.

남    그곳에서 아이들을 돌봐 주었니?

여    아니. 그곳에서 봉사활동을 하는 게 처음이라 그냥 방과 장난 감을 청소했어.

남    그렇구나.


## 05 ⑤

M    Wow, this place is really huge.

W    Yeah, it will take a day to go on every ride.

M    Let's decide what to ride first.

W    We should ride on the roller coaster first. Look! It looks exciting!

M    But look at that line. It's too long.

W    We can wait. It will take less than an hour to get on the roller coaster.

M    Okay. Let's wait in line, then.

---

남    와, 이곳은 정말 크다.

여    응, 놀이 기구를 다 타려면 하루가 걸릴 거야.

남    먼저 무엇을 탈지 결정하자.

여    우선 롤러코스터를 타야 해. 봐! 신나 보이잖아!

남    하지만 저 줄을 봐. 너무 길어.

여    기다리면 되지. 롤러코스터를 타는 데 한 시간은 안 걸릴 거야.

남    그래. 그러면 줄을 서자.


## 06 ③

M    Sora, I'm thinking of running for student president.

W    Oh, really? Good for you. I'm sure you will do a good job.

M    But my rival will be hard to beat. She's smart, pretty, and very popular among students.

W    You are as great as her. And even if you lose, you will learn a lot from this.

M    I agree on that.

W    Cheer up! You have my full support.

---

남    소라야, 나 학생회장에 출마할까 생각 중이야.

여    오, 정말? 잘됐다. 나는 네가 잘할 거라고 확신해.

남    하지만 내 경쟁자를 이기기 어려울 거야. 그녀는 똑똑하고, 예쁘고, 학생들 사이에서 인기가 많아.

여    너도 그녀만큼 훌륭해. 그리고 네가 지더라도, 너는 이번 일을 통해 많이 배울 거야.

남    나도 동의해.

여    힘내! 나는 너를 전폭적으로 지지해.


## 07 ⑤

M    Will you tell me about your school?

W    Okay, Dad. I have six classes a day, and the last class finishes at 3 o'clock.

M    Tell me more about your classes.

W    I learn twelve subjects a week, and I like most of them. Oh, except for one. I hate math.

M    Why is that?

W    It's too difficult for me. But I really like language classes like Korean, English, and Chinese. English is my favorite subject.

M    I'm glad to hear that.

---

남    학교생활에 대해서 말해 줄래?

여    네, 아빠. 저는 하루에 6개의 수업을 듣고, 마지막 수업은 3시에 끝나요.

남    수업에 대해 더 말해 주렴.

여    일주일에 12개의 과목을 배우고, 대부분의 과목을 좋아해요. 아, 하나만 제외하고요. 저는 수학이 싫어요.

남    왜지?

여    저에게 너무 어려워요. 하지만 저는 국어, 영어, 중국어와 같은 언어 과목을 정말 좋아해요. 영어는 제가 가장 좋아하는 과목 이에요.

남    그 말을 들으니 기쁘구나.


## 08 ①

[Telephone rings.]

W    Hi, Tony. What's up?

M    Mom. Are you busy at work right now?

W    No, I'm not that busy right now. Is there any problem?

M    I'm sick. I have a fever and I can't move at all.

W    Since when have you been sick?

M    I was cold and dizzy at school, but it's getting worse.

W    Okay. I'll be right there. It will take 20 minutes by taxi. Wait for me.

---

[전화 벨소리가 울린다.]

여    여보세요, Tony. 무슨 일이니?

남    엄마. 지금 직장에서 바쁘세요?

여    아니, 지금은 그렇게 바쁘지 않단다. 무슨 문제라도 있니?

남    저 아파요. 열이 나고 전혀 움직일 수가 없어요.

여    언제부터 아팠니?

남    학교에서 춥고 어지러웠는데, 점점 심해지고 있어요.

여    알겠다. 금방 갈게. 택시로 20분 정도 걸릴 거야. 기다리렴.

## 09 ③

M  Hajin, what are you going to do this summer vacation?

W  I'm going on a trip to Thailand with my family.

M  What are you going to do there?

W  Well, we will take a tour of the city and go to the local market.

M  I heard Thailand is famous for its massage services.

W  My parents want to get massages, but I don't.

M  I see. Oh, don't forget to go to the beach and enjoy the seafood.

W  I won't. I'm really looking forward to the trip.

- - - - - - - - - - - - - - - - - - - - - - - - - - - - -

남  하진아, 이번 여름 방학 때 무엇을 할 거니?

여  가족들과 태국에 여행을 갈 거야.

남  그곳에서 뭐 할 계획이니?

여  음, 도시 구경을 하고 현지 시장에 갈 거야.

남  내가 듣기로 태국은 마사지 서비스가 유명하다던데.

여  부모님께서는 마사지를 받고 싶어 하시는데, 나는 그렇지 않아.

남  그렇구나. 아, 해변에 가서 해산물 먹는 것을 잊지 마.

여  잊지 않을게. 여행이 너무 기대가 돼.

## 10 ④

M  Do you have trouble going to sleep at night? Here are some tips for you. First, try to go to sleep at the same time every day. Then your body will be ready to sleep at that time. Second, take a warm bath before you go to bed. It will help your body and mind relaxed. Another good way is doing some simple stretching. Then you will fall asleep more easily.

- - - - - - - - - - - - - - - - - - - - - - - - - - - - -

남  여러분은 밤에 잠이 드는 데 어려움을 겪고 있나요? 여러분을 위한 몇 가지 조언을 해드리겠습니다. 첫째, 매일 같은 시간에 잠자리에 들도록 노력하세요. 그러면 여러분의 몸은 그 시간에 잘 준비를 할 것입니다. 둘째, 잠자리에 들기 전에 온욕을 하세요. 그것은 여러분의 몸과 마음을 편안하게 하는 데 도움을 줄 것입니다. 또 다른 좋은 방법은 간단한 스트레칭을 하는 것입니다. 그러면 더 쉽게 잠들 수 있을 것입니다.

## 11 ③

W  Hello, students. This is your principal. Tomorrow, we are going to have a fire drill. Morning classes will end ten minutes earlier each. We will have the drill before lunchtime, and it will take about 40 minutes. After the fourth period ends, everyone should stay at their seats and listen carefully to the announcement.

- - - - - - - - - - - - - - - - - - - - - - - - - - - - -

여  안녕하세요, 학생 여러분. 교장입니다. 내일, 우리는 소방 훈련을 할 예정입니다. 오전 수업은 10분씩 일찍 끝날 것입니다. 점심시간 전에 훈련을 할 것이고, 훈련은 약 40분 정도 걸릴 것입니다. 4교시가 끝나면, 모든 학생은 자리에 그대로 계시고 방송에 귀를 기울이셔야 합니다.

## 12 ④

[Telephone rings.]

W  Hello, Ace Mall customer service.

M  I'd like to return a jacket.

W  I'm sorry you were not happy with our item. When did you buy it?

M  I bought it last Wednesday.

W  Did you buy it online or at the store?

M  Online.

W  Then you'll have to make a request for the return online. I'll tell you how to do it.

- - - - - - - - - - - - - - - - - - - - - - - - - - - - -

[전화 벨소리가 울린다.]

여  안녕하세요, Ace Mall 고객 센터입니다.

남  재킷을 반품하고 싶습니다.

여  저희 상품이 마음에 들지 않으셨다니 죄송합니다. 언제 구매하셨나요?

남  지난주 수요일에 샀습니다.

여  인터넷에서 사셨나요, 아니면 매장에서 사셨나요?

남  인터넷이요.

여  그러면 인터넷으로 반품을 요청하셔야 할 것 같습니다. 어떻게 하는지 알려 드릴게요.

## 13 ①

W  Did you enjoy our food, sir?

M  Yes, we are all satisfied with the food and service.

W  I'm happy to hear that. So, there were four adults in your party, right?

M  No, there were only three.

W  Oh, sorry. There's a mistake in the bill. Let me check. [Pause] You're right. Three adults.

M  So is the bill 60 dollars?

W  No, it isn't. We are currently offering ten percent discount for parties of three or more.

M  Really? That's good. Here's my credit card.

| 여 | 식사 맛있게 하셨습니까, 선생님? |
|---|---|
| 남 | 네, 저희 모두 음식과 서비스에 만족합니다. |
| 여 | 그 말씀을 들으니 기쁩니다. 그럼, 일행이 성인 네 분 맞으시죠? |
| 남 | 아니요, 세 명뿐입니다. |
| 여 | 오, 죄송합니다. 계산서가 잘못되었군요. 확인해 보겠습니다. *[잠시 후]* 선생님 말씀이 맞습니다. 성인 세 분입니다. |
| 남 | 그럼 60달러를 내면 되나요? |
| 여 | 아뇨, 아닙니다. 저희는 지금 세 명 이상의 일행에게는 10퍼센트 할인을 해드리고 있습니다. |
| 남 | 정말요? 좋네요. 여기 제 신용카드입니다. |

## 14 ②

| M | How can I help you, ma'am? |
|---|---|
| W | I'd like to open a bank account. |
| M | What kind of account would you like to open? |
| W | I need a checking account. |
| M | Would you also like to open a savings account? |
| W | No, that's fine. |
| M | Please fill out this form and show me your identification card. |

| 남 | 무엇을 도와드릴까요, 부인? |
|---|---|
| 여 | 은행 계좌를 개설하고 싶습니다. |
| 남 | 어떤 종류의 계좌를 개설하고 싶으신가요? |
| 여 | 당좌 예금 계좌가 필요합니다. |
| 남 | 저축 예금 계좌도 개설하시겠어요? |
| 여 | 아니요, 괜찮습니다. |
| 남 | 이 양식을 작성하시고 신분증을 보여 주세요. |

## 15 ③

*[Telephone rings.]*

| M | Hi, Jenny. What's up? |
|---|---|
| W | Dad, when are you coming back? |
| M | I'm driving home now. I'll be back in 20 minutes. |
| W | Can I ask you something? |
| M | Of course, sweety. Just tell me. |
| W | Can you drop by the grocery store and get me some cookies and milk? |
| M | Of course I can. Is there anything else you need? |
| W | That's all. Thanks. |

*[전화 벨소리가 울린다.]*

| 남 | 여보세요, Jenny. 무슨 일이니? |
|---|---|
| 여 | 아빠, 언제 돌아오세요? |
| 남 | 지금 운전해서 집에 가는 길이란다. 20분 안에 도착해. |
| 여 | 부탁 좀 해도 될까요? |

| 남 | 물론이지, 애야. 말해 보렴. |
|---|---|
| 여 | 식료품점에 들러서 저에게 쿠키와 우유를 사다 주실 수 있으세요? |
| 남 | 물론이지. 더 필요한 건 없니? |
| 여 | 그게 다예요. 감사해요. |

## 16 ⑤

| W | Why are you still awake, Mike? It's almost 2 a.m. |
|---|---|
| M | I can't sleep because of the test. |
| W | But the test is next week. |
| M | I'm stressed out because of it. I really want to do well this time. |
| W | Mike. Just relax. If you have too much pressure on the test, you won't get a good score. |
| M | Is it true, Mom? |
| W | Of course it is. So relax, and get some sleep. |

| 여 | 왜 아직도 깨어 있니, Mike? 거의 새벽 두 시야. |
|---|---|
| 남 | 시험 때문에 잠을 못 자겠어요. |
| 여 | 하지만 시험은 다음 주잖아. |
| 남 | 시험 때문에 스트레스를 받아요. 이번엔 정말 잘하고 싶어요. |
| 여 | Mike. 마음을 편히 가지렴. 시험에 너무 큰 부담감을 느끼면, 좋은 성적을 받을 수 없어. |
| 남 | 그게 정말이에요, 엄마? |
| 여 | 물론이지. 그러니 긴장 풀고, 잠을 좀 자렴. |

## 17 ①

| ① W | Excuse me, sir. You dropped your wallet. |
|---|---|
| M | Oh, I didn't know that. Thank you so much. |
| ② W | Could you lend me some money? |
| M | How much do you need? |
| ③ W | What present do you have in mind? |
| M | What about a wallet? |
| ④ W | Can you show me the way to the subway station? |
| M | Sure. Go down two blocks. |
| ⑤ W | Do you have the time? |
| M | It's three thirty right now. |

| ① 여 | 실례합니다, 선생님. 지갑을 떨어뜨리셨어요. |
|---|---|
| 남 | 오, 몰랐어요. 정말 감사합니다. |
| ② 여 | 돈 좀 빌려줄 수 있나요? |
| 남 | 얼마가 필요한데요? |
| ③ 여 | 어떤 선물을 생각하고 있나요? |
| 남 | 지갑 어때요? |
| ④ 여 | 지하철역 가는 길 좀 알려 주시겠어요? |
| 남 | 물론이죠. 두 블록 걸어 내려가세요. |

⑤ 여  지금 몇 시인지 아세요?
   남  지금은 3시 30분입니다.

## 18 ④

M  Good afternoon, passengers. This is your captain speaking. First I'd like to welcome everyone on ABC Flight 75A. It is 1:25 p.m. now, and the weather looks good. We are expecting to land in London approximately fifteen minutes ahead of schedule. The weather in London is clear and sunny. I'll talk to you again before we reach our destination. Enjoy your flight. Thank you.

남  안녕하세요, 승객 여러분. 기장입니다. 우선 ABC 항공사의 75A 여객기에 탑승하신 것을 환영합니다. 현재 시각은 오후 1시 25분이고, 날씨는 좋아 보입니다. 저희는 일정보다 약 15분 일찍 런던에 도착할 것으로 예상됩니다. 런던의 날씨는 맑고 화창합니다. 목적지에 도착하기 전에 다시 말씀드리겠습니다. 즐거운 비행 되십시오. 감사합니다.

## 19 ②

M  Excuse me. Could you help me?
W  Certainly. What can I do for you?
M  I'm looking for a T-shirt.
W  What about this one over here? It sells very well.
M  Well. Actually, I want a striped T-shirt.
W  Then, how about this one?
M  I really like it. It's so nice.
W  Would you like to try it on?
M  I'd love to, but it looks a little small for me.

남  실례합니다. 도와주시겠어요?
여  네. 무엇을 도와드릴까요?
남  저는 티셔츠를 찾고 있어요.
여  이쪽에 있는 이것은 어떠세요? 매우 잘 나갑니다.
남  음. 사실, 저는 줄무늬 티셔츠를 원해요.
여  그러면, 이건 어떠세요?
남  정말 마음에 들어요. 아주 멋지네요.
여  입어 보시겠어요?
남  그러고 싶은데, 저에게는 조금 작아 보이네요.

## 20 ⑤

W  Hi, Paul. It's a surprise to see you here.

M  Hi, Mina. It's been a long time. How have you been?
W  Pretty good. Thanks. How about you?
M  I've been great, too. Oh, I'm leaving for China next month.
W  Why? To study?
M  No. I got a job there.

여  안녕, Paul. 여기서 너를 보다니 놀랍다.
남  안녕, 미나야. 오랜만이다. 어떻게 지냈니?
여  잘 지냈어. 고마워. 너는 어때?
남  나도 잘 지냈어. 오, 나 다음 달에 중국으로 떠나.
여  왜? 공부하러 가니?
남  아니. 그곳에서 직장을 얻었어.

>> 03회 듣기 실전 모의고사          pp. 128~135

| 01 ① | 02 ⑤ | 03 ② | 04 ④ | 05 ⑤ | 06 ⑤ | 07 ② | 08 ⑤ |
| 09 ③ | 10 ③ | 11 ③ | 12 ⑤ | 13 ② | 14 ④ | 15 ② | 16 ④ |
| 17 ④ | 18 ④ | 19 ③ | 20 ④ | | | | |

### Dictation Test

**01** areas, stop, sunny, high  **02** go abroad, shelf, mermaid  **03** finish, playing, ends, put off  **04** stayed home, cultivate, fed, picked  **05** noise, close look, at least  **06** awful, by accident, break, guilty, depressed  **07** wild plants, named, small  **08** starving, make, freezer, nearby  **09** saving energy, ways, examples, in use, unplug  **10** attention, author, sign copies, invite  **11** contains, changing, health, fresh, choose  **12** left, turned in, leather, anytime  **13** studying together, hour earlier, make it  **14** ready, scene, best, lines  **15** packing, drive, broke down, wake, up  **16** tennis, another, started  **17** going fishing, dangerous, Hold, leaves  **18** due to, held, same, refund  **19** eat out, again, reasonable  **20** opened, cool, facilities, go there

## 01 ①

**M** Good morning. I'm Jim Clark from the weather center. Today, it's going to be cloudy and rainy in some areas. The rain will stop by tonight. Tomorrow it will be sunny all around the country with a high of 30 degrees Celsius in the afternoon. Don't forget to wear a hat when you go out.

---

**남** 안녕하세요. 날씨 센터의 Jim Clark입니다. 오늘 몇몇 지역은 흐리고 비가 내리겠습니다. 비는 오늘밤에 그치겠습니다. 내일은 전국적으로 화창하고 오후에는 최고 기온이 30도가 되겠습니다. 밖에 나가신다면 모자를 쓰는 것을 잊지 마세요.

## 02 ⑤

**M** Wow, look at these mugs. Are they all yours?

**W** No, they're my parents'. They buy mugs every time they go abroad.

**M** So they're all from different countries. Fantastic! I really like the one on the top of the shelf.

**W** You mean with stars and the moon on it?

**M** No, the one right next to it.

**W** Ah, the one with a mermaid on it, right?

**M** That's it. It's so pretty.

---

**남** 와, 이 머그컵들 좀 봐. 이것들은 다 네 거니?

**여** 아니, 우리 부모님 거야. 부모님은 해외에 가실 때마다 머그컵을 사시거든.

**남** 그러면 다 다른 나라에서 온 거네. 멋지다! 나는 선반 제일 위에 있는 저 머그컵이 진짜 마음에 들어.

**여** 별들과 달이 있는 거 말이야?

**남** 아니, 그 바로 옆에 있는 거야.

**여** 아, 인어가 있는 거, 맞지?

**남** 바로 그거야. 정말 예쁘다.

## 03 ②

**W** Did you finish your homework, Andy?

**M** Not yet. I'll do it after watching this program.

**W** But you said you would do it after playing games in the morning.

**M** This program ends only in 20 minutes, Mom.

**W** Don't put off your work. How many times do I have to tell you?

**M** Okay, Mom. I got it.

**W** I'm warning you. Turn off the TV and go to your room now.

---

**여** 숙제 다 했니, Andy?

**남** 아직요. 이 프로그램을 보고 나서 할게요.

**여** 하지만 아침에는 게임을 한 후에 숙제를 하겠다고 말했잖아.

**남** 이 프로그램은 겨우 20분 뒤면 끝나요, 엄마.

**여** 할 일을 미루지 마라. 몇 번을 말해야 하니?

**남** 알겠어요, 엄마. 알아들었어요.

**여** 경고하는 거야. 텔레비전을 끄고 당장 방으로 가거라.

## 04 ④

**M** What did you do last weekend?

**W** I stayed home watching movies and reading books. What about you?

**M** I went to my grandmother's to help her with the farm work.

**W** Farm work? Sounds tough. Did you cultivate a field?

**M** No, nothing like that. I just fed the farm animals and picked some fruits.

**W** That must be exciting.

---

**남** 지난 주말에 뭐 했니?

**여** 집에 있으면서 영화도 보고 책도 읽었어. 너는?

**남** 나는 할머니 댁에 가서 농장 일을 도와드렸어.

**여** 농장 일? 힘들겠다. 밭을 간 거니?

**남** 아니, 그런 건 아니야. 그냥 농장 동물들에게 먹이를 주고 열매를 땄어.

**여** 그건 재미있겠다.

## 05 ⑤

**M** What can I do for you?

**W** I think there's a problem with my car. Sometimes it makes a lot of noise when I start the engine.

**M** Umm... there must be something wrong. Let me take a close look.

**W** How long will it take?

**M** It will take at least half an hour.

**W** Then I will be back in 30 minutes.

**M** Okay.

---

**남** 무엇을 도와드릴까요?

**여** 제 자동차에 문제가 있는 것 같아요. 가끔 제가 시동을 걸 때 소음이 많이 나요.

**남** 음… 분명 뭔가가 잘못되었네요. 자세히 볼게요.

**여** 얼마나 걸릴까요?

**남** 적어도 30분은 걸릴 거예요.

**여** 그러면 30분 뒤에 올게요.

**남** 그러세요.

## 06 ⑤

**W**  You look gloomy. What's wrong?

**M**  Oh, I feel awful.

**W**  What happened? Tell me about it.

**M**  I was cleaning my teacher's desk, and I dropped her cell phone by accident.

**W**  Oh, that's too bad. Did the cell phone break?

**M**  The cell phone works but the screen is cracked. She says it's okay, but I feel guilty about it.

**W**  Don't be so depressed. It was an accident.

---

**여**  너 우울해 보인다. 무슨 일 있어?

**남**  아, 나 기분이 최악이야.

**여**  무슨 일 있었어? 나에게 말해 봐.

**남**  선생님의 책상을 청소하고 있었는데, 실수로 선생님의 휴대전화를 떨어뜨렸어.

**여**  오, 그거 안됐다. 휴대전화가 부서졌니?

**남**  휴대전화는 작동되지만 액정에 금이 갔어. 선생님께서는 괜찮다고 하시는데, 나는 그것에 대해 죄책감을 느껴.

**여**  너무 우울해하지 마. 그건 사고였잖아.

## 07 ②

**M**  Did you hear that the Butterfly Garden opened last week?

**W**  Yeah. Actually, I went there with my family last weekend.

**M**  Really? How was it? They say they have a lot of wild plants there.

**W**  That's right. There were many I had never seen before. And there were lots of butterflies, too.

**M**  That's why they named it the Butterfly Garden. So, was everything great?

**W**  Yes, except for one thing. The parking lot was too small. We had to wait for an hour to park the car.

**M**  Um. That's a problem.

---

**남**  나비정원이 지난주에 개장했다는 얘기 들었어?

**여**  응. 사실, 나는 지난 주말에 가족과 함께 그곳에 갔어.

**남**  정말? 어땠어? 그곳에 야생 식물들이 많다고 하던데.

**여**  맞아. 내가 전에 보지 못한 식물들이 많았어. 그리고 나비도 많았고.

**남**  그래서 나비정원이라고 이름 붙인 거네. 그럼, 모든 것이 좋았어?

**여**  응, 한 가지만 빼고. 주차장이 너무 작았어. 차를 주차하려고 한 시간 동안 기다려야 했어.

**남**  음. 그거 문제구나.

## 08 ⑤

**M**  Mom. I'm starving.

**W**  Do you want me to make you some sandwiches?

**M**  That would be nice.

**W**  Oh, there's no butter in the freezer.

**M**  I'll go get some butter at the nearby supermarket.

**W**  Will you? Take the money on the table.

**M**  Okay, Mom.

---

**남**  엄마, 저 너무 배고파요.

**여**  내가 샌드위치를 좀 만들어 줄까?

**남**  그게 좋겠어요.

**여**  오, 냉장고에 버터가 없구나.

**남**  제가 근처 슈퍼마켓에 가서 버터를 좀 사 올게요.

**여**  그럴래? 탁자 위의 돈을 가져가렴.

**남**  네, 엄마.

## 09 ③

**M**  I have to write a report about saving energy at home. But I don't have any ideas.

**W**  There are many easy ways you can save energy at home.

**M**  Like what? Give me some examples.

**W**  Well, you can turn off the lights and electrical appliances when they are not in use.

**M**  That's right. Anything else?

**W**  You can also close the curtains at night and unplug battery chargers when the batteries are fully charged.

**M**  Wow! There are a lot of simple ways to save energy.

---

**남**  집에서 에너지를 절약하는 것에 대한 보고서를 써야 하는데, 아이디어가 떠오르지 않네.

**여**  집에서 에너지를 절약할 수 있는 쉬운 방법들이 많아.

**남**  어떤 거? 예를 좀 들어 줘.

**여**  음, 전등과 가전제품을 쓰지 않을 때 끌 수 있어.

**남**  맞다. 다른 거는?

**여**  밤에 커튼을 치고, 배터리가 충전이 다 됐을 때 배터리 충전기의 플러그를 뽑을 수도 있어.

**남**  와! 에너지를 절약할 수 있는 간단한 방법들이 많이 있구나.

## 10 ③

**M**  Hello, this is the manager speaking. Can I have

your attention for one minute, please? For this month's special event, the author of the best-seller, Sally Brown will be coming to our bookstore. She will sign copies of her books. The event will be at 2 p.m. this Saturday. We would like to invite you to come and talk with her. Thank you.

남 안녕하세요. 매니저입니다. 잠시만 주목해 주시겠습니까? 이번 달의 특별 행사로, 베스트셀러의 저자인 Sally Brown이 저희 서점에 올 것입니다. 그녀는 자신의 책에 사인을 할 것입니다. 행사는 이번 주 토요일 2시에 있을 것입니다. 오셔서 그녀와 대화를 나누시도록 여러분을 초대하고 싶습니다. 감사합니다.

## 11 ③

W Many people think fast food is bad for one's health. In general, fast food contains a lot of fat and salt. These days, however, fast food restaurants are changing. More and more customers are concerned about their health. Therefore, fast food restaurants are offering healthy food like low-fat, low-salt meals and fresh salads. Customers can even choose ingredients and make their own burgers and sandwiches.

여 많은 사람들이 패스트푸드는 건강에 좋지 않다고 생각합니다. 일반적으로, 패스트푸드는 지방과 소금을 많이 함유하고 있습니다. 하지만, 요즘에는 패스트푸드 식당들이 변화하고 있습니다. 점점 더 많은 손님들이 자신의 건강에 대해 걱정하고 있습니다. 따라서 패스트푸드 식당들이 저지방, 저염 식사와 신선한 샐러드와 같은 건강한 음식을 제공하고 있습니다. 손님들은 심지어 재료를 골라서 자신만의 버거와 샌드위치를 만들 수도 있습니다.

## 12 ⑤

*[Telephone rings.]*
M Best Dining Restaurant. How can I help you?
W Hello. I ate brunch at your restaurant this morning and I think I left my wallet there.
M Let me check if anyone turned in a wallet. Just a moment.
W Okay.

M Is it a leather wallet in wine color?
W That's it. I'm glad someone found it.
M Drop by here anytime to get it.

*[전화 벨소리가 울린다.]*
남 Best Dining 식당입니다. 무엇을 도와드릴까요?
여 안녕하세요. 오늘 오전에 그 식당에서 브런치를 먹었는데, 그곳에 지갑을 놓고 온 것 같아요.
남 누군가 지갑을 가져왔는지 확인해 보겠습니다. 잠시만요.
여 네.
남 검붉은색의 가죽 지갑인가요?
여 맞아요. 누군가가 찾았다니 기쁘네요.
남 언제든 들르셔서 가져가세요.

## 13 ②

M How about studying together at the public library tomorrow?
W Okay. What time shall we meet?
M Let's meet in front of the library at 9:30 in the morning.
W But there will be too many students at that time.
M Then how about an hour earlier?
W Let's make it at 8 o'clock. Is it okay?
M All right, then.

남 내일 공공 도서관에서 함께 공부하는 게 어때?
여 좋아. 몇 시에 만날까?
남 도서관 앞에서 오전 9시 30분에 만나자.
여 하지만 그 시간에는 학생들이 너무 많을 거야.
남 그러면 한 시간 더 일찍은 어때?
여 8시에 만나자. 괜찮아?
남 좋아, 그럼.

## 14 ④

W Sorry to keep you waiting. Are you ready to shoot the scene?
M Of course I am.
W Good. In this scene, your role is very important.
M I'll try my best.
W I know that you're a good actor. Just don't forget the lines.
M I won't.
W Okay. Let's go.

| 여 | 기다리게 해서 죄송해요. 장면을 찍을 준비가 되셨나요? |
|---|---|

**여** 기다리게 해서 죄송해요. 장면을 찍을 준비가 되셨나요?

**남** 물론 됐습니다.

**여** 좋아요. 이 장면에서, 당신의 역할이 매우 중요해요.

**남** 최선을 다하겠습니다.

**여** 당신이 좋은 배우라는 걸 알아요. 단지 대사만 잊지 마세요.

**남** 안 잊을게요.

**여** 좋아요. 갑시다.

---

*[전화 벨소리가 울린다.]*

**여** 안녕, 지호야? 나 수진이야.

**남** 오, 안녕. 무슨 일이야?

**여** 너 어제 테니스 수업에 오지 않았잖아. 아팠니?

**남** 그건 아니야. 사실은, 나 다른 운동을 해 보기로 결정했어.

**여** 정말? 그게 뭔데?

**남** 나 아이스 스케이팅을 배우기 시작했어. 미리 너에게 말하지 않아서 미안해.

**여** 괜찮아. 나중에 보자.

---

### 15 ②

**M** Did you finish packing your stuff?

**W** Almost. I'm so excited.

**M** What time do you need to be at the airport?

**W** I have to be there by 9 a.m. Dad, can you drive me to the airport tomorrow?

**M** I wish I could. But, you know, my car broke down.

**W** Oh, I forgot. Then, could you wake me up tomorrow morning?

**M** Okay, I will.

---

**남** 짐은 다 쌌니?

**여** 거의요. 저 너무 신나요.

**남** 공항에 몇 시까지 가야 하니?

**여** 오전 9시까지 가야 해요. 아빠, 내일 저를 공항까지 태워다 주실 수 있으세요?

**남** 그럴 수 있으면 좋겠다. 하지만 너도 알다시피 자동차가 고장 났잖니.

**여** 오, 깜빡했어요. 그러면, 내일 아침에 저를 깨워 주실 수 있으세요?

**남** 그래, 그럴게.

---

### 17 ④

① **M** How about fish and chips for lunch?

  **W** Sounds great!

② **M** What do you usually do in your free time?

  **W** I like going fishing with my father.

③ **M** Let's go swimming to the lake.

  **W** I don't think it's a good idea. It's too dangerous.

④ **M** Look! I caught a fish.

  **W** Wow. It's big. Hold tight! It might get away.

⑤ **M** We should hurry. The boat leaves in ten minutes.

  **W** Okay. Let's run.

---

① **남** 점심으로 피시앤칩스 어때?

  **여** 좋지!

② **남** 너는 여가 시간에 보통 무엇을 하니?

  **여** 나는 아버지와 낚시하러 가는 것을 좋아해.

③ **남** 우리 호수에 수영하러 가자.

  **여** 좋은 생각이 아닌 것 같아. 너무 위험해.

④ **남** 봐! 내가 물고기를 잡았어.

  **여** 와. 크다. 꽉 잡아! 도망칠지도 몰라.

⑤ **남** 우리 서둘러야 해. 배가 10분 뒤에 떠나.

  **여** 그래. 우리 뛰자.

---

### 16 ④

*[Telephone rings.]*

**W** Hello, Jiho? This is Sujin.

**M** Oh, hi. What's up?

**W** You didn't come to the tennis lesson yesterday. Were you sick?

**M** Not really. Actually, I decided to try another sport.

**W** Really? What's that?

**M** I've started learning ice-skating. I'm sorry I didn't tell you earlier.

**W** That's okay. See you later.

---

### 18 ④

**W** We are sorry to tell you that the jazz festival will be postponed. This is due to the storm that is moving toward this area. The event will be held on July 15th instead of July 8th. The venue will be the same. If you wish to get a refund for the tickets, you can do so on the website.

---

**여** 재즈 축제가 연기된다는 말씀을 드리게 되어 유감입니다. 이는 이 지역을 향해 오고 있는 폭풍 때문입니다. 행사는 7월 8일

대신에 7월 15일에 개최될 것입니다. 장소는 같을 것입니다. 입장권을 환불받고 싶으시다면, 홈페이지에서 하실 수 있습니다.

## 19 ③

W Let's eat out for dinner.

M That's a good idea. Which restaurant do you want to visit?

W How about the new Italian restaurant we went to last week?

M I don't want to go there again.

W Why not? You said the food was great.

M Yeah, I liked the food and the price was reasonable.

W Then, what's the problem?

---

여 저녁으로 외식하자.

남 좋은 생각이야. 어떤 식당에 가고 싶니?

여 지난주에 갔던 그 새로 생긴 이탈리아 음식점 어때?

남 나는 그곳에 다시 가고 싶지 않아.

여 왜 싫은데? 음식이 훌륭하다고 했잖아.

남 응, 음식은 마음에 들었고, 가격도 합리적이었어.

여 그러면 뭐가 문제인데?

## 20 ④

M A new shopping mall opened yesterday.

W I know. Have you been there?

M Not yet. But people say it's really cool.

W Yes. My sister went there with her friends, and she said all the facilities were nice.

M Why don't we go there sometime?

W When?

---

남 새로운 쇼핑몰이 어제 문을 열었어.

여 알아. 너 거기에 가 봤니?

남 아직. 그런데 사람들 말로는 정말 멋지대.

여 응. 언니가 친구들과 가 봤는데, 모든 시설이 좋다더라고.

남 언제 같이 가는 게 어때?

여 언제?

>> 04회 듣기 실전 모의고사    pp. 136~143

| 01 ② | 02 ⑤ | 03 ② | 04 ④ | 05 ④ | 06 ③ | 07 ⑤ | 08 ⑤ |
| 09 ④ | 10 ② | 11 ⑤ | 12 ① | 13 ③ | 14 ② | 15 ⑤ | 16 ③ |
| 17 ③ | 18 ④ | 19 ④ | 20 ① | | | | |

### Dictation Test

**01** region, all day, beach  **02** selling, prefers, especially  **03** go, curious, first prize  **04** tanned, lifeguard, meaningful  **05** front, back, discount, both  **06** out, mood, comedy, next time  **07** place, ready, confirm, later  **08** accessories, over, withdraw  **09** here, leave, message, call back  **10** magician, achieved, questions, auditorium  **11** looking for, curly, sweater, customer, first  **12** reserved, book, How long, stay  **13** each, free, many, change  **14** practice, unwell, able to, game  **15** farewell, transferring, pick, up, say hello  **16** so long, opposite, wrong  **17** raising, better, seen, while, allergic  **18** five to, entrance, cost, inside, touch  **19** difficult, knowing, teaching, like  **20** changed, Neither, graduate school

## 01 ②

M Here is the world weather forecast. First, let's look at the Asia-Pacific region. In China, it's very windy and cold. The temperature is around 1 degree Celsius. In Japan, it's drizzling now, and it's going to rain all day today. In South Korea, the weather is cloudy, but there will be no rain today. In Australia, the sun is shining and it's a perfect weather to go to the beach.

---

남 세계의 날씨를 말씀드리겠습니다. 우선, 아시아 태평양 지역을 보도록 하겠습니다. 중국은 바람이 많이 불고 춥습니다. 기온은 약 섭씨 1도가량입니다. 일본은 현재 이슬비가 내리고 있고, 오늘은 종일 비가 내리겠습니다. 한국은 흐리지만, 오늘 비가 내리지는 않겠습니다. 오스트레일리아는 햇살이 빛나고 있고 해변에 가기에 완벽한 날씨입니다.

## 02 ⑤

M Excuse me. Can I get some help?

W Sure. What do you need?

M Today is my wife's birthday, so I need a present for her.

W How about this scarf? It's selling very well.

M Do you mean the black one over there? It looks

good, but she prefers a bright color.

W  Then how about this one with ivory color?

M  It's nice. I especially like the pink rose pattern.

---

남  실례합니다. 좀 도와주시겠어요?

여  물론이죠. 무엇이 필요하세요?

남  오늘이 아내의 생일이라, 그녀를 위한 선물이 필요해요.

여  이 스카프는 어떠세요? 아주 잘 팔려요.

남  저기 있는 검정색 스카프 말씀이세요? 좋아 보이지만, 아내는 밝은색을 선호해요.

여  그러면 이 아이보리색 스카프는 어떠세요?

남  좋네요. 저는 특히 분홍색 장미 무늬가 마음에 들어요.

## 03 ②

W  How did the science fair go, Chris?

M  It was great, Mom. There were so many good science projects.

W  How did your robot do?

M  Everyone there really liked it. Actually, I have good news for you.

W  What is it? I'm really curious.

M  I got first prize with my robot!

W  Amazing! That's my boy!

---

여  과학 박람회는 어땠니, Chris?

남  멋졌어요, 엄마. 훌륭한 과학 프로젝트들이 아주 많았어요.

여  너의 로봇은 어땠니?

남  거기 있는 모든 사람이 정말 마음에 들어 했어요. 사실, 엄마께 전해드릴 좋은 소식이 있어요.

여  뭔데? 정말 궁금하구나.

남  제 로봇으로 1등상을 받았어요!

여  굉장하구나! 역시 내 아들이야!

## 04 ④

W  Minho, you look tanned. Did you go to the beach last weekend?

M  Yeah, but I didn't go swimming there.

W  Then why did you go to the beach?

M  You know I am a good swimmer. I started doing volunteer work as a lifeguard.

W  Really? It sounds like fun.

M  It's not only fun but it is also meaningful.

---

여  민호야, 너 탄 것 같아 보인다. 지난 주말에 해변에 갔니?

남  응, 하지만 그곳에 수영을 하러 간 게 아니었어.

여  그럼 해변에 왜 갔어?

남  너 내가 수영 잘하는 거 알잖아. 나 인명 구조원으로 자원봉사 활동을 시작했어.

여  정말? 그거 재미있겠다.

남  재미있을 뿐만 아니라 의미 있어.

## 05 ④

M  Hi, I'd like two tickets for *Spiderman*, please.

W  Would you prefer to sit at the front, middle or the back?

M  The back please. Oh, do you offer a student discount?

W  Yes, we do. Are you both students?

M  Yes, here are our student cards.

W  Okay, that'll be 14,000 won.

M  Here you are.

---

남  안녕하세요, 〈스파이더맨〉 표 두 장 주세요.

여  앞쪽, 가운데, 뒤쪽 중 어디에 앉는 것을 선호하세요?

남  뒤쪽이요. 오, 학생 할인을 해주시나요?

여  네, 해드려요. 두 분 다 학생이세요?

남  네, 여기 저희의 학생증이요.

여  좋아요, 14,000원입니다.

남  여기 있습니다.

## 06 ③

M  Are you busy tonight?

W  Not really. What's up?

M  Let's go to the movies. There's a new movie just out today.

W  Well, I'm not in the mood for a movie today.

M  Come on. It's a comedy. You'll love it.

W  Today is not the day. Maybe next time.

---

남  오늘 밤에 바쁘니?

여  그렇지는 않은데. 무슨 일이야?

남  영화 보러 가자. 오늘 새 영화가 개봉해.

여  음, 오늘은 영화를 볼 기분이 아니야.

남  가자. 코미디 영화야. 분명 좋아할 거야.

여  오늘은 날이 아니야. 다음에 가자.

## 07 ⑤

*[Telephone rings.]*

M  Hello. Fine View Restaurant. May I help you?

W  Yes, can I place an order before we arrive for dinner today?

M  Sure, ma'am. If you order now, we can have your order ready when you arrive.

W That's nice. We are just three people and we will arrive at 7:30 this evening. We would like to have roasted chicken, shrimp cream spaghetti, and fresh salad.

M Just a minute. Let me confirm your order. Roasted chicken, shrimp cream spaghetti, and fresh salad for three people. Is that right?

W Correct. I want to order drinks later at the restaurant.

M Okay. See you this evening.

---

*[전화 벨소리가 울린다.]*

남 여보세요. Fine View 식당입니다. 도와드릴까요?

여 네, 오늘 저녁을 먹으러 가기 전에 미리 주문을 할 수 있을까요?

남 물론이죠, 부인. 지금 주문을 하시면, 도착하실 때 음식을 준비해 놓을 수 있습니다.

여 그거 좋네요. 저희는 세 명이고 오늘 저녁 7시 30분에 도착할 것입니다. 닭구이, 새우 크림 스파게티, 그리고 신선한 샐러드를 먹겠습니다.

남 잠시만요. 주문을 확인하겠습니다. 세 분이시고, 닭구이, 새우 크림 스파게티, 그리고 신선한 샐러드를 주문하셨죠? 맞나요?

여 맞습니다. 음료는 나중에 식당에서 주문하고 싶습니다.

남 알겠습니다. 오늘 저녁에 뵙겠습니다.

---

**08** ⑤

W Are you going to come to Sora's birthday party?

M Yes, I am.

W I'm thinking of buying her a necklace. She really likes accessories. What are you going to buy?

M I haven't decided yet.

W Then why don't we buy the necklace together? In fact, it's a little over my budget.

M Okay. But I need to go to the bank first to withdraw some money.

W Let's hurry, then.

---

여 너 소라의 생일 파티에 올 거니?

남 응, 갈 거야.

여 나는 소라에게 목걸이를 사 줄까 생각 중이야. 소라는 액세서리를 정말 좋아하거든. 너는 뭘 살 거야?

남 나는 아직 결정하지 못했어.

여 그러면 목걸이를 같이 사는 게 어때? 사실, 그건 내 예산을 좀 초과하거든.

남 좋아. 그런데 나는 먼저 은행에 가서 돈을 좀 인출해야 해.

여 그러면 서두르자.

---

**09** ④

*[Telephone rings.]*

M Hello, this is John speaking.

W Hello, can I speak to Mary?

M Sorry, but she's not here.

W Can I leave a message?

M Sure.

W This is Susan. Please tell her to call back to me. My number is 555-1234.

M Okay. I'll tell her.

W Thanks a lot.

---

*[전화 벨소리가 울린다.]*

남 여보세요, John입니다.

여 여보세요, Mary와 통화할 수 있을까요?

남 미안하지만, 그녀는 여기에 없어요.

여 메시지를 남겨도 될까요?

남 물론이죠.

여 저는 Susan인데요. Mary에게 저한테 전화 좀 해 달라고 말해주세요. 제 번호는 555-1234입니다.

남 알겠습니다. 그녀에게 말할게요.

여 정말 고맙습니다.

---

**10** ②

W Listen carefully, students. Tomorrow, we are going to have a special event. A world-famous magician, Chanwoo Kim is going to visit our school. He's going to speak about his job and how he achieved his dream. Then, you can ask him questions about his life as a magician. There will be no class, so please come to the auditorium. Thank you.

---

여 경청해 주세요, 학생 여러분. 내일, 우리는 특별한 행사를 열 예정입니다. 세계적으로 유명한 마술사인 김찬우 씨가 우리 학교를 방문할 것입니다. 그는 자신의 직업과 그가 어떻게 꿈을 이루었는지에 대해 말해 줄 것입니다. 그리고 나서 여러분은 마술사로서의 그의 삶에 대해서 질문할 수 있습니다. 수업은 없을 것이니, 강당으로 와 주세요. 감사합니다.

---

**11** ⑤

W Ladies and gentlemen, may I have your attention, please? We are looking for a four-year-old girl named Lucy. She's about 100 centimeters tall and has curly brown hair. She is wearing a yellow sweater and blue jeans. If you see her, please bring her to the customer center on the first floor. Thank you.

---

여  신사 숙녀 여러분, 주목해 주시겠습니까? 우리는 Lucy라는 이름의 네 살 된 여자아이를 찾고 있습니다. 그녀는 키가 약 100센티미터이고 갈색 곱슬머리입니다. 그녀는 노란색 스웨터와 청바지를 입고 있습니다. 그녀를 발견하시면, 1층에 있는 고객 센터로 데려와 주세요. 감사합니다.

## 12  ①

*[Telephone rings.]*

M  Hello, Cloud Travel Agency.

W  Hello. This is Linda Marcus. I reserved a flight to Washington D.C. with you.

M  Yes, Ms. Marcus. I remember you. How may I help you?

W  I want to book a hotel room. Can you help me with that?

M  Of course I can. How long are you going to stay?

W  I'm going to stay for two nights. And I prefer a hotel near the subway station.

M  I found the perfect one for you.

*[전화 벨소리가 울린다.]*

남  여보세요, Could 여행사입니다.

여  여보세요. 저는 Linda Marcus입니다. 그쪽을 통해 워싱턴행 항공기를 예약했어요.

남  네, Marcus 씨. 기억합니다. 무엇을 도와드릴까요?

여  호텔 방을 예약하고 싶은데요. 도와주실 수 있나요?

남  물론이죠. 얼마나 머무르실 건가요?

여  2박을 할 거예요. 그리고 지하철역 근처 호텔을 선호합니다.

남  당신에게 딱 맞는 호텔을 찾았습니다.

## 13  ③

W  Wow, these hairpins are so pretty! How much are they?

M  They're 1,000 won each, but if you buy seven, you can get one free.

W  Seven hairpins? I don't need that many.

M  You can give them to your friends. Christmas is next week.

W  That's a great idea. Then I will buy seven, and get one free. Here is 10,000 won.

M  Okay, here's your change.

---

여  와, 이 머리핀들 너무 예쁘네요! 얼마인가요?

남  각각 천 원이지만, 7개를 사시면 하나는 그냥 드려요.

여  머리핀 7개요? 그렇게 많이는 필요 없는데요.

남  친구들에게 주면 되죠. 크리스마스가 다음 주잖아요.

여  그거 좋은 생각이네요. 그러면 7개를 사고 하나는 그냥 받을게요. 여기 만 원이요.

남  네, 여기 거스름돈이요.

## 14  ②

*[Telephone rings.]*

M  Hello, Richard Rogers speaking.

W  Hello, Mr. Rogers. This is Tom's mother.

M  Hello. Ms. Parker. What's the matter?

W  I'm sorry to say this, but Tom can't go to the soccer practice today.

M  Is he sick?

W  No, he's not. But his grandfather is unwell. I have to take Tom to the hospital to visit him.

M  Oh, I see. Do you think he will be able to be at practice tomorrow? We have an important game next week.

W  Of course he will.

*[전화 벨소리가 울린다.]*

남  여보세요, Richard Rogers입니다.

여  여보세요, Rogers 선생님. Tom의 엄마입니다.

남  안녕하세요. Parker 부인. 무슨 일이신가요?

여  이런 말씀드려서 죄송합니다만, Tom이 오늘 축구 연습에 못 갈 것 같습니다.

남  Tom이 아픈가요?

여  아니요, 안 아파요. 하지만 그의 할아버지께서 편찮으세요. Tom을 병원에 데려가서 할아버지를 방문해야 해요.

남  오, 그렇군요. 내일은 Tom이 연습에 올 수 있을까요? 다음 주에 중요한 시합이 있어서요.

여  물론 갈 거예요.

## 15  ⑤

W  Have you heard that they are going to hold a farewell party for Yumi this Saturday?

M  Yes, I have. I'm sorry to hear that she's transferring to another school. But I can't come to the party.

W  Why not?

M  My cousins from Canada are visiting Korea. I have to pick them up at the airport.

W  Oh, I see.

M  Please say hello to her for me.

W  Of course I will.

---

여　이번 주 토요일에 유미를 위한 송별회를 할 예정인 거 들었니?

남　응, 들었어. 그녀가 다른 학교로 전학을 간다니 유감이다. 하지만 나는 송별회에 못 가.

여　왜 못 가는데?

남　캐나다에서 사촌들이 한국을 방문해. 나는 공항에 그들을 마중 나가야 해.

여　오, 그렇구나.

남　나 대신 그녀에게 안부 전해 줘.

여　물론 그럴게.

## 16 ③

W　You're late again. Did you get up late?

M　I'm so sorry. But I woke up on time.

W　Then what took you so long?

M　I took the subway on the opposite side. I realized my mistake when it was too late.

W　Oh, come on. This isn't the first time you took the wrong subway.

M　You're right. I keep making the same mistakes.

W　Let's go get something to eat. I'm starving.

---

여　너 또 늦었어. 늦게 일어났니?

남　정말 미안해. 하지만 나는 제시간에 일어났어.

여　그러면 왜 늦었어?

남　지하철을 반대편에서 탔어. 너무 늦게 실수를 깨달았어.

여　오, 제발. 네가 지하철을 잘못 탄 게 이번이 처음은 아니잖아.

남　네 말이 맞아. 나는 계속 같은 실수를 하고 있어.

여　뭐 좀 먹으러 가자. 나 배가 너무 고파.

## 17 ③

① W　Do you have a pet?

　M　Yes, I'm raising a dog.

② W　Do you prefer cats or dogs?

　M　I like cats better than dogs.

③ W　Have you seen this dog?

　M　No, I'm sorry.

④ W　Can you take care of my dog for a while?

　M　Okay.

⑤ W　I'm allergic to dog hair.

　M　Really? I didn't know that.

---

① 여　너는 애완동물이 있니?

　남　응, 나는 개를 한 마리 키우고 있어.

② 여　너는 고양이와 개 중 어느 쪽을 선호하니?

　남　나는 개보다 고양이가 더 좋아.

③ 여　이 개를 보신 적이 있나요?

　남　아니요, 죄송해요.

④ 여　잠깐만 내 개를 돌봐 줄 수 있니?

　남　그래.

⑤ 여　나는 개털 알레르기가 있어.

　남　정말? 몰랐어.

## 18 ④

M　Attention, please. We are going to open at 10 a.m. It is five to ten now. You can buy tickets by the entrance. Tickets cost ten dollars for adults and five dollars for children. You can't take any food or drinks inside the museum. You may take pictures, but please do not touch any exhibits. We hope you enjoy the exhibition.

---

남　주목해 주세요. 저희는 오전 10시에 개장하겠습니다. 지금은 10시 5분 전입니다. 입구 옆에서 입장권을 구입하실 수 있습니다. 입장권은 성인은 10달러, 어린이는 5달러입니다. 박물관 안으로는 어떤 음식이나 음료도 가져가실 수 없습니다. 사진은 찍으셔도 되지만, 전시품을 만져서는 안 됩니다. 전시회를 즐기시기를 바랍니다.

## 19 ④

W　You know what? History is too difficult for me.

M　Who is your history teacher at school?

W　Mr. Park teaches me history.

M　I heard that he knows a lot about history.

W　Yeah. But knowing is one thing, and teaching is another. Who's your history teacher?

M　Ms. Lee, the new teacher.

W　What's she like?

---

여　있잖아? 역사는 나에게 너무 어려워.

남　학교에서 역사 선생님이 누구시니?

여　박 선생님이 역사를 가르쳐 주셔.

남　그 선생님은 역사에 대해 많이 알고 계시다고 들었는데.

여　맞아. 하지만 아는 것과 가르치는 것은 다르잖아. 너의 역사 선생님은 누구시니?

남　이 선생님이야. 새로 오신 선생님이셔.

여　그녀는 어떤 분이니?

## 20 ①

M　Wow, Claire! It's been a long time since I've seen you.

W  It really has.

M  You haven't changed a bit.

W  Neither have you. What do you do these days?

M  I'm still studying at the graduate school. What about you?

W  I'm a lawyer now.

---

남  와, Claire! 너를 본 지 정말 오랜만이다.

여  정말 그러네.

남  너는 하나도 변하지 않았구나.

여  너도 그래. 너는 요즘 뭐 하니?

남  나는 아직 대학원에서 공부를 하고 있어. 너는 어때?

여  나는 지금 변호사야.

**Dictation Test**

**01** until, clear up, throughout  **02** contain, easily lose, pictures    **03** finished, straight, honest, more than, quit  **04** called, see, off, doing, works    **05** surprise, first time, working, shape    **06** fight, lend, bad, apologize    **07** decided, underwear, toothbrush, flashlight, go hiking    **08** even, together, middle  **09** music, whether, single, pianist  **10** indoors, racket, across, ground    **11** introduce, teenager, courage, film    **12** ask, volunteer, arranging    **13** pick, up, waiting, half    **14** hurts, pain, push, turn around  **15** favor, take, way    **16** taking part, helping out, role    **17** was taken, ahead, photographer, no idea  **18** aboard, restrooms, second, drinks    **19** fancy, anything, pair of    **20** forgot, send, address

---

**01** ①

M  It's Monday morning, and here's the weather report for this week. It's raining now and the rain will continue until Wednesday. On Wednesday, a typhoon is expected to hit the city so please take precautions for it. On Thursday, the sky will clear up and the sun will be shining throughout the weekend.

---

남  월요일 아침입니다, 그리고 이번 주 일기 예보를 전해드리겠습니다. 현재는 비가 내리고 있고, 이 비는 수요일까지 계속되겠습니다. 수요일에는 태풍이 도시를 강타할 것으로 예상되니, 그에 대한 예방 조치를 취하십시오. 목요일에는 하늘이 갤 것이고 주말 내내 햇살이 빛나겠습니다.

---

**02** ③

M  Do you need help?

W  Yes, I'm looking for a water bottle.

M  Okay. What about this one? It can contain a lot of water.

W  It looks nice. But I need one with a strap. I easily lose my stuff.

M  I see. What about this one? It has a strap, and a handle as well.

W  I like it. But I don't want any pictures on it.

M  Then this is what you're looking for.

W  I love it. I'll take it.

---

남  도와드릴까요?

여  네, 저는 물병을 찾고 있어요.

남  네. 이건 어떠세요? 물을 많이 담을 수 있어요.

여  좋아 보이네요. 하지만 저는 끈이 있는 것을 원해요. 저는 물건을 쉽게 잃어버리거든요.

남  알겠습니다. 이건 어떠세요? 끈이 있고, 손잡이도 있어요.

여  마음에 들어요. 하지만 그림이 없으면 좋겠어요.

남  그러면 이것이 당신이 찾고 있는 것이군요.

여  너무 마음에 들어요. 그것을 살게요.

---

**03** ⑤

M  Sora, did you read my novel?

W  Yeah, I've just finished reading it.

M  What do you think of it? Please talk straight to me.

W  Well. To be honest, there are some parts that I didn't understand. Maybe you should make some changes.

M Thanks for being frank. But you know, I've read and rewrote the novel more than three times. Maybe I'm not good enough to be a writer.

W No way! You're good enough.

M No, I'm not. I think I should quit.

남 소라야, 내 소설 읽었니?

여 응, 이제 막 다 읽었어.

남 어떻게 생각해? 솔직히 말해 줘.

여 음, 솔직히, 내가 이해하지 못한 부분들이 좀 있어. 아마도 조금 수정해야 할 것 같아.

남 솔직히 말해 줘서 고마워. 하지만 너도 알다시피 난 세 번 이상 그 소설을 읽고 수정했어. 아마도 난 작가가 될 자격이 없나 봐.

여 말도 안 돼! 너는 충분히 훌륭해.

남 아니, 그렇지 않아. 난 그만둬야 할 것 같아.

## 04 ②

M Where were you going yesterday? I saw you at the train station.

W Did you?

M Yes. I called out your name, but you didn't hear me.

W I didn't go anywhere. I went there to see my grandmother off. She stayed at my house for a week.

M I see.

W What were you doing at the train station?

M I went there to see my father. He works there.

W Really? I didn't know that.

남 너 어제 어디 가고 있었니? 나는 기차역에서 너를 봤어.

여 그랬니?

남 응. 네 이름을 불렀는데, 너는 듣지 못하더라.

여 나는 아무 데도 가지 않았어. 나는 할머니를 배웅해드리러 그곳에 갔어. 할머니께서 일주일 동안 우리 집에 머무르셨거든.

남 그렇구나.

여 너는 기차역에서 뭐 하고 있었니?

남 나는 아버지를 뵈러 갔어. 그곳에서 일하시거든.

여 정말? 몰랐어.

## 05 ④

M Susan. What a surprise to see you here!

W Jason. It's you. Long time no see.

M Is it your first time here?

W Yes, it is.

M I've been working out here for more than a year.

W I can see that. You look to be in shape.

M Thanks. I'm going to run on the treadmill now. See you later.

남 Susan. 여기서 너를 보게 되다니!

여 Jason. 너구나. 오랜만이야.

남 여기에 처음 온 거니?

여 응, 처음이야.

남 나는 일 년 넘게 여기에서 운동을 해오고 있어.

여 그런 것 같다. 너는 건강해 보여.

남 고마워. 이제 트레드밀에 뛰러 가야겠다. 나중에 보자.

## 06 ②

M Are you all right, Mina? You look depressed.

W I got into a fight with my younger sister this morning.

M Why did you have a fight with her?

W She asked me to lend her my new jacket but I said no.

M Come on, what are sisters for? You wear her clothes sometimes.

W You're right. Now I feel so bad about it.

M I think you should give her a call and apologize to her right now.

남 너 괜찮니, 미나야? 우울해 보인다.

여 오늘 아침에 여동생과 싸웠어.

남 여동생과 왜 싸웠는데?

여 동생이 내 새 재킷을 빌려달라고 했는데, 내가 싫다고 말했어.

남 그러지 말고, 자매 좋다는 게 뭐야? 너 가끔 동생의 옷을 입잖아.

여 네 말이 맞아. 지금은 그 일 때문에 마음이 너무 안 좋아.

남 내 생각에는 네가 당장 동생에게 전화를 걸어서 사과를 해야 할 것 같아.

## 07 ⑤

W Jim, are you ready to go on the school field trip tomorrow?

M Yes, I am. I finished packing my bag. I also decided on what to wear tomorrow.

W Did you pack your underwear? Last time, you didn't bring any.

M Yes, I did. I put my underwear, socks, toothbrush, toothpaste, and everything I need in my bag.

W Are you going to take a flashlight? It's in the garage.

M The teacher said we don't need it. We're not going to go hiking at night this time.

W That's a relief.

---

여 Jim, 내일 수학여행에 갈 준비가 됐니?

남 네, 준비 됐어요. 가방을 다 쌌어요. 내일 무엇을 입을지도 결정했어요.

여 속옷 챙겼니? 지난번에, 너는 속옷을 하나도 가져가지 않았잖아.

남 맞아요, 그랬죠. 가방에 속옷, 양말, 칫솔, 치약, 그리고 필요한 모든 것을 넣었어요.

여 손전등도 가져갈 거니? 그것은 차고에 있어.

남 선생님께서 필요 없다고 말씀하셨어요. 이번에는 밤에 산행을 하지 않을 거예요.

여 그거 다행이구나.

## 08 ①

*[Telephone rings.]*

M Hello, Jina? This is Minho.

W Hello, Minho. What's up?

M Did you finish the art homework?

W No, I didn't even start.

M Why don't we do it together? You can come to my house or I can go there.

W Well, then can you come to my house? I was in the middle of cleaning my room. I have to finish it first.

M Okay. I'll be there in 30 minutes.

---

*[전화 벨소리가 울린다.]*

남 여보세요, 지나니? 나 민호야.

여 안녕, 민호야. 무슨 일이야?

남 미술 숙제 끝냈니?

여 아니, 아직 시작도 못 했어.

남 같이 하는 게 어때? 네가 우리 집에 오거나 내가 그쪽으로 갈 수 있어.

여 음, 그러면 우리 집으로 올래? 나는 방을 청소하는 중이었거든. 그걸 먼저 끝내야 해.

남 좋아. 30분 뒤에 갈게.

## 09 ①

W Hey, did you hear about the new teacher?

M Yes, she's our new music teacher. She's from New York, and she went to a college in Austria.

W Awesome! Do you know whether she's married or not?

M She's single. She's only 28 years old. Oh! She majored in piano.

W Really?

M Yeah. You want to be a pianist. I bet you'll love her.

W I can't wait to see her.

---

여 있잖아, 너 새로 오신 선생님에 대해 들었니?

남 응, 그녀는 우리의 새로운 음악 선생님이셔. 그녀는 뉴욕 출신이고, 오스트리아에서 대학을 다니셨대.

여 멋지다! 결혼을 하셨는지 안 하셨는지 알아?

남 미혼이셔. 그녀는 겨우 스물여덟 살이셔. 오! 그녀는 피아노를 전공하셨어.

여 정말?

남 응. 너는 피아니스트가 되고 싶어 하잖아. 너는 분명 그녀를 좋아할 거야.

여 빨리 뵙고 싶다.

## 10 ⑤

M This is a sport that two teams play indoors. Each team has one or two members. To play the sport, the players need a table with a net, a racket, and a light-weight ball. Players should pass the ball across the net to the other side of the table. The ball should not get out of the table or fall to the ground.

---

남 이것은 두 팀이 실내에서 하는 운동입니다. 각 팀에는 한 명이나 두 명의 선수가 있습니다. 경기를 하기 위해서 선수들은 네트가 달린 탁자, 라켓, 그리고 가벼운 공이 있어야 합니다. 선수들은 공을 네트 너머의 탁자 반대편으로 보내야 합니다. 공은 탁자를 벗어나거나 바닥에 떨어지면 안 됩니다.

## 11 ③

W Hello, everyone. Today, I want to introduce you to a popular novel, *Bridge to Terabithia*. It was written by Katherine Paterson, and won a medal for children's best novel. A teenager boy is the main character, and the writer talks about friendship, courage, and hope through his story. It was also made into a film with the same title. I highly recommend this novel.

---

여 여러분, 안녕하세요. 오늘, 저는 여러분께 인기 있는 소설인 〈Bridge to Terabithia〉를 소개해드리고자 합니다. 그것은 Katherine Paterson이 썼고, 아동 문학상을 받았습니다. 한 10대 소년이 주인공이고, 작가는 그의 이야기를 통해 우리에게 우정, 용기, 그리고 희망에 대해 이야기합니다. 그것은 같은 제목의 영화로도 만들어졌습니다. 저는 이 소설을 강력히 추천합니다.

## 12 ⑤

*[Telephone rings.]*

W  Hello. Namsan Public Library. How may I help you?

M  Hello. I called you to ask something.

W  Yes, what is it?

M  Is it possible to volunteer at your library?

W  Of course. There are a lot of different types of volunteer jobs like cleaning or arranging bookshelves.

M  Nice. So how do I apply?

W  First, can I have your name? Then tell me when you can begin.

*[전화 벨소리가 울린다.]*

여  여보세요. 남산 공공 도서관입니다. 무엇을 도와드릴까요?

남  여보세요. 뭐 좀 여쭤보려고 전화드렸어요.

여  네, 무엇입니까?

남  그 도서관에서 봉사활동을 할 수 있을까요?

여  물론입니다. 청소나 책장 정리와 같은 다양한 종류의 봉사활동 업무가 많이 있습니다.

남  좋네요. 그러면 어떻게 신청하죠?

여  우선 이름을 말씀해 주실래요? 그러고 나서 언제 시작할 수 있는지 말씀해 주세요.

## 13 ④

M  When are you coming back today?

W  The bus will arrive at the express bus terminal at 6:50 p.m. Could you pick me up, Dad?

M  Of course. I can pick you up if you don't mind waiting for me for a while.

W  How long?

M  The meeting will finish around 6:40 but it will take about half an hour to get to the bus terminal. Is it okay?

W  That's fine with me.

남  오늘 몇 시에 돌아오니?

여  버스가 고속버스 터미널에 저녁 6시 50분에 도착할 거예요. 저를 마중 나와 주실 수 있어요, 아빠?

남  물론이다. 만일 네가 나를 잠깐 기다려도 괜찮으면 마중 갈 수 있어.

여  얼마나 오랫동안이요?

남  회의는 6시 40분쯤 끝날 건데 버스 터미널까지 가는 데 30분 정도 걸릴 거야. 괜찮니?

여  저는 괜찮아요.

## 14 ⑤

M  Ouch! It hurts.

W  Don't be nervous. Tension will make your muscles stiff, and it will cause more pain.

M  All right. I'll try to be relaxed.

W  If I push you too hard, just tell me.

M  It's okay now.

W  Now I'll massage your back. Please turn around.

남  아야! 아파요.

여  긴장하지 마세요. 긴장감은 근육을 뻣뻣하게 만들고, 그것은 더 심한 고통을 야기할 거예요.

남  알겠어요. 긴장을 풀도록 노력할게요.

여  제가 당신을 너무 세게 누르면 말씀해 주세요.

남  지금은 괜찮아요.

여  이제 등을 마사지해드릴게요. 뒤로 도세요.

## 15 ⑤

W  Where are you going, Minjun?

M  I'm going to the park to play basketball with my friends.

W  Okay. Can you do me a favor?

M  What is it, Mom?

W  I made strawberry jam for your grandmother. Can you take it to her on your way to the park?

M  No problem. Grandma will love it.

W  Thanks.

여  어디 가니, 민준아?

남  공원에 가서 친구들과 농구를 할 거예요.

여  그렇구나. 부탁 하나 들어줄래?

남  뭔데요, 엄마?

여  할머니를 위해 딸기잼을 만들었어. 공원에 가는 길에 할머니께 그것을 가져다드릴 수 있니?

남  문제없어요. 할머니께서 좋아하시겠어요.

여  고맙구나.

## 16 ④

M　Mom, I'm going to school.

W　School? But it's Saturday. Are you going to study?

M　No. The school festival is next week.

W　Oh, are you taking part in the festival?

M　Yeah, I'm helping out as a staff member.

W　I see. You're playing an important role.

M　Thank you for telling me.

---

남　엄마, 저 학교에 가요.

여　학교? 하지만 토요일이잖니. 공부를 할 거니?

남　아니요. 학교 축제가 다음 주예요.

여　오, 축제에 참가하는 거니?

남　네, 저는 구성원으로 돕고 있어요.

여　그렇구나. 중요한 역할을 맡고 있구나.

남　말씀 감사해요.

## 17 ③

① M　What do you usually do in your free time?

　W　I usually take pictures.

② M　Who took this picture?

　W　It was taken by my father.

③ M　Could you take a picture of me in front of the statue?

　W　No problem. Go ahead.

④ M　What do you want to be in the future?

　W　I want to be a photographer.

⑤ M　Do you know who built the statue?

　W　I have no idea.

---

① 남　너는 여가 시간에 주로 무엇을 하니?

　여　나는 보통 사진을 찍어.

② 남　누가 이 사진을 찍었니?

　여　우리 아빠가 찍으셨어.

③ 남　동상 앞에서 제 사진 좀 찍어 주실 수 있을까요?

　여　문제없어요. 가 보세요.

④ 남　너는 장래에 무엇이 되고 싶니?

　여　나는 사진작가가 되고 싶어.

⑤ 남　너는 누가 이 동상을 세웠는지 아니?

　여　모르겠어.

## 18 ⑤

W　Welcome aboard Blue Star Ferry. The time is now 10:15 a.m. and it will take about 30 minutes to get to Salt Spring Island. The restrooms are on the first and the second floor, and the snack bar is on the second floor. You can enjoy hot and cold drinks there as well. We hope you have a wonderful trip. Thank you.

---

여　Blue Star 여객선에 탑승하신 것을 환영합니다. 현재 시각은 오전 10시 15분이고 Salt Spring 섬까지는 약 30분이 걸릴 예정입니다. 화장실은 1층과 2층에 있고, 간이식당은 2층에 있습니다. 그곳에서 따뜻한 음료와 차가운 음료도 즐기실 수 있습니다. 즐거운 여행하시기를 바랍니다. 감사합니다.

## 19 ②

M　How was it like shopping at the new shopping center?

W　It was great. There were a lot of fancy restaurants, so I had wonderful lunch with my friends.

M　Didn't you buy anything?

W　Of course I did. I bought a shirt, a pair of jeans, and a cap.

M　Is that all?

---

남　새로운 쇼핑센터에서 쇼핑 어땠니?

여　좋았어. 멋진 식당들이 많이 있어서, 친구들과 훌륭한 점심을 먹었어.

남　아무것도 사지 않았니?

여　물론 샀지. 셔츠 한 장, 청바지 한 벌, 그리고 모자 하나를 샀어.

남　그게 다야?

## 20 ③

[Telephone rings.]

W　Hi, John. This is Jessy.

M　Hi, Jessy. What's up?

W　You forgot it, didn't you?

M　What are you talking about?

W　You were supposed to send me the book list by e-mail.

M　Oh, I'm so sorry. What was the address?

---

[전화 벨소리가 울린다.]

여　안녕, John. 나 Jessy.

남　안녕, Jessy. 무슨 일이야?

여　너 그거 잊었지, 그렇지 않니?

남　무슨 소리야?

여　서적 일람표를 나에게 이메일로 보내기로 했잖아.

남　오, 정말 미안해. 주소가 뭐였지?

soobakⒸ | visang

최상위권*** 증가
**3.9**배

성적*향상률
**99.1**%

성적장학생** 증가
**227**%

중등 업계 유일!
메타인지 학습 솔루션
# 수박씨닷컴

**7일
무료체험**

*알파ON클래스를 이용한 1,986명 회원 전수조사 결과 6개월~1년 6개월 만에 1,968명 성적 향상
 (2021.04 기준) (회원들이 자발적으로 제출한 성적에 근거한 자료로서, 성적표 결과와 완전히
 일치하지 않을 수 있습니다.)
**2012년 985명 / 2021년 2,237명 (전교1등부터 평균 93점 이상)
***최상위권 : 내신 전과목 평균 95점 초과

☑ **업계 유일!** 시작부터 확실하게 앞서나가는 **수준별 맞춤 학습 강좌**

 전 과목 전 출판사
**학교별 맞춤 강좌**

 중등 베스트셀러
**비상교재 독점 강의**

 메타인지 맞춤!
**개념/교재별 콕 강의**

 **초등 와이즈캠프**
초~중등 동시수강

☑ 메타인지 향상을 위한 **과목별 메타학습 솔루션 & 1:1 메타코칭**

 사회/역사 과학 키워드 중심의 구조화 학습
**한눈에 쏙쏙 마인드맵**

 수학 이해도 진단 및 보충 학습
**스마트 매쓰 솔루션**

 영어 전략적인 단어 암기 학습
**내신 VOCA 마스터**

 메타 코칭 집중 모니터링 및 피드백
**실시간 화상·원격 학습 관리**

중등인강 1위* 수박씨닷컴만의 메타학습 솔루션
**지금 바로! 7일 무료체험하고, 성적 향상을 경험해보세요!**
* 2022 대한민국 퍼스트브랜드대상 중등인강 부문 수상

**문의 1544-7380 | www.soobakc.com**

**All that** 올댓·중학·영어　중학영어의 모든 것이 들어 있는 올댓으로 학교 시험 완벽 대비!

**대표전화** 1544-0554
**주소** 서울특별시 구로구 디지털로33길 48 대륭포스트타워 7차 20층
**협의 없는 무단 복제는 법으로 금지되어 있습니다.**